# New Headway

Advanced for Business, Arts Student's Book

Liz and John Soars

**OXFORD**
UNIVERSITY PRESS

# CONTENTS

| LISTENING | SPEAKING | THE LAST WORD | WRITING |
|---|---|---|---|
| Two brothers from Kenya – an interview with Vijay and Bhikhu Patel p14<br>National stereotypes p15 | Discussion – immigrants and emigration p11<br>Discussion – nationality stereotypes p15 | British and American English<br>*We've got a small **flat**.*<br>*We **have** a small **apartment**.*<br>p16 | Formal and informal letters p117 |
| 'The Importance of Being Earnest' – a scene from Oscar Wilde's play p23 | Information gap – finding out about Iris Murdoch p18<br>Acting out a scene from a play p23 | Sounds and spelling – a poem about pronunciation<br>*tough, bought, cough, dough*<br>p26<br>Homophones<br>*through, threw* p26 | Storytelling p118 |
| An interview with Anita Roddick, founder of *The Body Shop* p34 | Simulation – planning an advertising campaign p35<br>Discussion – the role of advertising p35 | Word linking and intrusive sounds<br>*English is an international language*<br>*blue eyes*<br>/w/<br>*my office* p36<br>/j/ | A business report p120 |
| An interview with Hollywood star Liza Minnelli p44 | Maze – how to become an A-list celebrity p44 | Tags and replies<br>*'I like Cabaret.' 'Oh, you do, do you?'*<br>*You haven't seen my car keys, have you?*<br>*You're a star, you are.* p46 | Expressing a personal opinion p122 |
| A romantic meeting – another couple tell the story of how they met p48<br>When love lasts forever – an interview with 102-year-old Olive Hodges p53 | Discussion – do you believe in fate? p48 | Getting emotional<br>Sounding anxious, grateful, etc.<br>*Get this heap of old metal out of my drive! Now!*<br>*You mean more to me than words could ever say.* p54 | Discussing pros and cons p123 |
| An interview with foreign correspondent Simon Winchester p61 | Discussion – how television reports the news p61 | Responding to news<br>*'Guess what! I won £5 million.'*<br>*'You're kidding!'* p62<br>Sounding sarcastic<br>*'Pete. I crashed your car. Sorry.'*<br>*'Great. That's all I needed. Thank you very much.'* p62 | A letter to a newspaper p124 |
| Words of wisdom – ten people talk about advice they have been given in their lives p68 | Prediction game – Dilemma! How well do you know your classmates! p67<br>Discussion – words of wisdom p68 | Breaking the rules of English<br>*'Ending a sentence with a preposition is something up with which I will not put.'* p70 | Describing a personal experience p126 |

3

OXFORD
UNIVERSITY PRESS

Great Clarendon Street, Oxford OX2 6DP

Oxford University Press is a department of the University of Oxford. It furthers the University's objective of excellence in research, scholarship, and education by publishing worldwide in

Oxford New York

Auckland Cape Town Dar es Salaam Hong Kong Karachi Kuala Lumpur Madrid Melbourne Mexico City Nairobi New Delhi Shanghai Taipei Toronto

With offices in

Argentina Austria Brazil Chile Czech Republic France Greece Guatemala Hungary Italy Japan South Korea Poland Portugal Singapore Switzerland Thailand Turkey Ukraine Vietnam

OXFORD and OXFORD ENGLISH are registered trade marks of Oxford University Press in the UK and in certain other countries

© Oxford University Press 2003

The moral rights of the author have been asserted

Database right Oxford University Press (maker)

First published 2003
2009 2008 2007 2006 2005
10 9 8 7 6 5

**No unauthorized photocopying**

All rights reserved. No part of this publication may be reproduced, stored in a retrieval system, or transmitted, in any form or by any means, without the prior permission in writing of Oxford University Press, or as expressly permitted by law, or under terms agreed with the appropriate reprographics rights organization. Enquiries concerning reproduction outside the scope of the above should be sent to the ELT Rights Department, Oxford University Press, at the address above

You must not circulate this book in any other binding or cover and you must impose this same condition on any acquirer

Any websites referred to in this publication are in the public domain and their addresses are provided by Oxford University Press for information only. Oxford University Press disclaims any responsibility for the content

ISBN-13: 978-0-19-436930-5
ISBN-10: 0-19-436930-7

Printed and bound in China

ACKNOWLEDGEMENTS

*Writing section*: written by Jayne Wildman

*The authors and publisher are grateful to those who have given permission to reproduce the following extracts and adaptations of copyright material*: p9 H.G. Wells quote from *The Future in America*, Harper & Bros., New York © H. G. Wells 1906. Reproduced by permission of A P Watt Limited; p10 William Williams quote from William Williams Papers, Manuscripts and Archives Division, The New York Public Library, Astor, Lenox and Tilden Foundations. Reproduced by permission; p10 Arnold Weiss quote from *Island of Hope, Island of Tears*, Viking Penguin, New York © David M. Brownstone, Irene M. Franck and Douglass L. Brownstone, 1979. Reproduced by permission; p11 Henry Curran quote from *Pillar to Post*, Charles Scribner's and Sons, New York © Henry H. Curran, copyright renewed 1969; p19 Interview with Iris Murdoch by Joanna Coles © Joanna Coles, *The Guardian* 21 September 1996. Reproduced by permission of Guardian Newspapers Limited; p25 from *Fair Game* by Elizabeth Young, published by Heinemann. Reprinted by permission of The Random House Group Ltd; p28 'Eat, Sleep, Buy, Die' by Jonathan Rowe, *The New Internationalist* November 2000 www.newint.org. Reproduced by permission; p48 'Fateful Attraction' by Jenny Tucker, *Elle* January 2002. Reproduced by permission; p57 'Harry faces Eton drug test' by Charles Rae and Jammi Pyatt © News International Newspapers Limited, *The Sun* 14 January 2002. Reproduced by permission; p58 'Prince Harry sent to rehab over drink and drugs' by Claire Hill, *The Independent* 13 January 2002. Reproduced by permission; p64 Extract from *Letters to Daniel* by Fergal Keane. Reproduced by permission; p76 'Walt Disney: The man behind the mouse' by Melissa Burdick-Harmon, *Biography Magazine* February 2002; p82 Extract from *Letters of the Younger Pliny* translated by Betty Radice (Penguin Classics, 1963) © Betty Radice 1963. Reproduced by permission; p83 'The First Radio Signal Across the Atlantic, 12 December 1901' by Guglielmo Marconi, in *Scrapbook 1900-1914* by Leslie Bailey; p84 'The First Channel Flight, 25 July 1909' by Louis Bleriot, in *Scrapbook 1900-1914* by Leslie Bailey; p85 *First on the Moon: A Voyage with Neil Armstrong, Michael Collins, Edwin E. Aldrin Jr.* written with Gene Farmer and Dora Jane Hamblin; p92 'Worshipping the body at the altar of sport' by Martin Jacques © Martin Jacques, *The Observer* 13 July 1997. Reproduced by permission of Guardian Newspapers Limited; p110 from *Pip Pip* by Jay Griffiths. Reprinted by permission of HarperCollins Publishers Ltd. © Jay Griffiths; p116 'Stop being coy' by Bryan Heath from *The Sunday Times* 29 June 1980. Reproduced by permission of Times Newspapers Ltd.

*Sources*: p9 Statue of Liberty National Monument/Ellis Island Immigration Museum Brochure

*Tapescript*: p87 'The Christmas Truce, 1914 – Oh what a lovely war! Interview'. Reproduced by permission of Richard Carrington; The following are reproduced by permission of BBC Worldwide Ltd: p44 Interview with Liza Minelli; p53 Interview with Olive Hodges; p64 *Letter to a newborn son* by Fergal Keane; p114 'The Miracle Men'

*Illustrations by*: Jamel Akib p105; Mark Duffin p121; Rose Hardy p35; Darren Hopes p95; Mike Moran p53; Oxford Designers and Illustrators p64; Ali Pellatt p43; Geoff Waterhouse/Just for Laffs pp36, 62, 80, 86, 90, 98

*Commissioned photography by*: Gareth Boden: pp33, 46, 79 (hotel room), 112; MM Studios pp17–18 (book covers), 25, 37 (camera, champagne, sunglasses, OK Magazines), 56, 57, 58

*We would also like to thank the following for permission to reproduce*: p71 (*in order from l to r*): Georges Seurat, French 1859–1891, *A Sunday on La Grande Jatte*, 1884, 1884-86, oil on canvas, 207.6 x 308 cm. The Art Institute of Chicago, Helen Bartlett Memorial Collection, 1926.224; *The Afghan Girl*, photographed in 1985 © Steve McCurry/Magnum Photos; *TGV Avignon Station*, 2001. Architects J.M.Duthilleul, F.Bonnefille and E. Tricaud. Photo Rafal Tomasik, The European Railway Picture Gallery: http://tgv.kielce.tpnet.pl; *Casablanca*, 1942. Humphrey Bogart and Ingrid Bergman. Director Michael Curtiz. Warner Bros Casablanca. Photo: The Kobal Collection; Henry Moore, *Draped Reclining Mother and Baby*, 1983 (LH822) The Henry Moore Foundation, bronze , length 265.5 cm. Reproduced by permission of the Henry Moore Foundation; Tracey Emin *My Bed*, 1998, mattress, linens, pillows, rope, various memorabilia 31 x 83 x 92 in ( 79 x 211 x 234 cm) Courtesy of Jay Jopling/ White Cube, London © the artist. Photo courtesy of The Saatchi Gallery, London/Photo: Stephen White

*Photographs*: Action Plus p91 (G.Kirk/horse racing & javelin); AKG London p109 (Musées Royaux des Beaux-Arts, Brussels: Pieter Bruegel, *Landscape with the Fall of Icarus*, (1525/30–1569) 74 x 112 cm); Alamy pp28 (Stock Connection Inc/container port), 29 (D.Hoffman Photo Library/landfill site), 63 (Popperfoto/Confucius); Bryan and Cherry Alexander pp100 (Greenland), 101 (woman and child, harbour & plane); By kind permission of Apple Computer, Inc p27; Axiom Photographic Agency p15 (C.Caldicott/Indian women), (D.Constantine/South American men at bar), (H.Kutomi/Japanese woman), (C.Parker/ British on beach); BBC Photographic Archives p64 (M.Robinson); By kind permission of BMW Group p16 (Mini Cooper); Manuel Bauer/www.lookat.ch pp100, 102; By kind permission of The Body Shop p27 & 34 (© Copyright: The Body Shop International PLC); © Bill Bryson by arrangement with Transworld Publishers p17 (*The Lost Continent: Travels in Small-town America*, Black Swan, 1999); Camera Press pp7 (R.Gillard/Prince Philip), 18 (Jane Brown/Iris Murdoch portrait), 20 (N. Rangoy), 77 (older Disney), 96 (N.Norrington/ballet performance); Cartoon Bank, The New Yorker cartoons pp12 (© 2003 Frank Cotham from cartoonbank.com. All rights reserved), 41 (Leo Cullum), 66 (Mike Twohy), 116 (Aaron Bacall), 116 (Bernard Shoenbaum); Cartoon Stock pp13b (Fran), 30 (Harley Schwadron), 33 (Arnaldo Almeida), 60 (John Morris), 88 (Mike Baldwin), 89 (Alan De la Nougerede), 94 (Kes), 97 (Carroll Zahn), 115 (Stan Waling); Collections pp106-107 (bridge); Donald Cooper/Photostage p23; Corbis pp7 (© Archivo Iconigrafico, S.A./Van Gogh), (Bettmann/Karl Marx), (L.Goldsmith/Bob Marley), 9 (Bettmann/Ellis Island 1917), (Bettmann/procession of immigrants & medical examination), 10 (German boy), 22 (Bettmann/both), 37 (L.Vincent/Corbis Sygma/Oscar), 40 (J.Blair/Robert Redford), (Reents/Siemoneit/ Sygma/Leonardo di Caprio), 63 (Gianni Dagli Orti/Socrates), (C.Bland/Eye Ubiquitous/Buddha), (F.G.Mayer/Washington), (Bettmann/ Parker), (Bettmann/Luther King), (Bettmann/ Austen), 74 (J.Cornfield/hand), 77 (Bettmann/with wife and Mickey Mouse), 81 (K.Su/Great Wall of China), (Gianni Dagli Orti/Mona Lisa), (C.Collins/World Trade Centre attack), 82 (Bettmann/Pompeii figures); 83 (Schenectady Museum; Hall of Electrical History Foundation/Marconi), 84 (Hulton-Deutsch Collection/Bleriot), (sea), (Bettmann/ Titanic), 85 (NASA/Neil Armstrong/man on the moon), 87 (Bettmann/trenches), 96 (M.Carraro/Darcy Bussell), 103 (D. G. Houser/women), (M. S. Lewis/child in doorway), (B.Brecelj/man and cloves), 113 (Bettmann/at easel & with Gala), (J.Bryson/Sygma/Dali staring eyes); Corbis Royalty-free p83 (sea); Courtesy of Daimler Chrysler UK Ltd p16 (Chrysler PT Street Cruiser); By kind permission of Daimler Chrysler for Mercedes-Benz p27; Joe Downing p72 (as a young man), 72-73 (Gallas/Le Thor/ Downing in his studio), 73 (left) (Joe Downing painting, 1997, oil on canvas, 162 x 130 cms , Private Collection Photo Andre Morain), 73 (right) Joe Downing painting, 1992, oil on canvas, 162 x 130 cms, Private Collection; Getty Images/The Bridgeman Art Library p82 (Italian School, Vesuvius); Getty Images/Photographer's Choice p30 (T.Russell/newspaper presses), (J.Hunter/scuba); Getty Images/Rubberball Productions p37 (bouncer); Getty Images/Sport pp38 (S.Barbour), 91 (B.Stickland/wrestling), (C.Brunskill/canoeing), (R.Kinnaird/rugby), 92–3 (M.Tama/runners), (J.Herbert/big screen), 96 (G.M.Prior/Steve Redgrave), (R.Kinnaird/rowing); Getty Images/Stone pp29 (H.Kingsnorth/girl in supermarket), 39 (J.Lamb), (S.Murphy/elderly couple), 51 (R.Elliott), 54 (S.McClymont), 74 (R.H.Wetmore II/storm), 79 (D.H.Endersbee), 91 (J.Lamb/yoga ), 108 (J.McBride); Getty Images/Taxi pp13 (S.Sullivan/ snowboarding), 29 (I.Mckinnell/crowded supermarket), 31 (D.Sacks/John), 47 (Microzoa/cat), (S.Joester/ woman & mirror), (Colorstock/hands & rosary), (J.Copeau/couple touching noses), (G.Ceo/woman on phone), 74 (J.Wilkes/water), (C.Franklin/crossroads), 110 (G.Buss/all seasons); Getty Images/The Image Bank pp8 (A.Caulfield), 31 (J.Lamb/David), 36 (R.Lockyer), 47 (P.Molnar/father & toddler), (Yellow Dog Productions/fans), 67 (A.Edwards), 91 (R.McVay/rockclimbing), 130 (C.Lucas Abreu); Getty Images/PhotoDisc pp25, 37 (woman), 37 (dollars & jewels), 47 (two girls & wedding), 104, 119, 120, 125, 129; Getty Images /Thinkstock p37 (limousine); Reprinted by permission of HarperCollins Publishers Ltd ©J.R.R.Tolkein 2003 p17 (J.R.R.Tolkein, *The Lord of the Rings, Part I, The Fellowship of the Ring*, 2002); Chris Heads p49 (from Elle Magazine, January 2002); Courtesy of Professor John Hodges p53 Olive and Fred Hodges February 2002, aged 102 years, married 77 years and Olive Hodges in 1919 aged 20; Hulton Archive p7 (APA/Archive Photos/Al Capone), 11 (Museum of the City of New York/Jacob A. Riis/Archive Photos/Polish baby), 81 (Hiroshima), (American War of Independence), 81 (E.Levick/Archive Photos/plane), 114 (painting of pilgrims at shrine), (St Bernadette); The Imperial War Museum, London p87 (ref Q70075: British and German soldiers together on Christmas Day 1914); Katz p61 (Gamma Presse Images); The Kobal Collection p24 (Duck Soup, 1933. Director Leo McCarey, Paramount Collection), 76, 77 (Disney with drawings), 127 (*Road to Perdition*, 2002. Tom Hanks and Tyler Hoechlin. Director Sam Mendes. 20th Century Fox/ Dreamworks/Francois Duhamel); Ken Lennox p14; Macmillan Children's Books p69 (Lewis Carroll *Alice's Adventures in Wonderland* images created by Sir John Tenniel and coloured by Diz Wallis); Magnum Photos p68 (Cornell Capa photograph of Grandma Moses, c. 1960); Mary Evans Picture Library p81 (Darwin); By kind permission of McDonald's Restaurants Ltd p27; National Pictures p57; New York Public Library p10 (Art Resource, NY/Russian girl – ID 801540); Peter Nicholls/NI Syndication 19; By kind permission of Nike p27; PA Photos pp7 (D.Giles/Martina Navratilova), (ABACA Press/Nicole Kidman), 34 (J.Green), 40 (Y. Mok/Jade Jagger), (ABACA Press/Cher), 42 (Deutsche Presse-Agentur), 57 (A.Parsons), 61 (EPA); Reproduced by permission of Penguin Books Ltd p18 (Iris Murdoch *Jackson's Dilemma*, Michael Joseph, 1996); Powerstock p15 (Atlantide S.N.C./four men with arms over shoulders), (Y. Levy/African men playing game), 91 (EPA/skateboarding); By kind permission of Qantas Airways p27 (further information can be found at www.qantas.com.au); Reprinted by permission of The Random House Group Ltd p17 (John Grisham, *A Time to Kill*, Arrow, 1992), (Elizabeth Young, *Fair Game*, Arrow, 2001), (Laurie Lee, *Cider with Rosie*, Vintage Classics, 2002), 18 (Iris Murdoch, *Under the Net*, Vintage Classics, 2202; *The Sea, The Sea*, Vintage Classics, 1999); Retna p40 (Larry Laszlo/Mena Suvari); Rex Features p37 (jewelled shoe), 40, 75, 81 (Berlin Wall), 14 (St Bernadette's grotto & sick pilgrims), 7 (Mother Teresa), 44 (T.O'Neill/Liza Minnelli with Judy Garland), (Snap/Liza Minnelli Cabaret Poster), (Sipa Press/Liza Minnelli with David Gest), 45 (A.Krusberg/Liza Minnelli in performance with Ray Charles); David Robinson p102 (aerial); Scala p81 (Olympic Games); Scala p113 Salvador Dalí, *The Persistence of Memory*, 1931. Oil on canvas, 9 1/2 x 13" (24.1 x 33 cm). The Museum of Modern Art, New York. Given anonymously. © Salvador Dali, Gala-Salvador Dali Foundation, DACS, London 2003; Science Photo Library p85 (John Sandford/lunar surface), p95 (Mehau Kulyk/body photomontage); "Shell" emblem reproduced with the permission of Shell International Petroleum Company Limited (Shell Property only)/"The trademarks used in these materials are reproduced with the permission of the trademark owners." p27; Liz & John Soars p85 (Justin); Stanley Gibbons Ltd p102 (stamps); Still Pictures p28 (R.Giling/shoe factory); Courtesy of Sunderland Echo pp106 (docks); By kind permission of Toyota (GB) PLC p27; Chris Tubbs p50 (from Elle Magazine, January 2002); Vin Mag Archive p37 (OK Magazines); By kind permission of Vodaphone p27; Simon Winchester p105; Zefa p99 (G. Schuster), 100 (R.Wareham/Zanzibar)

Although every effort has been made to trace and contact copyright holders before publication, this has not been possible in some cases. We apologize for any apparent infringement of copyright and if notified, the publisher will be pleased to rectify any errors or omissions at the earliest opportunity

# 1 Our land is your land!

**STARTER**

**1** Why are these people famous? What do they have in common? Discuss with a partner, then with the class.

**1** Al Capone

**2** Mother Teresa

**3** Van Gogh

**4** Karl Marx

**5** Martina Navratilova

**6** Bob Marley

**7** Nicole Kidman

**8** Prince Philip

**2** Match each person with their country of birth and the country they died in or live in now.

Australia    **Czech Republic**    England    **France**    **Germany**    Greece

India    **Italy**    Jamaica    The Netherlands    The United States    **Macedonia**

**3** Do you know why any of these people emigrated?

**1** Look at the photograph. What things can you identify? What is their significance?

**2** Read the introduction to Ellis Island. Choose the numbers you think are correct. Then answer the questions.

1 Check the numbers with your teacher. Do any surprise you?

2 Which countries do you think the immigrants came from?

3 Why is Ellis Island a symbol of 'the American dream'?

**Ellis Island** is a symbol of America's immigrant heritage. For more than six decades – 1892 to 1954 – this island, about one mile south west of New York City, saw an estimated (1) 5 / 7 / 12 million immigrants pass through it. Today their descendants account for almost (2) 10% / 20% / 40% of the population of the United States. During peak periods as many as (3) 500 / 2,000 / 5,000 people each day would be checked, and questioned. Ellis Island, like its neighbour the Statue of Liberty, is a symbol of the American dream of freedom and opportunity.

**3** Read an extract from the British writer and journalist H.G. Wells. Use a dictionary if necessary.

Answer the questions.

1 Why does Wells call Ellis Island 'this filter of immigrant humanity'?
2 What words and images does Wells use to illustrate the huge numbers of people?
3 What do you learn about the way the people were processed?
4 How would you answer Wells' final question? What has it all amounted to?

*Medical Examination, Ellis Island 1910*

# TALES FROM ELLIS ISLAND

I VISITED ELLIS ISLAND YESTERDAY. It chanced to be a good day for my purpose. For the first time in its history this filter of immigrant humanity has this week proved inadequate to the demand upon it. It was choked with twenty thousand or so from Ireland, and Poland, and Italy, and Syria, and Finland, and Albania. Men, women, children, dirt, and bags together. All day long, the long procession files, step by step, bearing bundles and trunks and boxes, past this examiner and that, past the quick, alert medical officers, and the clerks. It is a daily procession that would stretch over three miles, that in any week in the year could put a cordon of close-marching people round London or New York, that could populate a new Boston. **What in a century will it all amount to?**

**H.G. Wells 1907**

*Ellis Island 1917*

**4** Read about some individual immigrants. Work in three groups.

**Group A** Read about the Russian girl on p10.
**Group B** Read about the German boy on p10.
**Group C** Read about the Polish baby on p11.

Answer the questions.

1 Who is telling the story?
2 What is the problem?
3 What is the role of the commissioners? How do they treat the immigrants?
4 What do you learn about the families and background of the immigrants?
5 Is there a happy ending?

**5** Find partners from the other two groups. Compare the three stories, using your answers to exercise 4.

# RUSSIAN GIRL
## AGE 20

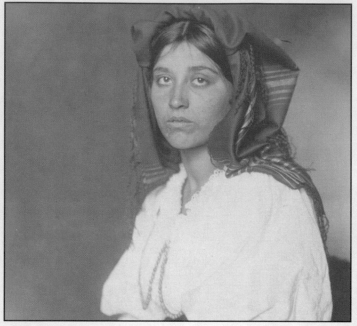

A HANDSOME, CLEAR-EYED RUSSIAN GIRL of about twenty-years, the daughter of a farmer comes in and sits down before us. She is clean and intelligent looking. She nervously clasps and unclasps her hands and the tears are welling in her eyes.

'That girl,' says one commissioner, 'is an interesting and puzzling case. Her father is a farmer in moderate circumstances. A young man with whom she grew up, the son of a neighbor, came here two years ago, and last year wrote to her father that the girl could come over and he would marry her. So she came, alone. But the prospective bridegroom didn't show up. I wrote to him – he lives somewhere in New Jersey – and last week he appeared and looked her over. Finally he said he'd changed his mind. He wasn't sure whether he wanted to marry her or not. Naturally her pride was somewhat wounded. She says she doesn't want to go back to be laughed at by her family, and I can't let her land. So everything is at a standstill. She could work, look at her strong arms! A nice girl, too. Well, I don't know what to do. You don't know any lady who wants a servant, do you? No? Well, I just don't know what to do with her.'

He turns again to the girl.

'Are you willing to marry Peter if he comes again?'

The girl nods and says, 'I am', the tears brimming over.

'Well, I'll write to the fellow again and tell him he's a fool. He'll never have such a chance again.'

**William Williams Papers, Ellis Island Commissioner, March 1910**

# GERMAN BOY
## AGE 13

THEY ALSO QUESTIONED PEOPLE ON literacy. My uncle called me aside.

He said, 'Your mother doesn't know how to read.' I said, 'That's all right.'

For the reading you faced what they called the commissioners – like judges on a bench. I was surrounded by my aunt and uncle and this other uncle who's a pharmacist – my mother was in the center. They said she would have to take a test of reading.

So one uncle said, 'She can't speak English.'

A commissioner said, 'We know that. We will give her a siddur.'

You know what a siddur is? It's a Jewish book. The night they said this, I knew that she couldn't do that and we would be in trouble. Well, they opened up a siddur. There was a certain passage there they had you read. I looked at it and I saw right away what it was. I quickly studied it – I knew the whole paragraph. Then I got underneath the two of them there – I was very small – and I told her the words in Yiddish very softly. I had memorized the lines and I said them quietly and she said them louder so the commissioner could hear it. And that served the purpose. She looked at it and it sounded as if she was reading it, but I was doing the talking underneath.

ARRIVING AT ELLIS ISLAND

**Arnold Weiss, 1921**

# POLISH BABY

## AGE 0

THE POLISH WIFE OF A Pennsylvania coal miner, both admitted a year before, had gone back suddenly to Poland to visit her old father, who had taken sick and might soon die. The visit over, she returned to America. She would be admitted at once, for little visits do not count against quotas. Her husband was at Ellis Island, waiting for her. We told him everything would be all right, but he still looked extremely nervous. Then the ship came in, the *Lapland* of the Red Star line, from Antwerp, and we found out why he was so nervous. On the day before the ship made port, out on the high seas, a baby had been born to the returning mother. Mother and child were both doing well in the Ellis Island hospital, everyone was delighted, until the inspector admitted the mother, but excluded the baby.

'Why?' asked the father, trembling.

'Polish quota exhausted,' pronounced the helpless inspector.

They brought the case to me. Deport the baby? I couldn't. But somebody had to act quickly, for the mother was not doing well under the idea that her baby would soon be taken from her.

'The baby was not born in Poland,' I ruled, 'but on a British ship. She is chargeable to the British quota. The deck of a British ship is British soil.'

'British quota was exhausted yesterday,' replied the inspector. That was a blow. But I had another shot.

'Come to think of it,' I remarked, 'the *Lapland* hails from Antwerp. That's in Belgium.

The baby is Belgian. Use the Belgian quota.'

'Belgian quota ran out a week ago,' said the inspector. I was stumped.

'Oh, look here,' I began again. 'I've got it! It is clear to me that the mother was hurrying back, so the baby would be born here and be a native-born American citizen. No immigrant business at all. This baby had the intention to be born in America, only the ship was a day late and that upset everything. And – under the law – the baby, by intention, was born in America. It is an American baby – no baby Pole at all, no British, no Belgian – just a good American baby. That's the way I rule!'

**Henry Curran, Ellis Island Commissioner, 1922–26**

## Vocabulary work

**6** Find the words or phrases in your text which have similar meanings to these phrases. Explain them to your partners from the other groups.

**Text A**
1  plays nervously with her hands
2  her eyes are filling with tears
3  her pride was hurt
4  no progress can be made
5  she finally starts to cry

**Text B**
1  took me away from the group
2  stood opposite
3  particular
4  learnt … by heart
5  worked well

**Text C**
1  shaking slightly
2  that was a big disappointment
3  I made another attempt
4  comes from
5  I was not able to think of any answer at all

## What do you think?

- Read and comment on these quotes.

  1  *'No country has received a more diverse variety of immigrants than the United States.'*

  Do you think this is true? What other countries have received great numbers of immigrants? From where?

  2  *'Each successive group of arrivals, however, is viewed as less desirable than their predecessors.'*

  How do people generally react to immigrants? Why do you think they react like this?

- What's the difference between …?

  a refugee   an illegal immigrant

  **an asylum seeker**   an immigrant

  Are any of these groups in the news at the moment?

- Do you have many immigrants in your country? Which countries do they come from?
  Do you know of any that have become famous and/or successful?

- What causes people to emigrate? Is there any country you would like to emigrate to? Why?

# LANGUAGE FOCUS
## Avoiding repetition

There are several ways to avoid repeating words or phrases.

**1 Missing words out**
*The girl nods and says 'I am . . .'* ( = I am willing to marry Peter.)

What words have been omitted in these sentences?
*She told me to tidy up, but I already had.*
*Frank won the match. I didn't think he would.*
*A present for me? How kind. You shouldn't have.*

**2 Reduced infinitives**
Just *to* can be used instead of the whole infinitive when the meaning is clear from the context. Which words are omitted after *to* at the end of these sentences?
*'Your mother doesn't know how to read.' I said, 'That's right. She never learnt to.'*

*They said she had to take a test for reading. So one uncle said, 'Does she have to?'*

**3 Synonyms in context**
*bags . . . bundles . . . trunks . . . boxes*
*told her softly . . . said quietly*

Think of another word for these words.

| huge | rich | kill | injure | argument |

▶▶ **Grammar Reference p147**

## Missing words out

1 Complete the sentences with an auxiliary verb or a modal verb. Make the verb form negative where necessary.

1 I tried to repair my car, but I __couldn't__ . I didn't have the right tools.

2 'You look awful. Why don't you see a doctor?'
'I _____ . He just gave me some pills and told me to take things easy.'

3 'It's a long journey. Take care on the motorway.'
'Don't worry. We _____.'

4 I met your sister last night. She thought we'd met before, but we _____ .

5 'Have you read this report?'
'No, I _____ , but I _____.'

6 The weather forecast said that it might rain this afternoon. If it _____ , we'll have to call off the tennis.

7 My car's being mended at the moment. If it _____ , I'd give you a lift. Sorry.

8 I'm so glad you told Sue exactly what you thought of her, because if you _____ , I certainly _____ !

9 I got that job I applied for, so I was delighted. I really didn't think I _____ .

10 'Come on, John! It's time you were getting up!'
'I _____ ! I'll be down in a second.'

11 'I think I'll give Bob a ring.'
'You _____ . You haven't been in touch with him for ages.'

12 I went to a party last night, but I wish I _____ . It was awful.

13 My boyfriend insists on doing all the cooking, but I wish he _____ – it's inedible!

14 'Aren't you going to Portugal for your holidays?'
'Well, we _____ , but we're still not sure.'

15 'Andy got drunk at Anne's party and started insulting everyone.'
'He _____ ! That's so typical. He's always doing that.'

**T 1.1** Listen and check. Practise with a partner.

I DO!

GOOD ANSWER!

**2** Ask questions and try and find things that you have in common with other students in the class.

*Have you tried snowboarding?*

*Do you like …?*

*Who are your favourite …?*

*Have you ever …?*

*Where do you usually go …?*

*Did you go to the … exhibition?*

**3** Tell the class what you found out, using some of these expressions.

| Things in common | Things different |
| --- | --- |
| Juan's been to Russia, and **so have I**. | He's tried snowboarding, **but I haven't**. |
| He likes jazz, and **I do, too**. | He comes from a big family, **but I don't**. |
| He doesn't smoke, and **neither do I**. | He didn't see the film, **but I did**. |
| He isn't married, and **nor am I**. | He hasn't been to Paris. **I have, though**. |
| He can't drive, and **I can't, either**. | |

## Reduced infinitives

**4** Write the responses, using the verb in brackets and a reduced infinitive.

1 **A** Can you come round for a meal tonight?
  **B** <u>Thanks very much. I'd love to.</u> (love)

2 **A** Did you post my letter?
  **B** _____ (forget)

3 **A** I can't take you to the airport after all. Sorry.
  **B** _____ (agree)

4 **A** Was John surprised when he won?
  **B** _____ (not expect)

5 **A** Why did you slam the door in my face?
  **B** _____ (not mean)

6 **A** You'll be able to enjoy yourself when the exams finish.
  **B** _____ (intend)

**T 1.2** Listen and compare your answers.

## Synonyms in context

**5** Complete the sentences with a synonym of the word in *italics*. Change the word class where necessary, as in the first example.

1 I don't *trust* this government. I have no <u>faith</u> in them whatsoever.

2 She is not only a *skilled* painter, she is also a(n) _____ piano player.

3 You've managed to *persuade* me. Your argument is most _____.

4 Advertisements are not allowed to *lie*, but they _____ us in subtle ways.

5 Chess is a game of *tactics*. You have to plan your _____ well in advance.

6 The doctor read my notes *carefully*, then gave me a(n) _____ examination.

7 He has an *annoying* habit of always being late. It really _____ me.

8 It's *very important* that you don't tell anyone. In fact, it's _____.

9 Skiing can be *dangerous*, but I like to take a few _____.

10 She wasn't *scared* at all by the dog, but I was _____.

**6** Find synonyms, or near synonyms, for these words. Write sentences to illustrate their differences in meaning.

- enemy
- friend
- love
- hate
- talk
- laugh

**An enemy is who you're fighting against in a war.**
**A business wants to do better than its competitors.**
**We are rivals in love, but opponents in games.**

*'Sometimes, from time to time, now and again, occasionally, at times I wish I'd never been given this Thesaurus.'*

## LISTENING AND SPEAKING
### Two brothers from Kenya

**1** Read the newspaper extract. Who are the people? Why was there a newspaper story about them?

# From £5 to £250,000,000!

**The inspiring tale of two Asian brothers who fled to Britain from East Africa and made a fortune**

In 1967, at the age of 16, Vijay Patel and his brother Bhikhu fled to Britain from the village of Eldoret in Kenya. They arrived with £5 between them. They now own a pharmaceutical company which employs more than 600 people and is worth £250 million! This is the story of how they made their fortunes.

The Patel brothers receiving their 'Entrepreneur of the Year' awards

**2** Read the questions from the first part of an interview with Vijay and Bhikhu. What do you think their answers might be?

1 What was life like in Eldoret?
2 Did you come to England together?
3 What was it that made you come to England?
4 What were the steps from that point to actually starting your business?
5 Did you qualify as an architect?
6 There is a tradition among the Patels, certainly in East Africa, of business, isn't there?
7 Was your father a businessman?

**3** **T 1.3** Read and listen to part one of the interview on p132. Compare the brothers' answers with your ideas in exercise 2.

**4** **T 1.4** Listen only to part two. Are these statements true or false? Correct the false ones.

1 They both began their careers with corner shops.
2 Bhikhu wanted to give up his work as an architect.
3 Vijay didn't start his pharmacy business until Bhikhu joined him.
4 The two brothers working together in the same business often causes problems.
5 Their different strengths and weaknesses complement each other.
6 They are grateful to their mother for the sacrifices she made.
7 She worked 24 hours a day, seven days a week for thirteen years.
8 Both brothers have experienced racial discrimination.

**5** **T 1.5** Listen to part three. Complete the sentences with the exact words used.

1 We _____ for six hundred people directly.
2 We're not the sort of _____ or _____ people in any sense.
3 I mean, clearly, in terms of _____ in _____, one tends to sort of _____ oneself a little bit but not _____, I hope.
4 I would rather do some _____ work rather than _____ .
5 Chase your _____ and go for it, and that's _____ what I have done.

### What do you think?

- Which factors in Vijay and Bhikhu's lives do you feel have led to their success?
- Do you agree with the advice they give to young people? In what ways are they good role models?
- Asians form a large part of Britain's immigrant population. Why is this?
- The brothers have lived in England for many years and yet they still have Asian accents. Why might this be?
- How does family background influence lives? How has your family influenced your life?

# VOCABULARY AND SPEAKING
## Describing nationalities

**1** Complete the chart. Use a dictionary if necessary. Add two more countries of your choice.

| Country | Adjective | Person | People | Language(s) |
|---|---|---|---|---|
| Britain | British | a Briton* | the British | English, Welsh, Gaelic |
| Scotland | | | | |
| France | | | | |
| Belgium | | | | |
| The Netherlands/ Holland | | | | |
| Denmark | | | | |
| Sweden | | | | |
| Poland | | | | |
| Turkey | | | | |
| Spain | | | | |
| Switzerland | | | | |
| Argentina | | | | |
| Peru | | | | |
| Iceland | | | | |
| New Zealand | | | | |
| Afghanistan | | | | |
| | | | | |
| | | | | |

*Rather old-fashioned now. Used mainly to refer to *ancient Britons*.

**2** **T 1.6** Listen to six people of different nationality speaking English and try to identify where they come from. What do they say about their country and/or nationality?

**3** Work in small groups. Choose a few nationalities that you know. First describe them in stereotypical fashion, then discuss how much your experience of them fits the stereotype.

> *The British have a reputation for being cold and reserved, and they're always talking about the weather because it's so awful.*

> *Actually most of my English friends are very outgoing, they ...*

> *English food is considered to be dreadful – completely tasteless.*

> *Well, what I found when I was in England was ... ... and the weather was ...*

**4** What is your nationality stereotype? Are you like that?

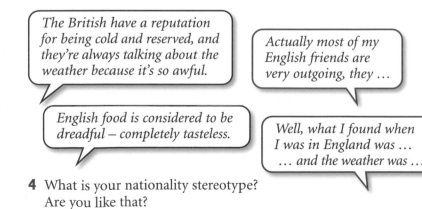

# THE LAST WORD
## British and American English

**1** `T 1.7` Read and listen to the conversations with a partner. Which is British English? Which is American English? What are the differences?

1   A   Where do you live?
      B   We've got a small flat. It's on the ground floor of a block of flats in the centre of town.
      A   Have you got a garden?
      B   No, we haven't, just a car park at the back.

2   A   Where do you live?
      B   We have a small apartment. It's on the first floor of an apartment building downtown.
      A   Do you have a yard?
      B   No we don't, just a parking lot in the back.

**2** `T 1.8` Read and listen to these conversations in American English. Try to convert them into British English.

1   A   Do you have the time?
      B   Yeah, it's five of four.
      A   Did you say five after?
      B   No, five *of* four.

2   A   What are you gonna do on the weekend?
      B   The usual stuff. Play soccer with the kids, and sweep the yard.

3   A   Did you enjoy the game?
      B   Yeah, it was great, but we had to stand in line for half an hour to get tickets.

4   A   Did you have a good vacation?
      B   Yeah, real good.
      A   How long were you away?
      B   Five days in all. Monday thru Friday.

5   A   Can you mail this letter and package for me?
      B   Sure thing.
      A   And can you stop by the liquor store and buy a six-pack of Michelob and some potato chips?
      B   Is that all?

6   A   Did you see *The Birds* on cable last night?
      B   Sure, even though I've seen it two times before.
      A   My third time. Isn't it just an awesome movie?
      B   Sure is. One of my favorites.

7   A   Did they bring the check yet?
      B   Yeah. They just did. But I can't read a thing. It's lighted so badly in here.

8   A   Do we need to stop for gas?
      B   Yeah, why not? I need to use the restroom anyway.

**3** `T 1.9` Listen and compare your ideas.

**4** What is the British English for these words? Use a dictionary if necessary.

| | | | | | |
|---|---|---|---|---|---|
| cellphone | bathrobe | drugstore | truck | fall (n) | windshield |
| garbage | cookie | closet | sidewalk | elevator | pants |

Do you know any more American English words or expressions?

▶▶ **Writing** Formal and informal letters **p117**

# 2 Never lost for words!

**Phrasal verbs · Tense review · Sounds and spelling**

**STARTER**

**1** Read the extracts. Match them with a cover and type of book. What helped you to identify them?

| a modern romance*     an autobiography     a fantasy     a classical drama     a thriller     a travel story |
|---|

*This is also known as 'Chick Lit.' = literature for 'chicks'/modern young women.*

**1**   Nothing prepares you for the Grand Canyon. No matter how many times you read about it or see it pictured, it still takes your breath away. Your mind, unable to deal with anything on this scale, just shuts down.

**2**   To be, or not to be – that is the question. Whether 'tis nobler in the mind to suffer the slings and arrows of outrageous fortune, or to take arms against a sea of troubles …

**3**   I never set out to pinch anyone's bloke, let alone Nina's. The day it all started, picking up a bloke was the last thing on my mind. Even I don't go out on the pull in manky old combats and a sweater that's seen better days.

**4**   The group stood silently, mesmerized by the two bodies, which, though dead, continued to spew blood. The thick smell of gunfire hung over the stairway.

**5**   As for Bilbo Baggins, even while he was making his speech, he had been fingering the golden ring in his pocket: his magic ring that he had kept secret for so many years. As he stepped down he slipped it on his finger, and he was never seen by any hobbit in Hobbiton again.

**6**   The last days of my childhood were also the last days of the village. I belonged to that generation which saw the end of a thousand years' life.

**2** What are your favourite types of book? Which books have you read recently? Why? Tell your partner about one of them.

**3** Have you read any books in English? Discuss them, and reasons for reading in English, with the class.

# READING AND SPEAKING
## Losing her words

1 Work with a partner. Ask and answer questions to complete the biodata of novelist Iris Murdoch.

Student A    Look at this page.
**Student B**    Look at the copy from your teacher.

*Where was she born?*

*Dublin.*

## MURDOCH, Iris Jean
### 1919–1999

She was born in (1)___Dublin___ , the only child of Anglo-Irish parents. She read (2) classics at Oxford University, then worked for four years in (3)_____. She returned to Oxford to teach philosophy. Her first novel *Under the Net*, published in (4) 1954 , was an immediate success. Other titles include *The Sandcastle*, *The Bell*, and *The Sea, The Sea*, for which she was awarded (5)_____. She said that in her novels she tried to convey (6) 'the unique strangeness of human beings' .

In 1956 she married John Bayley, a professor of (7)_____ at Oxford. They had a (8) long, happy, if unusual marriage, but no children.

Iris was still writing in her late 70s. Her 26th and last novel, *Jackson's Dilemma*, published in 1995, was written whilst she was suffering from the beginnings of (9)_____. She died in 1999.

The Oscar-winning film, *Iris* (2002), starring (10) Judi Dench and Kate Winslet , tells the story of her love affair with John Bayley and her tragic struggle with the disease.

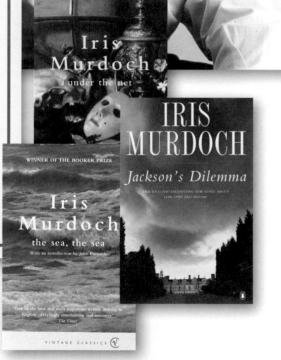

2 Read these three headings from an article about Iris Murdoch.

- Wild piles of books and papers
- Utterly at ease with each other
- Just a bit of writer's block?

What ideas do you get about Iris's house and its occupants? What is 'writer's block'?

3 Read part one of the article and answer the questions.

1 How is Joanna greeted when she arrives?

2 What impression do you get of John and Iris's house? Choose three key words from the text to describe it.

3 What are your first impressions of John and Iris? Likeable or unlikeable? Why?

4 What images do the words in *italics* convey? Use your dictionaries.
  a  … the *cheery face* of Professor John Bayley appears at the window, *chewing baked beans* …
  b  … *heaving* carrier bags, *spilling* their paper *guts* across the floor …
  c  … Iris Murdoch *spirals gracefully* into the room …
  d  … an *abandoned* glass of red wine *tucked away* under each armchair …

4 Read part two and answer the questions.
  1 Why has Joanna requested the interview with Iris?
  2 Why is Joanna worried?
  3 Both John and Iris try to explain her difficulty with writing.
     How do their explanations differ? Who is the most optimistic?
  4 How did Iris approach her writing in the past?
  5 In what ways does she show that she feels confused?

5 Read part three on p20.

# A VISIT TO IRIS MURDOCH

BY JOANNA COLES

The journalist Joanna Coles interviewed Iris Murdoch at her home in Oxfordshire shortly before the novelist was diagnosed as suffering from Alzheimer's Disease.

## PART ONE

### Wild piles of books and papers

'Bell not working. WE ARE HERE. Knock vigorously.' I do, and the cheery face of Professor John Bayley appears at the window, chewing baked beans. 'Come in, come in my dears,' he exclaims, opening the front door and waving a piece of toast. 'I find beans just the thing for lunch, don't you?'

He whisks us through a chaotic hall, past a vast, unsteady pyramid of books and into the most eccentric drawing room I have ever seen. There are heaving carrier bags, spilling their paper guts across the floor, and wild piles of books and papers. The walls are Georgian Green and though it is midday, it's dark, the window impenetrable to the light because of the fig leaves outside.

As we sit down, Iris Murdoch spirals gracefully into the room, and I suddenly notice there's an abandoned glass of red wine tucked away under each armchair, as if perhaps in case of emergency.

## PART TWO

### Just a bit of writer's block?

'Hello', Iris smiles, her eyes wide and friendly, and although I have already explained on the telephone, I explain again that I'm here because there are rumours she has given up writing for good. It's not the easiest of questions to ask such an intelligent and prolific author, and I am worried she may think me rude for even trying. But can it be true?

To my huge relief she smiles. 'Well, I'm trying to do something, but it hasn't, well ...' and then she starts laughing.

'Just a bit of writer's block I think,' interrupts Bayley, cheerfully.

'Yes, it's not ... well ... I certainly am trying,' she replies.

Iris Murdoch is without question one of the finest writers of her generation, producing 26 novels. Her last book, *Jackson's Dilemma*, was published last autumn, but nothing has followed. Has she suffered from this kind of block before?

'I think this is a very bad one,' she says absently.

'It has occurred before darling,' says Bayley, leaning towards her reassuringly.

'Perhaps,' she says flatly.

And do you still enjoy writing when you can?

'Well, I enjoy it, when I've found a way out, as it were. But, er ... otherwise ...' and she smiles apologetically.

'Otherwise ... I'm in a very, very bad, quiet place.'

We are all quiet for a moment before Bayley says to her:

'In the past, because of your philosophical mind perhaps, you've worked the whole novel out in advance, in meticulous detail, haven't you darling?'

He heads off to the kitchen to make coffee.

'I feel gloomy,' says Iris. 'The books I've written in the past I've done quite quickly. But I'm afraid at the moment that I'm just falling, falling ... falling as it were. But I may get better. I expect something will turn up. I hope so.'

## PART THREE

## Utterly at ease with each other

Bayley returns with a jug of coffee. 'You must pour,' says Iris patting his arm. 'You must pour.'

'Pour? Oh, I thought you meant 'paw'!'

And he starts scrabbling in the air as if he's a cat, and we all laugh. Their relationship is not only touching, it's still fresh and young, making sense of what marriage is for. Despite Iris's current problems, they seem utterly at ease with each other.

I wonder if they've missed having children?

'Iris has never shown the slightest interest in being a mum,' says her husband. 'And I'm not sure, but you could say that the best women novelists didn't have children. Jane Austen, George Eliot … I mean the really top notch ones.'

As Iris poses obediently for photos, he beckons me over to the kitchen table, where there appear to be two of everything, two honey pots, two mustard pots, two jam pots, and seven jars of coffee.

'We've been to see doctors, you know, and they say the old brain is very crafty. It can come up against a block and for a bit things are a bit strange, but then it finds its way around things again.'

**6** Answer the questions on part three.

1 How does Iris and John's relationship 'make sense of what marriage is for'?

2 How does John explain the fact that they never had children? Does he feel bitter about it?

3 What is John's final note of optimism?

**7** Answer these questions on the whole article.

1 In what ways do the house and its occupants reflect each other?

2 What instances are there that show he is proud of his wife's talent?

3 In what ways does he show his love for his wife?

4 Which adjectives would you use for John and which for Iris? Which describe both?

| | | |
|---|---|---|
| unconventional | loveable | loving |
| childlike | supportive | bewildered |
| distracted | gentle | cheerful |
| encouraging | dispirited | considerate |

### Vocabulary work

**8** Match the words and definitions.

| | | | |
|---|---|---|---|
| 1 | to whisk sb (away) | a | clever in an indirect way |
| 2 | rumour (n) | b | to gesture to sb to come here |
| 3 | prolific (adj) | c | information that is possibly not true |
| 4 | gloomy (adj) | d | to take sb somewhere quickly |
| 5 | top notch (adj) | e | likely to fall |
| 6 | crafty (adj) | f | to use your hands like an animal |
| 7 | to beckon sb | g | very productive |
| 8 | unsteady (adj) | h | dark and sad |
| 9 | to scrabble | i | to feel about roughly with the fingers |
| 10 | to paw | j | high quality |

### What do you think?

- Iris always said that she was very lucky to have found John. Why might she have said this? Do you think he felt the same about meeting her?

- How would John Bayley's role in her life differ before and after the onset of her illness?

- Alzheimer's Disease is a tragedy in any family. Why was it a particular tragedy for Iris Murdoch?

# VOCABULARY
## Phrasal verbs

---

**1** A phrasal verb can have more than one meaning. Some meanings are literal, some are metaphorical. In which of these sentences is *take in* used literally? Is it separable or inseparable?

1 My sister is always taking in stray cats.
2 These trousers are too big. I need to take them in.
3 She was completely taken in by his lies.
4 She likes to take in a gallery or two when she's in London.
5 They had so much news that I couldn't take it all in.

**2** Complete the phrasal verbs from the article about Iris Murdoch on pp19–20.

1 There's a glass tucked _____ under each armchair.
2 There are rumours she has given _____ writing.
3 In the past you've _____ the novel out in advance.
4 He heads _____ to the kitchen to make coffee.
5 I may get better. I expect something will _____ _____ .
6 (The brain) can come _____ _____ a block.

▶▶ **Grammar Reference p147**

---

**1** Complete the four sentences, using each phrasal verb twice in a suitable form.

| give away | give up |
|---|---|

1 'Guess how old I am.' 'I _____ . You'll have to tell me.'
2 They _____ a free CD with next month's magazine.
3 He tried to disguise himself, but I knew it was him. His voice _____ him _____ .
4 He handed his gun to the police officer and _____ himself _____ .

| work out | work up |
|---|---|

5 I can't _____ how to start this machine.
6 She _____ herself _____ into a terrible state about the exam next week.
7 All this physical works makes you _____ an appetite.
8 I keep fit by _____ regularly at the gym.

| put down | put up |
|---|---|

9 Stay with us. We can easily _____ you _____ for the night.
10 Let me _____ that date _____ in my diary or I'll forget it.
11 The shop _____ just _____ all its prices. I'm not going back.
12 He has a way of always _____ me _____ , and I feel so foolish.

| get on with | get up to |
|---|---|

13 The kids are very quiet. I wonder what they _____ ?
14 What page _____ we _____ in the last lesson?
15 How _____ you _____ your husband's family?
16 How _____ you all _____ last night's homework?

| go down with | go in for |
|---|---|

17 I can't understand why people _____ a career in politics.
18 I keep sneezing. I think I _____ a cold.
19 Her last novel _____ badly _____ the critics.
20 Our family _____ big celebrations at Christmas.

**2** Compare the pairs of sentences. What effect does the particle have?

1 I wrote a letter.       I wrote down his address.
2 I saw her at the station.   I saw her off at the station.
3 You used my toothpaste.   You've used up all the toothpaste.

**3** Complete the sentences with a verb and a particle.

| get (x2) | make | wear |
|---|---|---|
| work | settle | hand |
| hold | lie | |
| go | keep | |

| through | away (x2) | on |
|---|---|---|
| into | up | back |
| around | over | off |
| in | | |

1 My daughter spends the whole day _____ in front of the telly.
2 _____ from me. I've got a cold.
3 You told the teacher I cheated! I'll _____ you _____ for that! Just wait!
4 My tooth started hurting as the effects of the painkiller _____ .
5 We're off! _____ tight!
6 _____ _____ your homework carefully before you _____ it _____ .
7 The students were very quiet, _____ on their computers.
8 My son's a total mystery to me. I can't _____ to him at all.
9 You didn't believe what he said, did you? He _____ the whole thing _____ .
10 Have you _____ your new flat yet?

**4** **T 2.1** Listen and respond to the lines of conversation, using a phrasal verb from this page.

> *Do you want a cigarette?*

> *No, thanks. I've given up.*

**T 2.2** Listen and compare your answers.

## LISTENING AND SPEAKING
### I have nothing to declare but my genius!

1 Read these quotes from Oscar Wilde, a well-known Anglo-Irish writer famous for his sayings. What impression do you form of Oscar from them?

' To love oneself is the beginning of a lifelong romance. '

' There is no such thing as an immoral book. Books are well written, or badly written. '

' There is only one thing in the world worse than being talked about, and that is not being talked about. '

' I never travel without my diary. One should always have something sensational to read on the train. '

' I can resist anything but temptation. '

2 Are these statements about Oscar Wilde true or false? Discuss with a partner.
  1 He was a famous 20th century writer.
  2 He wrote plays, poetry, and prose.
  3 His most successful plays were comedies.
  4 He never married.
  5 He was imprisoned because of his political beliefs.

3 Read the biodata of Oscar Wilde and check your answers.
  Which play is considered to be his masterpiece?
  What is the meaning of the words *earnest* and *Ernest*?
  What is their pronunciation?

# OSCAR WILDE
## 1854–1900

An Irish-born English poet, novelist, and playwright. His greatest success was in the theatre with his shrewd and sparkling comedies, such as *Lady Windermere's Fan* (1892) and *An Ideal Husband* (1895). *The Importance of Being Earnest* (1895) is considered to be his masterpiece. Based on the double meaning of the name Ernest, it is an attack on people who take themselves too seriously. Wilde married in 1884 and had two sons. However, in 1895 he was imprisoned for two years for homosexual practices. On his release in 1897 he went to live in France. He died in Paris in 1900.

**4** **T 2.3** Listen to a scene from *The Importance of Being Earnest*. Lady Bracknell is interviewing a young man, Jack Worthing. Answer the questions.

1 Why is Jack being interviewed?
2 What's his occupation? Where does his money come from? Does he earn it?
3 Who is Gwendolen?
4 What pleases Lady Bracknell about Jack? What displeases her?
5 What do you learn of Jack's family background?
6 Is his interview successful?
7 What advice does Lady Bracknell give him?
8 Which of these adjectives would you use to describe Lady Bracknell?

| | | | | |
|---|---|---|---|---|
| reserved | aristocratic | snobbish | overbearing | timid |
| witty | prejudiced | earnest | inarticulate | arrogant |
| courteous | haughty | patronizing | | |

**5** **T 2.3** Your teacher will give you the scene. Read and listen to it again. Then answer the questions.

1 Give some examples to justify the adjectives you chose to describe Lady Bracknell.
2 How did Jack get the surname 'Worthing'?
3 What do you learn about the lives of the English upper classes in the 19th century? What was important to them? What were their attitudes to marriage, work, and property?
4 How does Oscar Wilde make the scene funny? Give some examples.

## Vocabulary work

**6** Find words in the scene to replace the words in *italics*.

1 There are far too many *lazy* men.
2 I do not approve of anything that *interferes* with natural ignorance.
3 As far as I can *see, the people who hunt animals illegally* are the only people *who earn money from it.*
4 A girl with a simple, *innocent* nature, like Gwendolen could hardly be expected to *live* in the country.
5 The *deceased* Mr Thomas Cardew, an old gentleman *with* a very *kind and generous personality.*
6 *Where* did this Mr James, or Thomas, Cardew *find* this ordinary handbag?
7 The line is *not important.*
8 I *admit* I feel somewhat *confused* by what you have just told me.
9 To be born, or at any rate, *reared* in a handbag, seems to me to *show no respect* for the ordinary decencies of family life.
10 Our only daughter – a girl *raised* with the utmost care …

## What do you think?

• Discuss these questions with a partner.
  1 How do you think Jack came to be in the handbag? Write down as many ideas as you can think of.
  2 Do you think Jack ultimately discovers his origins and marries Gwendolen?

• Discuss your ideas with the class. Your teacher will give you the answers. Read and compare them. Whose ideas were closest?

• Work with a partner and act out the scene together. Remember, it's a comedy, so make it as funny as possible! Perform the scene in front of the class.

# LANGUAGE FOCUS
## Tense review

**1** Which tenses are used in these sentences? Write the verb forms in the correct place in the charts. Fill any gaps with examples of your own.

1 You*'re being* very quiet. *Have* you *been silenced* by Oscar's wit?
2 Jack *was found* in a handbag while the cloakroom *was being cleaned*.
3 It's the first time I*'ve seen* you in ages. What *have* you *been doing*?
4 As soon as we *have* any news, you*'ll be* the first to know.
5 This room *is being used* for a meeting at the moment.
6 I wish I*'d realized* that he*'d been lying* to me all along.
7 He *didn't recognize* his home town. It *had been rebuilt* after the war.
8 We*'ll have been living* here three years this November.

| ACTIVE | Simple | Continuous |
|---|---|---|
| Present | | are being |
| Past | | |
| Future | | |
| Present Perfect | | |
| Past Perfect | | |
| Future Perfect | | |

| PASSIVE | Simple | Continuous |
|---|---|---|
| Present | | |
| Past | | |
| Future | | |
| Present Perfect | have been silenced | |
| Past Perfect | | |
| Future Perfect | | |

▶▶ **Grammar Reference p148**

## Simple and continuous

**2** Where possible, change the verb forms in these sentences from simple to continuous or continuous to simple. What is the change in meaning? Why is the change sometimes not possible?

1 Everyone's very nice to me. I don't know why.
2 I'll see Luis later.
3 I've cut my finger. It's really hurting.
4 David always gives Pam expensive presents.
5 What do you do?
6 He fired a gun.
7 She was dying.
8 I've been checking my emails.
9 The train leaves in five minutes.
10 That room is used as a study.

## Perfect and non-perfect

**3** Compare the use of tenses in these pairs of sentences. What are the differences in meaning?

1 They've been married for thirty years.
  They were married for thirty years.
2 I come from Scotland.
  I've come from Scotland.
3 When I've talked to him, I'll tell you.
  When I talk to him, I'll tell him.
4 The arrangements will be finalized on Friday.
  The arrangements will have been finalized by Friday.
5 Did you ever meet my grandfather?
  Have you ever met my grandfather?
6 I wish I knew the way.
  I wish I'd known the way.

**4** This is what the comedian Groucho Marx said to his host at the end of a party:

*I've had a perfectly wonderful evening, but this wasn't it.*

The joke rests on two different uses of the Present Perfect. What are they?

## Active and passive

**5** Correct these sentences.

1 In the extract from *The Importance of Being Earnest*, Jack is interviewing Lady Bracknell.
2 His money invests in stocks and shares.
3 Gwendolen can't expect to live in the country.
4 Jack gave the name Worthing.
5 The bag had found at Victoria Station.
6 Oscar Wilde imprisoned for two years.

## Tenses and verb forms

**6** **T 2.4** Close your books and listen to an extract from a modern romantic novel. You should recognize the opening lines. The speaker is Harriet Grey, a young woman who lives and works in London. What problems does she have?
What do you learn about her 'friend' Nina?

**7** **T 2.4** Read the text and put the verb in brackets into a suitable tense or verb form. Listen again and check and compare. What do you think happens next in the story?

FAIR GAME                                         25
_____

I never (1)_____ (set out) to pinch anyone's bloke, let alone Nina's. The day it all (2)_____ (start), picking up a bloke was the last thing on my mind. Even I (3)_____ (not go out) on the pull in manky old combats and a sweater that (4)_____ (see) better days. All I (5)_____ (think of), on that drizzly afternoon, was (6)_____ (find) a cab home. (7)_____ (start off) in mist-like fashion, the drizzle (8)_____ (move up) a gear, as if it (9)_____ (think) about (10)_____ (turn into) proper rain. At this point I was just up the road from Covent Garden, with drizzled–on hair and a jumper starting (11)_____ (smell) of a wet Shetland sheep. That was when I saw Nina (12)_____ (come) out of a smart little restaurant, with a bloke on her arm.

If I can misquote Jane Austen here, it is a truth universally (13)_____ (acknowledge) that if you are fated (14)_____ (bump into) someone like Nina when you (15)_____ (not see) her for four years, you (16)_____ (look) like a pig's breakfast. While she (17)_____ (look) like a *Sunday Times* fashion shoot in silk and cashmere. Only about six paces away, she (18)_____ (talk and laugh) in her silver-tinkle way to the bloke, who (19)_____ (hold) her umbrella up to stop her (20)_____ (get) wet. The last time I (21)_____ (see) her (at a wedding four years back) she (22)_____ (have) some tall, dark specimen in tow. Although everything about him was theoretically perfect, I (23)_____ (not be) particularly impressed – to me he (24)_____ (seem) just a bit plastic, somehow. I (25)_____ quite _____ (not know) what it was with this one – he wasn't classically good-looking exactly, but the spark (26)_____ (hit) me at once!

# THE LAST WORD
## Sounds and spelling

**1** Work with a partner. Write down all the English words you know which contain the letters *ough*. Tell the class, paying particular attention to the pronunciation.

**2** Read the poem and decide on the pronunciation of the words in *italics*. Use a dictionary if necessary.

### Hints on English Pronunciation

I take it you already know
Of *tough* and *bought* and *cough* and *dough*
Others may stumble but not you,
On *thorough*, *plough*, *enough* and *through*
Well done! And now you wish perhaps
To learn of less familiar traps.

Beware of *heard*: a dreadful word
That looks like *beard* and sounds like *bird*.
And *dead*: it's said like *bed* not *bead*
For goodness sake don't call it *deed*.
Watch out for *meat* and *great* and *threat*
(They rhyme with *suite* and *straight* and *debt*).

And *here* is not a match for *there*,
Nor *dear* and *fear*, for *bear* and *pear*.
And then there's *dose* and *rose* and *lose* –
Just look them up – and *goose* and *choose*
And *cork* and *work* and *card* and *ward*
And *font* and *front* and *word* and *sword*
And *do* and *go*, then *thwart* and *cart*,
Come, come! I've hardly made a start.

A dreadful language? Why man alive!
I'd mastered it when I was five.
And yet to write, the more I tried,
I hadn't learned at fifty-five.

**3** **T 2.5** Listen and check your pronunciation. Practise reading the poem aloud, taking turns to read a verse each.

**4** Write the words from the poem beside their phonetic transcription in column A.

▶▶ **Phonetic symbols chart on inside back cover**

|    |          | A       | B     |
|----|----------|---------|-------|
| 1  | /θruː/   | through | threw |
| 2  | /hɜːd/   |         |       |
| 3  | /miːt/   |         |       |
| 4  | /swiːt/  |         |       |
| 5  | /hɪə/    |         |       |
| 6  | /dɪə/    |         |       |
| 7  | /beə/    |         |       |
| 8  | /peə/    |         |       |
| 9  | /rəʊz/   |         |       |
| 10 | /tʃuːz/  |         |       |

**T 2.6** Listen to ten sentences with words that sound like those in column A, but have a different spelling and meaning. Write them in column B.

**5** The words in exercise 4 are all **homophones**. These are words with the same pronunciation but different meaning.

Here are some more homophones. Say the word in phonetics, then write the homophones.

|   |          | A    | B   |
|---|----------|------|-----|
| 1 | /pɔː/    | pour | paw |
| 2 | /biːn/   |      |     |
| 3 | /wɪtʃ/   |      |     |
| 4 | /weə/    |      |     |
| 5 | /wɔː/    |      |     |
| 6 | /θrəʊn/  |      |     |
| 7 | /kɔːt/   |      |     |
| 8 | /flaʊə/  |      |     |
| 9 | /piːs/   |      |     |

▶▶ **Writing** Storytelling **p118**

# 3 Big business

**STARTER**

**1** Work with a partner. Look at the logos of some multinational companies. What is the name of each company? What does it produce or sell?

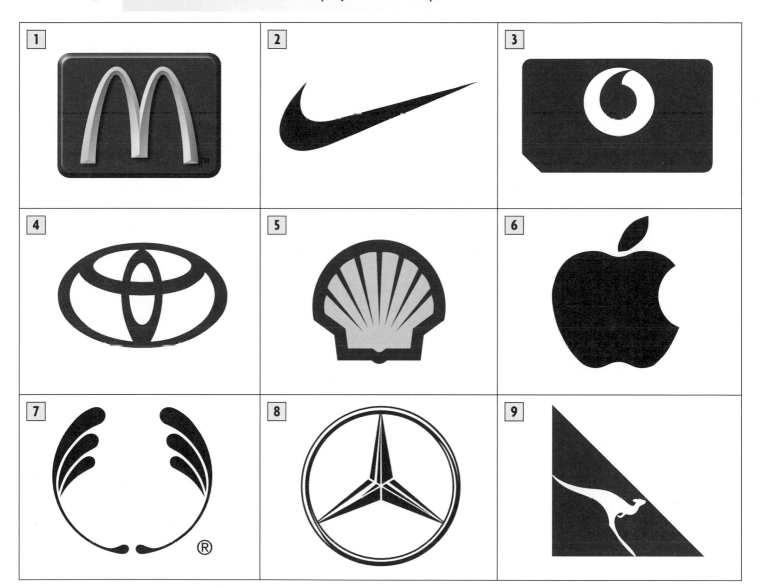

**2** Discuss these questions.
- Are these brand names well known in your country?
- Have you ever bought or used any of their products?
- Do you buy particular brands of food or clothes? Why/Why not?
- What are brands for?

# READING AND SPEAKING
## The global economy

**1** Work with a partner. What do you understand by globalization and consumerism? What are their pros and cons?

**2** Are these sentences facts (**F**) or opinions (**O**)?

1 There are severe environmental changes taking place in the world.
2 Globalization is synonymous with Americanization.
3 Only 20% of the world's population lives in rich countries, but they consume 86% of the world's resources.
4 The more people are in debt, the richer the banks become.
5 The United States is a target for the have-nots of globalization.
6 Debt repayments by developing countries are nine times as much as the aid they receive.
7 The global economy puts no value on morality, only profit.
8 Countries in the industrialized West exploit workers in poorer countries.

What is your reaction to the facts? Do you agree with the opinions? Compare your answers with the class.

**3** Look at the title of the article. What do you understand by it? Read the article. Which of the topics in exercise 2 are mentioned?

**4** According to the article, are these statements true or false?

1 'The economy' is not the same thing as the economy.
2 People feel optimistic because their lives are so prosperous.
3 The more we spend, the better life is.
4 If people stop spending, the economy collapses.
5 Companies respond to the needs of consumers.
6 It's good that we can buy cheap goods from around the world.
7 Many developing countries export food to pay back their debts.
8 We know how to solve some of these problems, but we don't want to do it.

**5** What do you understand by the words and phrases highlighted in the text?

## What do you think?

**1** What are some of the examples of craziness in the world that Jonathan Rowe mentions? Can you add any more?

**2** Is it economic colonialization to sell Kentucky Fried Chicken to the world, or is it just giving people what they want?

**3** What do you think are Jonathan Rowe's attitudes to the following? What are *your* attitudes?

- multinational corporations
- anti-globalization protesters
- economists
- public transport
- pollution and the environment
- supermarkets
- Western banks
- companies who use cheap labour in poor countries

The writer holds strong views on these issues. Can you present some counter-arguments?

**Multinational corporations keep prices down.**

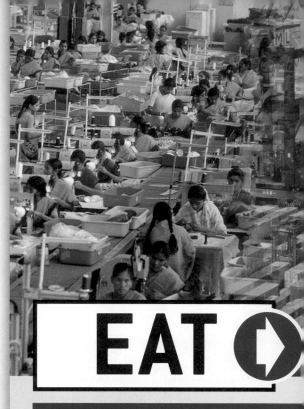

# EAT ▶

**Economic growth is the route t**

**I want to talk about the economy.** Not 'the economy' we hear about endlessly in the news each day and in politicians' speeches. I want to talk about the real economy, the one we live in day by day.

Most people aren't particularly interested in 'the economy'. 'Share prices are flying high, interest rates are soaring. The Dow Jones' index closed sixty-three points down on 8472.35.' We hear this and subconsciously switch off.

Notice that 'the economy' is not the same as the economy. 'The economy' is what men in suits play with to make vast personal wealth. The economy is where the rest of us live on a daily basis, earning our living, paying our taxes, and purchasing the necessities of life.

## Something wrong

We are supposed to be benefiting from all the advantages of a prosperous society. So why do we feel drained and stressed? We have no time for anything other than work, which is ironic given the number of labour-saving devices in our lives. The kids are always hassling for the latest electronic gadgets. Our towns become more and more congested, we poison our air and seas, and our food is full of chemicals.

# SLEEP ▶ BUY ▶ DIE

global prosperity. Or is it? Jonathan Rowe examines the price we pay for this growth

There's something wrong here. If times were truly good, then you'd think we'd all feel optimistic about the future. Yet the majority of us are deeply worried. More than 90 per cent of us think we are too concerned about ourselves and not concerned enough about future generations.

## Producing and consuming

The term 'economic expansion' suggests something desirable and benevolent, but expansion simply means spending more money.

More spending doesn't mean that life is getting better. We all know it often means the opposite – greed, deprivation, crime, poverty, pollution. More spending merely feeds our whole economic system, which is based on production and consumption. Unless money keeps circulating, the economy collapses. Airlines go bust, taking plane manufacturers and travel agents with them. If we don't keep consuming, then manufacturers and retailers go out of business. People don't buy houses, clothes, washing machines, cars. The whole system goes into stalemate.

## Creating need

As a leading economist put it, consumer societies are 'in need of need'. We don't need the things the economy produces as much as the economy needs our sense of need for these things. Why, in our supermarkets, do we have to choose from sixty different kinds of toilet paper and a hundred different breakfast cereals? Need is the miracle that keeps the engines of expansion turning relentlessly. In economics, there is no concept of enough, just a chronic yearning for more. It is a hunger that cannot be satiated.

There is so much craziness in the world. There is an American company that manufactures a range of food with a high fat content. This causes obesity and high blood pressure. By coincidence, the same company also makes products that help people who are trying to diet. Not only that, it even produces pills for those with high blood pressure.

Nearly all of my mail consists of bills (of course), banks trying to lend me money, catalogues trying to make me spend it, and charity appeals for the losers in this ecstasy of consumption — the homeless, the refugees, the

exploited, the starving. Why is it possible to buy strawberries from Ecuador and green beans from Kenya when these countries can hardly feed their own people? It is because these are cash crops, and the countries need the money to service their debts. Notice that servicing a debt does not mean paying it off. It means just paying the interest. Western banks make vast profits from third world debt.

## Making changes

How do we break the cycle? We need to become far more aware of the results of our actions. We buy clothes that are manufactured in sweat shops by virtual slaves in poor parts of the world. We create mountains of waste. We demand cheap food, mindless of the fact that it is totally devoid of taste and is produced using chemicals that poison the land. We insist on our right to drive our own car wherever we want to go.

The evil of the consumption culture is the way it makes us oblivious to the impact of our own behaviour. Our main problem is not that we don't know what to do about it. It is mustering the desire to do it.

# VOCABULARY AND SPEAKING
## Describing trends

**1** Look at these newspaper headlines describing trends. Are numbers going up or down?

P.O. PROFITS PLUMMET

Inflation soars to 10%

House prices shoot up

Microsoft market share tumbles

Ryanair leap in profits

Inflation rates plunge to 2%

Car industry predicts slump

Consumer spending picks up slightly

*'But on the positive side, money can't buy you happiness – so who cares?'*

**2** Look at the graph about the company, *Halico*. Talk about its profits, using the words in the boxes and in exercise 1.

| | Adjective | Noun |
|---|---|---|
| a | slight | |
| | gradual | fall |
| | steady | decrease |
| | sharp | rise |
| | dramatic | increase |
| | substantial | |

| Verb | Adverb |
|---|---|
| fall | slightly |
| drop | gradually |
| go down | steadily |
| decrease | sharply |
| rise | dramatically |
| go up | substantially |
| increase | |

**Halico enjoyed a steady rise in profits in January. Unfortunately, they fell ...**

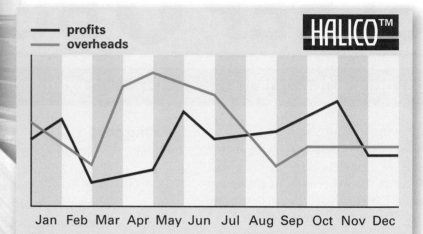

— profits
— overheads

HALICO™

Jan Feb Mar Apr May Jun Jul Aug Sep Oct Nov Dec

**T 3.1** Listen and compare your answers.

**3** Talk about *Halico*'s overheads in the same way.

When did overheads peak?
When did they reach their lowest point?
When did they level out?

**4** **T 3.2** Listen to information about the sales figures of another company, *Becom*, over the year. Complete the graph.

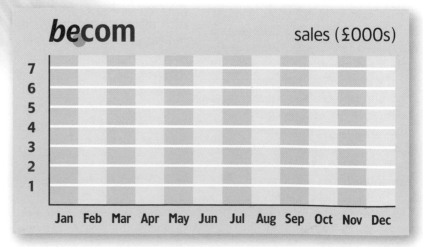

becom                                    sales (£000s)

7
6
5
4
3
2
1

Jan Feb Mar Apr May Jun Jul Aug Sep Oct Nov Dec

## Comparing statistics

**5** Look at the charts of two people's monthly expenditure, and compare them.

David spends twice / three times as much on ... as John does.

John doesn't spend anywhere near as much on ... as David does.

John spends 50% more / 20% less on ... than David does.

David spends a quarter / 25% of his salary on ...

John

| salary | expenditure per month | | | | | |
|---|---|---|---|---|---|---|
| €3,000 | €1,000 accommodation | €500 transport | €300 clothes | €315 going out | €250 food | €600 bills |

David

| salary | expenditure per month | | | | | |
|---|---|---|---|---|---|---|
| €8,000 | €2,000 accommodation | €1,400 transport | €200 clothes | €400 going out | €500 food | €2,400 bills |

**6** Your teacher will give you some statistics. In groups, prepare to give a presentation to the rest of the class using some of the vocabulary you have practised.

# LANGUAGE FOCUS
## Adverbs

### Adverb collocations

> Adverbs often go with certain verbs and adjectives. Look at the examples from the article on pp28–29.
>
> **verb + adverb**         **adverb + adjective**
> hear about **endlessly**    **deeply** worried
> turning **relentlessly**    **utterly** destroyed
>
> ▶▶ **Grammar Reference p150**

**1** Complete the sentences with an adverb from the box.

| | | | |
|---|---|---|---|
| severely | deeply | sorely | interminably |
| eagerly | desperately | highly | perfectly |
| virtually | distinctly | fatally | conscientiously |

1 I _____ need a holiday. I haven't had a break for three years.
2 The return of the Shakespearean actor Donald Bennett to the London stage is _____ awaited.
3 I work with a _____-motivated sales team. We all work hard.
4 It is _____ impossible to get away from mobile phones these days.
5 Bad weather has _____ affected the roads this weekend. Driving conditions are treacherous.
6 The politician's speech seemed to go on _____, but in fact it was only thirty minutes.
7 I hate cold climates. I am _____ tempted to emigrate somewhere warm.
8 I _____ remember you telling me not to phone before 2 p.m.
9 Having worked _____ for the same firm for forty years, he was awarded a gold watch.
10 In her anger she hit him. Later she _____ regretted this.
11 Two people escaped unhurt in the accident, but unfortunately the third passenger was _____ injured and died on the way to hospital.
12 Alison made her views on the subject of politicians _____ clear. She dislikes all of them.

**2** Match the verbs and adverbs. Make sentences using the adverb collocations.

| A | B |
|---|---|
| scream | passionately |
| gaze | profusely |
| love | longingly |
| break something | hysterically |
| work | conscientiously |
| apologize | deliberately |

### Adverbs with two forms

> Some adverbs have two forms, one with and one without -*ly*. Compare these examples.
>
> flying **high**      **highly** motivated
> doing **fine**      **finely**-chopped onions
>
> ▶▶ **Grammar Reference p150**

**3** Complete the sentences with the correct form of the adverb. In which examples does the meaning alter significantly?

| hard    hardly |

1 We all work extremely _____.
  Some countries can _____ feed their own people.

| easy    easily |

2 Manchester won the match _____.
  Relax! Take it _____!

| late    lately |

3 I hate it when people arrive _____.
  What have you been doing _____?

| sure    surely |

4 'Can you lend me some money?' '_____.'
  _____ you can see that your plan just wouldn't work?

| wrong    wrongly |

5 He was _____ accused of being a spy.
  At first everything was great, but then it all went _____.

| free    freely |

6 He talked _____ about his criminal past.
  The prisoner walked _____ after twenty years in jail.

| most    mostly |

7 What do you like _____ about me?
  She worked wherever she could, _____ in restaurants.

| wide    widely |

8 She has travelled _____ in Europe and Asia.
  When I got home, the door was _____ open.

*just*

**4** The adverb *just* is used in many different ways. What does it mean in these sentences? (Sometimes it doesn't mean very much!)

1 A new pair of socks for me! That's just what I wanted! Thank you.
2 'Who's that?' 'Don't worry. It's just me.'
3 You're just as beautiful as your sister.
4 I'm just putting the kettle on. Would you like a coffee?
5 I just caught the train with seconds to spare.
6 'I don't know what to do.' 'Why don't you just wait and see what happens?'
7 I wish you'd just listen to me for once!
8 We're just about out of sugar.
9 Just look at the children! Aren't they cute?
10 'What's the matter?' 'I don't know. It's just … it's just that I find it difficult to talk to you sometimes.'

▶▶ **Grammar Reference p150**
Adverbs are also dealt with in Units 10 and 12.

**5** Add *just* to these sentences. Match them to the definitions in the Grammar Reference.

1 Thanks for your advice. Listening to you makes me feel better.
2 I've read the most amazing book. You must read it.
3 Hang on a sec. I'm going to the loo.
4 The holiday was totally relaxing, which was what I needed.
5 My daughter is as hopeless with money as me.
6 I stood on tiptoe and managed to catch sight of Peter disappearing into the distance.
7 Do what I say. That's all I'm asking you to do.
8 We're about ten minutes or so away from the hotel.

*'I would like all of you to think of me as just one of the guys!'*

**6** **T 3.3** Listen to an interview with the Prime Minister. What is the latest crisis to hit the government? The word *just* is used five times. How many different uses can you remember?

**7** **T 3.3** The lines below are similar but not the same as some in the interview. Listen again and identify the differences.

1 We've been hearing at great length in the media about the latest crisis.
2 Polls show very clearly that the vast majority of the population fully support us.
3 My government deserves every penny of their payrise.
4 I have a lot of respect for our public sector workers, they are very hardworking.
5 Time and time again your ministers have urged workers to accept increases in line with inflation.
6 It seems absolutely clear to me.
7 The effectiveness of the nation's MPs is being greatly hindered by lack of funds.
8 Their salaries are ridiculously small compared to those people working in industry.
9 My own salary is being reviewed independently *and* it will be reviewed impartially.
10 I believe categorically in fair and just settlements for all working people.

Read the tapescript on p134 and check your answers. How many more adverbs can you find?

# LISTENING
## An interview with Anita Roddick

1 There are over 1,800 Body Shops worldwide. What do you know about the business? Do you know anything about Anita Roddick, who founded The Body Shop in 1976? What do you think she will be like?

2 **T 3.4** Listen to an interview with Anita Roddick. Which of these views does she express?

1 Business school teaches sound business practices.
Business school kills creativity.

2 Successful business people are ruthless.
They are compassionate.

3 Their god is profit.
Money is just a means to an end.

4 If the environment is damaged, so what?
It is vital to protect the environment.

5 Think globally.
Think locally.

6 Amass wealth and count it.
Amass wealth and give it away.

3 **T 3.4** Listen again and answer the questions.

**Part one**

1 What can you do at business school? What can't you do?

2 Why do immigrants make good entrepreneurs? What are the characteristics of a successful entrepreneur?

3 What, according to Anita Roddick, is the point of money?

4 What doesn't she want to be? What does she want to be?

**Part two**

5 What does business control?

6 Why are multinational corporations the big enemy?

7 What are her suggestions for honourable business practices?

**Part three**

8 What are her children's two reactions to her decision not to leave them any money?

9 What does she consider to be a great legacy?

10 What, for her, is the advantage of wealth?

## Language work

4 What do you understand by the following?

• I was saved . . . by not doing the traditional route.
• . . . they all dance to a different drum beat.
• . . . we don't give a darn about money.
• We vomit ideas.
• . . . multinational corporations bow down to nothing . . .

## What do you think?

• Do you agree that creative business people 'are terribly, terribly bad at managing'?

• What does Anita Roddick see her strengths as?

• Why do you think she has chosen not to leave her great wealth to her children?

# SPEAKING

## An advertising campaign

**1** Work in groups of six. Your teacher will give you roles.

**Students A, B, C,** and **D** work for a company called *StayWell*.
**Student E** works for a market research company.
**Student F** works for an advertising agency.

**FEELING GREAT SINCE 1989**

**StayWell** is having financial difficulties. Its most profitable product is a health drink called *Sogood*. Sales of this vitamin drink have been declining steadily for several years. You need to develop a strategy for the relaunch of the drink.

First look at the chart. It shows how you could structure your answer. It just shows *some* of the reasons for *one* potential strategy. It is not necessarily the right one.

|  | Who will you target? | What package? | What method of distribution? | Price of drink |
|---|---|---|---|---|
|  | Over 65s | New bottle | Stay with pharmacies | Increase |
| **Reason 1** | They already like *Sogood* so it will be easier to get them to like it. | It will be noticed more easily on the shelf. | It is proven that *Sogood* sells in pharmacies. | Research has shown they will pay. |
| **Reason 2** | The advertising needed to reach them is cheaper. | It will show that it is a new formula. | We have existing relationships with pharmacies. | The new formula justifies the increase. |
| **Reason 3** | It is less risky. |  | It shows that it is a true health drink, not a gimmick. |  |

Look at your role cards. Discuss what you know, and use your own ideas to plan a campaign.

**2** Present your proposals to the rest of the class.

### What do you think?

- What is the role of advertising in our lives? Does it inform us of what is available, or does it try to make us buy things we don't need?
- Does the enormous cost of advertising make goods more expensive?
- Think of an advertisement that you like or don't like. Tell the others about it. Why does/doesn't it achieve its aim?

# THE LAST WORD
## Word linking and intrusive sounds

**1** When a word begins with a vowel sound, it links with the sound before.

> English is an international language.

Mark the links in these sentences. Practise saying them.

1 We're in class learning English.

2 It's eight o'clock and time for a break.

3 I'm dying for a cup of coffee.

4 We've been in here for over an hour.

5 As a matter of fact, I think our teacher's asleep.

6 She doesn't understand that her English students are about to creep out.

**T 3.5** Listen and check.

**2** **T 3.6** When we link two vowel sounds, we add /w/ or /j/ when we speak. These sounds occur naturally.

| blue eyes | two oranges | go away |
|-----------|-------------|---------|
| /w/ | /w/ | /w/ |

| my office | the economy | three apples |
|-----------|-------------|--------------|
| /j/ | /j/ | /j/ |

Can you work out the rule? When do we add /w/ and when do we add /j/?

Sometimes we add /r/. Some people consider this to be bad pronunciation.

| law and order | Carla and Mike |
|---------------|----------------|
| /r/ | /r/ |

**3** **T 3.7** When we spell words out loud, for example our name, there is a lot of linking and intrusive sounds. Why is this?

| J O H N   S P E A R S |
|---|
| /dʒeɪ əʊ eɪtʃ en   es piː iː eɪ ɑː es/ |

 /j/ /w/        /j/ /j/ /j/ /r/

| M A N U E L   G O N Z A L E S |
|---|
| /em eɪ en juː iː el   dʒiː əʊ en zed eɪ el iː es/ |

  /j/      /w//j/       /j/ /w/      /j/   /j/

Practise spelling your name with speed and rhythm.

**4** When we spell names on the telephone, it is easy to confuse various sounds.

S sounds like F.     D sounds like T.
B sounds like P.     M sounds like N.

We can say things like **F for Freddie**, **S for sugar**, **L for London**, **V for Victor**. You can make them up as long as they're clear! You can also use the international alphabet.

A for Alpha     J for Juliet     S for Sierra
B for Bravo     K for Kilo       T for Tango
C for Charlie   L for Lima       U for Uniform
D for Delta     M for Mike       V for Victor
E for Echo      N for November   W for Whisky
F for Foxtrot   O for Oscar      X for X-ray
G for Golf      P for Papa       Y for Yankee
H for Hotel     Q for Quebec     Z for Zulu
I for India     R for Romeo

**T 3.8** Listen and write down the names you hear.

**5** Your teacher will give you a new identity and a new job. Ask other students what their name and company is.

▶▶ **Writing** A business report **p120**

# 4 Celebrity

**Synonyms and antonyms 1 · Discourse markers · Tags and replies**

**STARTER**

**1** Match the lines to make quotations about fame and success.

1 "A celebrity is a person who works hard all his life to become well known,

2 "I don't want to achieve immortality through my work.

3 "There is only one thing worse than being talked about,

4 "What goes up,

5 "Winning isn't everything,

6 "Whenever a friend succeeds,

7 "Genius is one per cent inspiration,

8 "If at first you don't succeed,

9 "Nothing succeeds

10 "Let me tell you about the rich.

☐ must come down." ANONYMOUS

☐ like success." PROVERB

☐ a little something in me dies." GORE VIDAL

☐ and that is not being talked about." OSCAR WILDE

☐ I want to achieve it through not dying." WOODY ALLEN

☐ and then wears dark glasses to avoid being recognized." FRED ALLEN

☐ try, try again." ROBERT BRUCE

☐ but it sure as hell beats losing." CHARLIE BROWN

☐ ninety-nine per cent perspiration." THOMAS EDISON

☐ They are different from you and me." F SCOTT FITZGERALD

**2** **T 4.1** Listen and check. Do you agree with any of them? What is *your* recipe for success?

## READING AND SPEAKING
### The cult of celebrity

**1** Discuss the questions as a class.

  1  Which celebrities are in the news at the moment?
What is the gossip about them? What is their claim to fame?
How do they spend their days? Which trendy places do they
go to? Where can you find out about them?

  2  *'We cannot avoid becoming entangled in what is called
"the cult of celebrity." The only question is to what degree
we want to pretend to resist.'*

     What do you understand by the term the 'cult of celebrity'?
Do you pretend to resist, or do you indulge your fascination
for celebrities? Who are you most interested in?

**2** Check you know these words and phrases.

- an icon
- a sitcom
- confessional TV
- the afterlife
- to ogle something/one

- fair game for criticism
- to scrutinize something/one
- to bestow fame on somebody
- a fly-on-the-wall documentary
- like a lamb to the slaughter

**3** Read the article and put these phrases in the correct place.

a  this life is our only one
b  are no more special than the rest of us
c  an endless supply of human-interest stories
d  everybody wants to claim a bit of you
e  I have indulged in small talk
f  by volunteering to be the subject
g  sometimes it lasts a lifetime
h  What can be done
i  undignified and unflattering
j  they want to do with their lives

**4** Would Jack Delaney agree or disagree with these viewpoints?
Find evidence in the article.

- Most fame is undeserved.
- It is possible to survive fame intact.
- The public is consistent in the way it treats celebrities.
- Newspapers used to be more respectful.
- Television subjects ordinary people to humiliation.
- Most people want to be famous.
- The cult of celebrity should make us feel ashamed.

Do *your* views differ?

**5** Answer the questions.

  1  Think of celebrities currently in the news who fit the
three categories of fame mentioned in the first paragraph.
  2  What two reasons does the writer provide to explain our
obsession? Do you agree?
  3  Why does Jay McInerney hate himself in the morning?
  4  What do you understand by the 'viciousness of voyeurism'?
What are the 'myths we too readily absorb'?

# cult of celebrity

**We are fascinated by their every move, we want to know everything about them. Jack Delaney asks why we are obsessed with the rich and famous.**

Some are born famous (like royalty), some achieve fame (like film stars) and some have fame thrust upon them (like crime victims). Sometimes their celebrity is short-lived, (1)___. In some rare cases, for example Diana, Princess of Wales, and Marilyn Monroe, it can be transformed by death into a sort of iconic status. But whatever the causes or circumstances, being a celebrity changes your relationship with the world. From being a private person, you become public property, and (2)___. You are the object of envy as well as admiration, fair game for criticism, interrogation, ridicule and spite.

## We make 'em, we break 'em

We treat the famous with a mixture of reverence and brutality. We adore them, praise them, scrutinize them and destroy them. We make them unable to tell where their real selves end and the PR-manufactured images begin. We have no mercy, we show no shame. It is easy to assume that all aspects of a celebrity life are free to be examined because he or she is on show, which means he or she doesn't have the same reality as everyone else. And it is precisely because many modern celebrities (3)___ that we feel justified in treating them with such contempt. We build them up and knock them down.

## So who are the famous?

It used to be the case that fame was bestowed only as a consequence of some mighty achievement or gruesome misdeed, when newspapers were filled largely with accounts of such things as earthquakes and wars, and when it was deemed contemptible for journalists to delve into the private lives of famous people, even the very famous.

It is now possible for people who are living ordinary private lives to become famous, for at least a short time, through the media – by appearing on game shows or confessional TV, for instance, or (4)___ of a fly-on-the-wall documentary. The readiness of people to let programme-makers into their homes, to answer the most intimate questions about their lives, and to allow themselves to be filmed in the most (5)___ situations, never ceases to amaze.

Given this ghastly invasion of one's life, why is fame so desirable? Ask an average bunch of 10-year-olds what (6)___, and a large proportion of them will say that they would like to be famous. Not for anything in particular. Just famous. Period. In the adult population, otherwise perfectly normal people think nothing of confessing all about their personal tragedies on daytime television.

## Why are we so obsessed?

The American writer Norman Mailer said that in an age without religion, celebrities are our new gods. If we have no faith in an afterlife and (7)___, then celebrity is the nearest any of us will get to immortality, and the pursuit of it becomes more urgent. At the pathological extreme of this motivation are murderers like Mark Chapman, who assassinated John Lennon partly, he said, to make himself famous.

Another feature of modern society is the power and omnipresence of the mass media. Its explosive expansion in the past couple of decades has created an insatiable need for new material. All the newspapers, magazines, television and radio programmes require (8)___. These are increasingly delivered in the form of

interviews, profiles, gossip columns, photoshoots at gatherings, and soundbites by or about people who are celebrated for something they have done, or for a position they occupy in society, or in some cases for just being a celebrity. There are some totally talentless people who are simply famous for being famous. As Andy Warhol said 'In the future, everyone will be famous for fifteen minutes.'

## Love it or loathe it?

The American writer, Jay McInerney, commented, 'I have enjoyed a little celebrity in my time, and I have ogled any number of models, (9)___ about popular film stars. But at least I hate myself in the morning. I fear as a nation we're losing our sense of shame in this regard.'

So how do you feel when you read a gossip magazine, or tune into confessional TV? Do you love it or loathe it? (10)___ to curb our fascination, particularly when the glittery sacrificial lambs go so willingly to slaughter? Probably not a lot. But perhaps we should be more aware of the viciousness of voyeurism and the myths we too readily absorb.

## What do you think?

**1** Discuss the questions.

- Why do we want to hear bad news about famous people more than good news? In what ways are celebrities unreal?

- What do you understand by 'reality TV'? Are there TV programmes in your country like the ones described in the article? What are they like?

- What is the mentality of stalkers? What makes someone want to kill the object of their obsession?

**2** Read what celebrities themselves say on the subject of fame. What do you think each quote means, and do you agree with it?

It was no great tragedy being Judy Garland's daughter. I had tremendously interesting childhood years – except they had little to do with being a child. **Liza Minnelli** *singer and actor*

For years I've been popular in America – not because of my talent, but because I'm famous. **Cher** *singer and actor*

# celebrities on celebrity

If you were me for a month, you might change it to two weeks. **Robert Redford** *actor and director*

People want you to be a crazy, out-of-control teen brat. They want you miserable, just like them. **Leonardo DiCaprio** *actor*

People create you and then you end up believing it. You become their soap opera. And what they want is not your success story but your failure. **Jade Jagger** *model and jewellery designer, daughter of Mick*

Sometimes I don't like the person I'm supposed to be. I don't feel like I deserve any of this. **Mena Suvari** *actor*

**3** Do you know …

- any other icons? What do they represent?
- someone who the press has built up and knocked down?
- an ordinary person who has become a celebrity?
- anyone who is famous simply for being famous?
- any children of celebrities who have had problems?

# VOCABULARY

## Synonyms

**1** Find words in the article on p39 that mean approximately the same as these.

| paragraph 1 | forced | |
| --- | --- | --- |
| | fame | |
| | respect (noun) | |
| paragraph 2 | great respect and admiration | |
| | cruelty | |
| | worship (verb) | |
| | examine | |
| | ruin (verb) | |
| | compassion, sympathy | |
| | guilt | |
| | suppose | |
| | exactly | |
| paragraph 3 | result (noun) | |
| | mainly | |
| | considered | |
| paragraph 6 | belief | |
| | killers | |
| | killed | |

**2** Complete the sentences with a synonym of the words in *italics*. Often the word class changes. The words appear in the article on p39.

1 She *succeeded* in building up a £50 million company. This _____ won her many awards.

2 She's always *finding fault with* her kids. She _____ them for their appearance, their laziness, everything.

3 He *admitted* murdering his employer. This _____ came after days of interrogation.

4 His recovery after the operation was *astonishing*. I was _____ to see him sitting up in bed when I visited him in hospital.

5 You simply must *control* your finances better. If you don't _____ your spending, you'll be in serious trouble.

## Antonyms

> Look at these examples of antonyms from the article on p39.
> Sometimes their celebrity is **short-lived**, sometimes **it lasts a lifetime**.
> From being a **private** person, you become **public** property.

**3** Complete the sentences with a word that has the opposite meaning to the words in *italics*. Sometimes the word class changes. The first three words appear in the article on p39.

1 You thought those stories about her were *real*, but she _____ them all.

2 His ability to make money is *admirable*. However, I have nothing but _____ for the appalling way he deals with his employees.

3 I know most people *love* travelling, but I _____ it. I'd rather stay at home.

4 I've always been *successful* at work, but my private life is a total _____ .

5 At first people thought it was a *genuine* Van Gogh, but later it turned out to be a _____ .

6 I find it difficult to *relax*. There is so much _____ in my life. So much to do, so little time to do it.

7 I was sure I had seen her before. I *didn't recognize* her face, but her voice was _____ .

8 This road is *straight* for a few kilometres, but then there are a lot of tight _____ , so be careful.

9 One of my cats is quite *tame and domesticated*. The other is totally _____ .

10 You thought she dropped the vase *accidentally*, but believe me, it was _____ .

*'It's not enough that we succeed. Cats must also fail.'*

# LANGUAGE FOCUS
## Discourse markers

**1** **T 4.2** Listen carefully to a woman speaking, and decide what she's talking about. Answer the questions.

1 What was the most important aspect of the occasion for the speaker?
2 What was special about the dresses?
3 How were the people from the press behaving?
4 What *wasn't* so important to the speaker?
5 What was the occasion?

**2** **T 4.3** Listen to another version of the monologue. What are the differences? Can you remember any?

---

**1** There are many adverbs and expressions which give the speaker's attitude to what he or she is saying.
  *Quite honestly*, I think you should pack in the job.
  *Admittedly*, you'd lose a lot of money.
  *Surely* job satisfaction is more important than money?

**2** These expressions can also structure and direct a piece of discourse.
  *As I was saying*, I'm still enjoying the work.
  *As a matter of fact*, I earn very little in my job.
  *Anyway*, who cares about money?
  *By the way*, do you know how much Justin earns now?

▶▶ **Grammar Reference p151**

---

**3** Complete the monologue with expressions from the box.

| | | | |
|---|---|---|---|
| anyway | apparently | mind you | as I was saying |
| at least | all in all, though | admittedly | of course |
| naturally | by the way | to tell you the truth | |
| still | no doubt | I mean | |
| obviously | so to speak | quite honestly | |
| actually | guess what? | as a matter of fact | |

❝All the A-list stars were there. That model, Angeline, (1)_____ I think it was Angeline, was there with her new boyfriend. (2)_____ they've been secretly going out for months. (3)_____, it was a glittering occasion. Stars everywhere and the crowds outside simply begging for autographs. (4)_____ I couldn't believe my eyes. And the dresses! (5)_____, I don't know how much they would have cost – a fortune, I imagine. All designer labels, (6)_____. The photographers were (7)_____ having a field day, and (8)_____ there were reporters everywhere, falling over each other (9)_____, to interview the biggest names. (10)_____ we didn't have the best seats, (11)_____ we were in the back row. (12)_____, we could still see everything. (13)_____, I was so busy star-spotting that I didn't take in the plot. (14)_____ you'd have been the same.

(15)_____, I'm not too keen on thrillers but it must have been good because at the end the whole audience rose to its feet and clapped. (16)_____, I'm not terribly sure what the story was about, but you really must go and see it when it's on general release.

(17)_____, it was an amazing evening and to top it off we went to Quaglino's for supper afterwards, and (18)_____ Sarah Jane Fox and Brad Brat were at the next table! How cool is that? (19)_____, Sarah Jane Fox has awful skin problems. (20)_____, who cares about that when you've got that much money!❞

---

**T 4.3** Listen again and check. Which expressions could be used in more than one place? Where?

**4** Complete the conversation, either with a discourse marker from exercise 3, or with appropriate words.

# HAVE YOU HEARD ...?

**ANNA** Have you heard that Jan is thinking of marrying Paul?

**BEN** (1) _Really?_ I don't know what she sees in him.

**ANNA** I know what you mean. Mind you, (2)_____ .

**BEN** Yes, I suppose having all that money does help.

**ANNA** Where did he get his money from?

**BEN** Apparently, (3)_____ .

**ANNA** He's been married three times before. Did you know that?

**BEN** (4)_____ , it's just the once, I think.

**ANNA** I suppose they'll have a big wedding.

**BEN** Of course (5)_____ .

**ANNA** Oh, well. Good luck to them.

**BEN** Absolutely. (6)_____ , did you hear that Sara and Jeff had a car accident?

**ANNA** Oh no! What happened?

**BEN** It wasn't serious. They skidded into a tree, but (7)_____ they weren't going fast. The car's a write-off , but (8)_____ no one was injured.

**ANNA** Thank goodness for that. I should get in touch with them, but I don't have their address.

**BEN** As a matter of fact, (9)_____ . I'll give it to you.

**ANNA** Great. Thanks a lot. (10)_____ , I must be going. I'm meeting Jan for lunch.

**BEN** Right. Nice to talk to you. Bye.

**T 4.4** Listen and compare your answers.

**5** Complete the sentences with your ideas.

1 **A** Hello. Your face looks familiar. Have we met before?
  **B** Actually, _____ .

2 **A** How come your business has been so successful?
  **B** Basically, _____ .

3 Why did the Prime Minister award himself a 50% pay rise? Surely _____ ?

4 Have you heard the latest about Cathy and Dave? Apparently, _____ .

5 I don't think Harry and Lucinda should get married. I mean, _____ .

6 I wish I was famous. All that money, all those parties every night. Mind you, _____ .

7 **A** Wasn't that a brilliant play last night!
  **B** To tell you the truth, _____ .

8 I agree, it was a great match, and they deserved to win it. By the way, _____ .

9 Why doesn't James ever phone me? Why is it always me who phones him? After all, _____ .

10 I don't have a clue what the answer is to all these problems. Anyway, _____ .

## SPEAKING
### How to become an A-list celebrity

1 Work in small groups. You have decided that it is your destiny in life to be famous. You want to get on the A list of celebrities who are invited to all the best parties, opening nights, balls and social events.

2 Read the situation on the card below and talk together until you all agree on what to do. Your teacher will give you your next card with more information and more decisions.

3 Keep discussing each situation until you get to the end of the activity. You might hit the big time or you might not!

---

⭐ It is time to start your journey on the road to fame and fortune. You want to make it to the big time as quickly as possible. You have identified two routes that could find you a way to join the rich and famous.

**Invent an interesting new past for yourself – become a new person! One that would make you newsworthy.**

**GO TO 7**

**Work your way into the elite groups of famous people by hanging out in the right places. Basically you will party your way to the top!**

**GO TO 2**

---

#### What do you think?

When you have finished, discuss these questions.

- In retrospect, did you make any wrong decisions? What should you have done?
- How did you make your decisions? Was everybody involved? Did one person dominate? Were your decisions democratic?
- Games such as these are used in management training to practise qualities of good leadership. What are the qualities of a good leader?

## LISTENING
### An interview with a Hollywood star

1 Work with a partner. Are these statements about Liza Minnelli, the singer and actor, true or false?
  1 She has been married five times.
  2 Her recent wedding had no guests.
  3 Her mother was Judy Garland.
  4 She has had similar health problems to her mother.
  5 She was born in England.

What else do you know about her? Tell the class.

**2** **T 4.5** Listen to part one of the interview. Correct the false statements in exercise 1. Answer the questions.

1 The song she sings is in three languages.
Do you recognize them? What is a cabaret?

> **Willkommen**, bienvenue, welcome
> Friend, étranger, stranger,
> Glücklich zu sehen, je suis enchantée, happy to see you,
> Bleiben, rester, stay…

2 Why does she love London and London audiences?
3 What does she mean when she says 'It's like a tennis match to sing to people in London'?
4 How does her voice change when she describes the school she went to?
5 How does she describe her current state of happiness?
6 In the second song, what is the thing that can change the world?

> How the world can change
> It can change like that
> To the one little word,
> **Married**
> See a palace rise,
> From a two-room flat,
> To the one little word,
> **Married**

**3** **T 4.6** Listen to part two. Complete the interviewer's questions.

1 Did it _____ to you?
2 I think yours _____, though, wasn't it?
3 How _____ all of that?
4 So you haven't _____ over it?

What are Liza Minnelli's answers to the questions? How does she explain the fact that all the guests at the wedding were famous?
What did Elton John say about David?

**4** **T 4.7** Listen to part three. How does Liza feel when she talks about …?

1 earning her own living in New York
2 her mother and father
3 the interviewer getting into trouble at school
4 the film *Cabaret*
5 Marisa Berenson

> I used to have this girlfriend known as Elsie
> With whom I shared four sordid rooms in Chelsea
> She wasn't what you'd call a blushing flower
> As a matter of fact she rented by the hour …
> Start by admitting from cradle to tomb
> It isn't that long a stay
> **Life is a cabaret, old chum**
> **It's only a cabaret, old chum**
> **And I love a cabaret.**

## Language work

**5** Try to remember the words from the interview. Compare with a partner, then check the tapescript on p136.

1 … the problems which _____ her mother, …
2 … she was looking _____ for a British audience.
3 The world … is like the inside _____.
   It _____ and _____.
4 … you know Elton … he was just _____.
5 Was it always expected that you would _____?
6 You clearly _____ a live audience, …

## What do you think?

• What is name dropping? Why does Liza Minnelli mention so many famous names?
• Is she a typical Hollywood star? Why/Why not?

## Final note

Liza Minnelli and David Gest separated after sixteen months.

Liza Minnelli Michael York *Cabaret*

# THE LAST WORD
## You did, did you?

**1** Read the lines below from the interview with Liza Minnelli.

**Interviewer** I like Cabaret.
**Liza Minnelli** Oh, you do, do you?

What kind of question tag is this? What is Liza Minnelli expressing?

**2** **T 4.8** Listen and underline the tags and replies in the conversation on the right. Do they rise or fall?

▶▶ **Grammar Reference p151**

**A** Liza Minnelli is just fantastic! Her concert was amazing.
**B** It was, wasn't it? And she puts so much energy into her songs, doesn't she?
**A** Yes, she does. Who wrote that song about marriage, and the way it changes the world?
**B** She did. It's one of the few songs she ever wrote, actually.
**A** So she can write as well as sing, can she? What a talent! Did you like her costumes?
**B** Yes, I did. I thought they were fantastic. I've seen most of them before.
**A** Have you? I haven't. She's playing again tomorrow, isn't she?
**B** Yes, I think so. Let's go again, shall we?
**A** All right. She's one of the all time greats, Liza Minnelli is.

**3** Work with a partner. Decide where tags and replies can naturally go in these conversations. Do they rise or fall?

1 **A** You haven't seen my car keys.
  **B** No. You had them this morning.
  **A** Yes. If I can't find them, I'll be late for work.
  **B** Panic over. Here they are!
  **A** Well done. You're a star.

2 **A** You didn't like that meal. You were pushing it around the plate.
  **B** No. Well, it hadn't been cooked properly. Your steak was all right?
  **A** Yes. It was fine. Let's get the bill and go home.
  **B** OK. We won't be coming back here in a hurry.

3 **A** You've forgotten the map?
  **B** Oh, dear. Yes.
  **A** But I put it next to the car keys.
  **B** Well, I didn't see it.
  **A** You're blind.
  **B** Oh, and you're perfect?

**T 4.9** Listen and compare. Practise the conversations with your partner.

**4** Respond to these statements in different ways.

1 Jeremy earns an absolute fortune!

   *He does, doesn't he?*
   *Does he? I had no idea. How much?*
   *So he's rich, is he? Well, well, well.*
   *He's a rich man, Jeremy is.*

2 Peter's new German girlfriend, Anna, is very beautiful.

**T 4.10** Listen and compare.

3 Jane and John are going to Florida on holiday. They're so lucky.
4 Zidane played really well in the match on Sunday, didn't he?
5 Harrods is a great shop. You can buy everything there.
6 I think our teacher is the best.
7 Simon's a very experienced traveller. He's been everywhere.

▶▶ **Writing** Expressing a personal opinion **p122**

# 5 Love is ...?

**Ways of adding emphasis · Proverbs and poetry · Getting emotional**

**1** Work with a partner. Look at the pictures. How would you describe the types of love portrayed? Which do you think are the deepest forms of love?

**2** Which have you experienced in your life? Share some experiences with the class.

**3** What is a *soul mate*? Have you found yours?! Do you know any couples who you would describe as *soul mates*?

# READING AND SPEAKING
## Fateful attraction

1 Do you know how your parents met? Tell the class.

2 Read about two couples who met in very unexpected circumstances. Work in two groups.

**Group A** Read about Tina and Andrew on this page.
Group B Read about Emma and Ross on p50.

In your groups, answer the questions.

1 How did their relationship start?
2 What stages were there in its development?
3 Did physical attraction play any part in their romance?
4 Do they believe in fate? Why/Why not?

3 Work with a partner from the other group. Compare the two stories using your answers from exercise 2. Which meeting do you think was most dependent on fate?

## Vocabulary work

4 Find these phrases in your article and try to work out their meaning from the context. Use a dictionary if necessary.

| Group A | Group B |
|---|---|
| 6 spur-of-the-moment | 2 burst out laughing |
| 12 messaging back and forth | 21 scrambled to my feet |
| 23 not overly impressed | 23 tore off along the path |
| 38 in the flesh | 43 blown away |
| 70 make a serious commitment | 59 mane of red hair |
| 71 knock sth on the head | 67 catapulted into a garden |

5 All the words in **A** and some in **B** appear in the texts. Match the synonyms.

**A** bizarre
random
stunning
guts
bashfully
dumbstruck
blush
mates
alleyway
retrieve

**B** lost for words
weird
striking
narrow path between buildings
fetch
pals
go red
shyly
courage
haphazard

6 **T 5.1** Listen to another couple, Martine and Jaap, who met in Provence in the South of France. Tell their story in your own words.

## What do you think?

• Which of the three couples had the most romantic meeting? Whose was most dependent on fate? Why?

• Do you believe in fate? Looking back on your life are there any events where you believe fate played a part?

• Do you believe fate is the best way to meet the love of your life? What alternatives can you think of?

# FATEF

## 'I SENT A RANDOM TEXT MESSAGE AND HE REPLIED!'

Tina Baldwin, 28, sent a random text message. Andrew, 21, instantly sent one back. A year later they were married.

**TINA** It was like any other day. I was chatting to my best friend in the kitchen. We were bored so I decided to send a text message to a random
05 number and see what happened. Don't ask me why – it was a real spur-of-the-moment thing. I typed in 'Feel like talking?' and waited to see if anyone would reply.
10 To my amazement, someone did – a guy. He just typed 'Yes'. From then on, we had a great hour or two, messaging back and forth. When he asked me to phone him, I didn't hesitate. We
15 both had the same sense of humour and, although it was odd at first, we talked just as easily as when we'd been texting.

I'd just come out of a relationship,
20 so I wasn't looking for a boyfriend. But over the next few months Andrew and I kept in touch every day.

Although I wasn't overly impressed by the photograph he sent of himself,
25 when we spoke on the phone I found myself becoming more and more attracted to him. It seems bizarre but I'm sure I fell in love with him before I ever saw him. We had so much in
30 common: we loved the same music, the same films, we laughed at the same jokes.

We met for the first time in a pub local to me in Somerset; he came
35 down from Hertfordshire. I was very nervous, and had a quick drink before I went to meet him. He was much better looking in the flesh and we hugged for ages. Holding him for
40 the first time is something I'll never forget. From then on we saw each

# JL ATTRACTION

## 'I'm sure I fell in love with him before I even saw him'

other constantly, meeting up on dates and getting together at weekends.

Ten months later we were married. 45 It was a great day – a proper big white wedding. Now I can't imagine life without Andrew and can't quite believe how we met. I guess he was just out there waiting for me.

50 **ANDREW** I've never believed in fate but when something like this happens, you realize that the odds are billions to one. At first, Tina and I were just having a bit of fun but, as time passed, 55 I saw that we had so much in common – we'd say the same thing at the same time, or I'd phone her and it would be engaged because she was trying to get through to me.

60 The thing I loved about Tina was her personality, and when, finally, I met her I thought she was stunning. That evening I drove back to Hertfordshire on my motorbike, knowing the 65 relationship wasn't going to end there.

During the following months, I'd make the four-hour journey to Somerset every weekend. It got to a point where it just wasn't practical any more and I 70 said to Tina, 'What we do is either make a serious commitment or knock it on the head.' I moved in a few weeks later.

I've left my family and friends in Hertfordshire but I've never regretted 75 the move for a second. On our wedding day I was ecstatic. There was nothing I wanted more.

ARTICLE B

## 'HE KNOCKED ME OFF MY BIKE!'

Emma Allen, 31, cycled into Ross, 39, during a bike ride in south-west London. Two years later they were married.

**EMMA** Whenever anyone asks us how we met, we burst out laughing – it's such a ridiculous story. I had gone out on my bike to meet a friend. I always
05 ride too fast and what happened this time was, as I rounded a corner, an arm appeared out of nowhere. The next minute, I was flying through the air into someone's garden.
10 Not only was I confused – I didn't know where I was for a moment and I could hear people saying 'What have you done, Ross? Do you think she's all right?' I was incredibly embarrassed.
15 After all, I was lying in a flowerbed with a bicycle on top of me.

I just wanted to crawl away and, being a redhead with fair skin who blushes really easily, I could feel this
20 heat rising up over my face. So I scrambled to my feet, saying crossly, 'I'm fine, I'm fine,' got on my bike and tore off along the path, hoping never, ever to see the guy I'd hit and his pals
25 again.

I did though. In a weird stroke of double fate, on my way back, I passed them again. And, hideously, my baseball cap flew off my head right in front of
30 them. It took all my courage to go back, bashfully, and retrieve it.

I'd seen Ross around before but I'd never spoken to him. So when, the next day, a bunch of flowers arrived on my
35 doorstep with a note saying, 'Have a happening day,' I knew who they were from. The florist confirmed it: yes, he was tall and blonde, and he worked as a landscape gardener.
40 It took a lot of guts but I knew I had to go and thank him in person. And I was glad I did – although my knees turned to jelly. I was blown away. We chatted for ages and a few weeks later
45 he invited me for dinner. That was it. We've now been married 11 years.

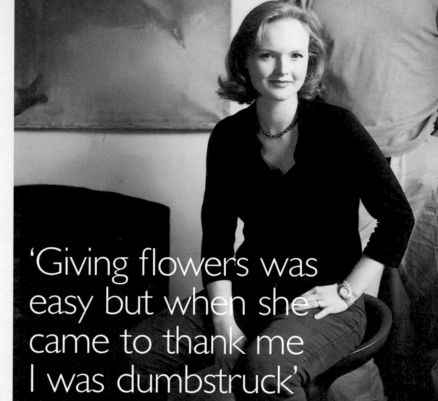

'Giving flowers was easy but when she came to thank me I was dumbstruck'

I'm a total believer in fate but, what I think is that you have to build your own destiny. If Ross hadn't sent me
50 flowers and if I hadn't gone to thank him, none of this would have happened.

**ROSS** I had just come back from travelling, surfing and hitching round
55 South America when I met Emma. I was feeling quite low having been mugged at gunpoint in Panama.

What I remember is seeing this very striking girl with a wonderful mane
60 of red hair. I'd seen her around before but we'd never spoken. One day I was with two mates, walking down this little alleyway and recalling some travelling tale. I must have gesticulated
65 too wildly because, the next thing I knew, this girl was coming for me on a bike and was suddenly catapulted into a garden. On the one hand I felt dreadful but on the other I couldn't believe how
70 gorgeous she was – this gorgeous red hair lying underneath a bicycle. I couldn't take my eyes off her.

For me the meeting was pure romance. What I did was go straight to
75 the local florist and, because she was so identifiable, they knew who she was and delivered flowers to her the next day.

Giving flowers was easy but when she came to thank me, I was dumbstruck.
80 I had never felt like this before – I knew she was the one.

Finally, I did find the courage to ask her out – and the rest, as they say, is history.

# LANGUAGE FOCUS
## Ways of adding emphasis

**1** Find similar sentences to these in your article. How exactly do they differ? What is the effect of the differences? Compare answers with a partner from the other group.

---

**ARTICLE A**

I'll never forget holding him for the first time. L39

---

I loved Tina's personality. L60

---

We either make a serious commitment or knock it on the head. L70

---

I wanted nothing more. L76

---

**ARTICLE B**

I think you have to build your own destiny. L47

---

I remember seeing this very striking girl. L58

---

I went straight to the local florist. L74

---

Finally I found the courage to ask her out. L82

---

There are many ways of emphasizing part of a sentence.

**1 Structures which add emphasis**

a I love Tina's personality. (base sentence)

| What |  |
| The thing | I love about Tina is her personality. |
| Something |  |

It's Tina's personality that I love.
It's Tina who I love.

b He criticizes/criticized me constantly. (base sentence)

| What |  |  |
| The thing | he does is / he did was | criticize me constantly. |
| Something |  |  |

**2 Negative inversion**

Certain negative expressions can be put at the beginning of a sentence for emphasis.

I'll never forget holding him for the first time.
***Never will I forget*** holding him for the first time.
People rarely fall in love at first sight.
***Rarely do people fall in love*** at first sight.

**3 Emphatic *do / does / did***

Finally I ***did*** find the courage to ask her out.

**4 Emphatic structures must sound emphatic!**

Practise saying the sentences from exercises 1, 2, and 3 above.

▶▶ **Grammar Reference p152**

**2** **T 5.2** Listen and identify the ways in which the speakers add emphasis to these base sentences.

1 I do my homework immediately after class.
2 It was love at first sight.
3 Most couples don't realize how difficult married life can be.
4 I blame the parents for badly-behaved kids.
5 The values of society are at risk and the very survival of our nation is threatened.
6 I understood what she meant then.
7 Sam broke the blue vase.
8 I won't marry anybody.

**3** Make this sentence more emphatic using these expressions.

**We like walking in Scotland.**

1 What we …
2 One thing …
3 Scotland is where …
4 It's …
5 … is something …
6 There's nothing …
   more than …

**T 5.3** Listen and check. What are the lines that stimulate the different responses? Practise the conversations with your partner, paying particular attention to the stress and intonation.

**4** Rephrase these sentences to make them more emphatic.

1 Love changes the course of your life.
2 She repeatedly contradicts me.
3 First you have to decide your priorities.
4 I admire Bill's courage.
5 You should go to Spain for your holiday.
6 **A** Why didn't you tell Peter the news?
   **B** I told him – honestly!
7 I've never been so humiliated in my life.
8 We eat out only occasionally.

**5** Complete these sentences with your own ideas, using an emphatic structure. Compare answers with the class.

1 What I can't *stand* about …
2 What surprises me *every* time …
3 The thing that annoys me *most* …
4 What we did after class yesterday …
5 It's our *teacher* who …
6 Something I've *never* told you …
7 What the *government* should …
8 *Never* in my *life* have I …

**T 5.4** Listen and compare your ideas.

## VOCABULARY AND SPEAKING
### Proverbs and poetry

**1** Match a line in **A** with a line in **B** to make proverbs. Do you have similar ones in your language?

| A | B |
|---|---|
| 1 Love is | through his stomach. |
| 2 The course of true love | repent at leisure. |
| 3 All the world loves | the heart grow fonder. |
| 4 Cold hands, | never to have loved at all. |
| 5 All's fair in love | contempt. |
| 6 Hell hath no fury like | and war. |
| 7 The way to a man's heart is | blind. |
| 8 Marry in haste, | never did run smooth. |
| 9 Better to have loved and lost than | you good. |
| 10 A little of what you fancy does | warm heart. |
| 11 Absence makes | a lover. |
| 12 Familiarity breeds | a woman scorned. |

**2** Complete the replies with a suitable proverb from exercise 1.

1 D'you know, when he left her, she threw all of his belongings out onto the street!
**You know what they say – hell hath no fury like a woman scorned.**

2 They're back together again but their relationship's had a bumpy ride.
**You know what they say –**

3 Go on then. I'll have one more. But that's the last one.

4 Good heavens! You? Going to cookery classes? You *must* be in love!

5 But I don't want you to go off to Borneo for six months. How'll I survive?

6 Oooh! Take your hands off my back! They're freezing!

**T 5.5** Listen and check. Write more conversation openers for the remaining proverbs. Ask another pair of students to respond with the correct proverb.

**3** Shakespeare added more proverbs to the English language than anyone else. Which two do you think *sound* like his from the list above?

**4** **T 5.6** Close your books and listen to one of Shakespeare's most famous love sonnets. Which season is he comparing his loved one to? Can you remember any words or phrases?

**5** **T 5.6** Work with a partner. Choose the correct word to complete the lines of the poem. Listen again and check. Then read the poem aloud.

# Sonnet xviii
## William Shakespeare 1609

a Shall I compare thee to a _____ day?

b Thou art more _____ and more temperate:

c _____ winds do shake the darling buds of May,

d And summer's lease hath _____ too short a date:

e Sometime too hot the eye of heaven _____,

f And often is his gold _____ dimmed,

g And every fair from fair sometime declines,

h By chance, or nature's changing course untrimmed;

i But thy eternal summer shall not _____,

j Nor lose possession of that fair thou ow'st,

k Nor shall death _____ thou wander'st in his shade,

l When in eternal lines to time thou _____;

m So long as men can _____, or eyes can see,

n So long lives this, and this gives life to thee.

**6** Which line or lines from the poem mean the following?

1 ☐ You are more beautiful and tranquil than a summer's day.

2 ☐ Summer doesn't last for a long time.

3 ☐ Summer is sometimes too hot and sometimes cloudy.

4 ☐ Everything beautiful in nature declines and becomes ugly with time.

5 ☐ You possess such beauty that it will last forever.

6 ☐ You will never die because you are immortalized in poetry.

7 ☐ As long as people exist who read this poem you will have eternal life.

**7** What other things could you compare a loved one to? Discuss with the class.

sunny/summer's/perfect
lovely/attractive/stunning
heavy/rough/soft
all/far/way
scalds/shines/burns
complexion/hair/chariot

fade/ebb/wither

boast/brag/proclaim
shrink'st/grow'st/wrinkl'st
write/breathe/think

**Glossary**
thee/thou = you
art = are
summer's lease = summer season
hath = has
fair = beauty
untrimmed = made ugly
thy = your
fair thou ow'st = beauty you own
eternal lines = immortal verse
this = this sonnet
life = immortality

# LISTENING AND SPEAKING
## When love lasts forever

**1** What and when is St Valentine's Day? Is it celebrated in your country?

**2** **T 5.7** Olive Hodges is 102 years old. She is being interviewed on St Valentine's Day. The lines below are taken from the interview. Listen and answer the questions.

1 *'She had been looking forward to her 77th wedding anniversary this year.'*
Why is she not looking forward to it now?

2 *'He came through without a scratch.'*
Who came through what?

3 *'… he did this about six times.'*
What did he do?

4 *'I'll put him out of his misery.'*
What did Olive mean by this?

5 *'I didn't see any need for a hurry.'*
Any hurry for what?

6 *'I think it was stronger.'*
What was stronger? When?

7 *'I had a job to reassure him.'*
What did Fred need reassurance about?

**3** Answer the questions.
1 How did Olive and Fred's relationship start?
2 What course did their courtship take?
3 What is Olive's recipe for a long marriage?
4 How do we know that they never took their love for granted?
5 How does the presenter show he is moved by the story?

## What do you think?

- What's your reaction to Olive's story? How common is her experience?
- Do you know any other couples who have enjoyed such a long marriage?

# THE LAST WORD
## Getting emotional

1 **T 5.8** Read and listen to these lines of conversation. Then discuss with a partner. Who could be speaking? What might the situation be? Discuss with the class.

1 Get this heap of old metal out of my drive! Now!

2 You mean more to me than words could ever say.

3 I could be wrong, but I think someone not a million miles from here is to blame for this.

4 Wow! I could never do anything like that. Stick men are my limit.

5 I'll have to consult my diary. Life's just so hectic at the moment. You know me, I'm so much in demand.

6 Come on, you can tell me. I won't breathe a word to anyone. I promise.

7 Could you *not* keep getting at me in front of our friends? It looks so awful.

8 Thank God you're here. When I couldn't get you on your mobile, I thought you'd had an accident.

9 He came in the top two per cent in the country. So his father and I are thrilled to bits.

10 Well, I think you did very well to come third. Keep up the good work and you'll win next time.

11 Oh, come on now, don't cry. You'll be fine. It's only a graze. Hardly bleeding at all.

12 It was nothing. Anybody would have done the same.

13 I can't tell you how much I appreciate everything you've done for me. I'd have been so lost here on my own.

14 I'm out of here right now! I don't like the look of that lot.

15 You're kidding me. Nobody gets hitched wearing green wellies!

16 What d'you mean I'm a couch potato?! I go to the gym twice a week.

2 Which of these emotions are expressed by the lines in exercise 1? Sometimes more than one is suitable.

| | | | |
|---|---|---|---|
| admiration | boastfulness | gratitude | reassurance |
| adoration | curiosity | indignation | relief |
| amusement | encouragement | irritation | sarcasm |
| anxiety | fear | modesty | suspicion |
| astonishment | fury | pride | |

3 **T 5.8** Say the lines to your partner according to the emotion. Listen again and compare the stress and intonation.

4 **T 5.9** Listen to someone asking the same question in several different ways. Try and identify the emotions.

▶▶ **Writing** Discussing pros and cons **p123**

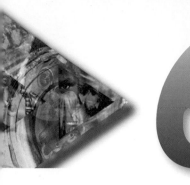

# 6 Newspeak

**Distancing the facts • Nouns formed from phrasal verbs • Responding to news**

**1** The words in the box are commonly used in newspaper headlines. Why do you think these words are often short and dramatic?

Complete the headlines with the words.

| | | | | | | | |
|---|---|---|---|---|---|---|---|
| haul | swoop | blow | havoc | cops | fury | raid | axe |
| orgy | cons | dumps | bid | row | ban | probe | |

**1** NEIGHBOURS' ☐ OVER HEDGE ENDS IN COURT

**2** BA to ☐ 5,000 jobs in ☐ to break even

**3** OAPs' ☐ at measly 1.5% rise in pensions

**4** £50 MILLION HUBBY PUTS BANK ☐ ON MISSUS

**5** SWORD MANIAC SHOT BY ☐

**6** NEW ☐ INTO MURDERS REVEALS FRESH CLUES

**7** WIFE ☐ HUSBAND IN SEX ☐

**8** Police ☐ on crack factory – huge drug ☐

**9** PC shot in bank ☐ dies

**10** New inflation figures deal ☐ to recovery hopes

**11** BOGUS VICAR ☐ WIDOW OF LIFE SAVINGS

**12** AIR TRAFFIC CONTROL STRIKE THREAT SPELLS ☐ FOR HOLS

**2** **T 6.1** Listen to five people talking about which newspapers they read and why. Put numbers 1–5 next to the correct newspaper(s). What do they like about the newspaper(s) they read?

☐ Financial Times  ☐ Sun  ☐ Independent  ☐ Guardian  ☐ Observer

☐ Daily Mail  ☐ Daily Mirror  ☐ Times  ☐ International Herald Tribune

**3** In Britain the main newspapers are national, not regional. Is it the same in your country?
Do your newspapers have a political bias?
Do you read a newspaper regularly? Which one? Why do you choose that one?

# READING AND SPEAKING
## Tabloid and broadsheet newspapers

**1** Look at the front pages of two different newspapers, *The Sun* and *The Independent on Sunday.*

Which is the tabloid newspaper, and which is the broadsheet? What are your immediate impressions of the different coverage?

Think of …

- the size of the headline
- the content of the headline (Eton is an expensive private school)
- the photograph
- the layout of the front page
- the use of the word *exclusive*
- the length of the text on the front page

**2** Read the two articles on pp57–8. Summarize each story in three or four sentences. Which newspaper … ?

- is more factual and objective
- is more sensational
- has longer, more complex sentences
- uses more informal, idiomatic, conversational language
- uses more formal, controlled, concise language

**3** Where did the reporters obtain their information? Who did they speak to? Which newspaper attributes its sources more? Why, do you think?

**4** This is the structure of the article in *The Sun.*

Harry admitted taking drugs ➡ his father's reaction ➡ his school's reaction ➡ a twist in the last two paragraphs

What is the structure of the article in *The Independent*?

**5** What are the different ways that Harry is referred to in each paper?

**6** Who or what are these in the articles? Can you remember?

**from *The Sun***
- John Lewis
- Highgrove, Gloucs
- *The News of the World*
- the Berkshire college

**from *The Independent***
- Featherstone Lodge
- the Rattlebone Inn
- St James's Palace
- David Baker

## Language work

**7** Make questions for these answers, using the words in brackets.
1  He might be expelled. (fail)   **What happens if he fails the drugs test?**
2  A member of staff told him. (find out)
3  To give him a short, sharp shock. (insist)
4  Yes, he learned a lot. (instructive)
5  It can lead to hard drugs such as cocaine and heroin. (potential danger)
6  It is very strict. It gives lectures about their dangers. (policy)
7  He is reported to have verbally abused an employee. (What … Harry said … done at the Rattlebone Inn?)
8  He turned it down immediately. (react)

**8** Find informal words or idioms in *The Sun* and formal words in *The Independent* that have similar meanings to these.

| The Sun – informal words for . . . | The Independent – formal words for . . . |
|---|---|
| cannabis | came out, became known |
| has been warned | warned, made aware |
| alcohol | very distressing or shocking |
| a person who is difficult to control | results |
| behaving in an uncontrolled fashion | happening in many places |
| stopped at a very early stage | given in to temptation |
| everyone will be watching | buildings and land of a business |

# THE Sun

Monday January 14th     **30p**     www.thesun.co.uk

## SUN EXCLUSIVE

# HARRY FACES ETON DRUGS TEST

**TROUBLED Prince Harry is facing drugs tests at Eton after admitting he took pot.**

He has been allowed to stay at the school by head John Lewis.

But the teenager risks being **EXPELLED** if he fails a random urine check in future.

A source said last night: "Harry has had the yellow card. If he ever tests positive he'll be out."

The youngster told Prince Charles he smoked cannabis and had booze binges at Highgrove, Gloucs, and a nearby pub when he was 16.

Harry, now 17, also went drinking at a pub on New Year's Eve. Eton insiders said the Prince "can be a handful."

A source added: "People are genuinely concerned he may be going off the rails.

"He also has a habit of spitting in the street – quite distasteful."

The News of the World told yesterday how Charles responded to Harry's cannabis confession by ordering him to visit a rehab unit – to frighten him into turning his back on drugs.

And Eton has told him that even though he never smoked pot at the school, its anti drug rule applies at home.

A senior source at the Berkshire college said: "The cannabis matter was brought to the attention of the head by Prince Charles.

"Obviously the Prince is extremely concerned about those who mix with his son in case any of them has been a bad influence on him.

### BORED

"The smoking of cannabis and the drinking of alcohol is widespread at Eton College and the headmaster operates a strong policy against it.

"But the difficulty is that you have a large number of boys with a huge weekly disposable income who get very bored and become easy prey for drug-dealers."

The source said Eton was "totally satisfied" with the way Prince Charles had handled Harry's drug use.

He went on: "It would seem the problem has been nipped in the bud."

*Warned ... Harry arriving at Highgrove yesterday* **Picture: DAVID BEBBER**

"However, the headmaster informed Charles his son could be made to take random urine samples in the future.

"The headmaster hates having to expel anybody – but he is very tough on drugs.

"All eyes at Eton will be on Harry to ensure he does not stray."

### ABUSE

Eton pupils are all given lectures about drugs by a counsellor.

They are warned how drugs affect the body and mind.

Staff are also trained to spot signs of drug abuse in the boys.

Eton rules say: "The school prospectus is explicit about the headmaster's right to dismiss any boy involved with illicit drugs.

"The headmaster also has the power to treat as a breach of school discipline behaviour during the holidays which brings the school into disrepute."

Meanwhile, a pupil who was expelled for having cannabis said he once offered a joint to Harry's brother William.

He added: "William was not amused. He politely turned it down immediately."

# Prince Harry sent to rehab over drink and drugs

### BY CLAIRE HILL

Prince Harry was sent to a drugs rehabilitation clinic after he admitted to smoking cannabis and drinking alcohol, it emerged last night.

His father, the Prince of Wales, sent his son to Featherstone Lodge Rehabilitation Centre in Peckham, south London. Prince Charles took the decision after learning his son had taken drugs during private parties at Highgrove, and had drunk alcohol at the nearby Rattlebone Inn in Sherston, reports said.

These incidents are reported to have happened last June and July when Harry was 16. It is believed that Prince Charles was alerted to the problem when a senior member of staff noticed a smell of cannabis. In the late summer, he visited the rehabilitation centre for what was intended to be a "short, sharp shock."

Bill Puddicombe, the chief executive of Phoenix House Treatment Service For Drug Dependency, confirmed Prince Harry's visit to the lodge. "The visit was at the request of the Prince of Wales, who is our patron," he said. "Prince Harry came for a couple of hours on a day in late summer and talked to several people in recovery, heroin and cocaine addicts mostly.

"They told him what had happened in their lives, which must have been quite harrowing for him. Prince Harry was friendly and relaxed and the residents liked him and responded very warmly to him.

"I spoke to the Prince in November and was pleased to hear that Harry had enjoyed his visit and learnt a lot.

"It was an opportunity for the Prince of Wales to teach Prince Harry about our work and the consequences of taking drugs. Featherstone has helped an enormous number of people, and we are pleased if the visit helped Prince Harry too."

Prince Harry was reportedly shown the residential and detox areas and sat in on a communal therapy group and heard stories of addicts moving from cannabis to cocaine and heroin.

A spokesman for St James's Palace said last night: "This is a serious matter which was resolved within the family, and is now in the past and closed." It is expected there will be widespread praise for the Prince of Wales's actions.

Prince Harry, now at Eton public school and planning to go to agricultural college after his A-levels, is the latest in a line of young aristocrats and

Prince Harry, who was sent to a drink and drugs rehabilitation unit by his father    PA

politicians' children who have succumbed to drug-taking. The Hon. Nicholas Knatchbull, a godson of Prince Charles, was in a rehabilitation clinic last year. Camilla Parker-Bowles's son, Tom, and Lord Frederick Windsor have also admitted using cocaine. Tony Blair's son, Euan, was found drunk in Leicester Square in 2000 when he was 16.

The *Mail on Sunday* also reported last night that the prince was at the centre of a police investigation into after-hours drinking at the Rattlebone Inn. He verbally abused a French employee and was ordered to leave the premises, the report said. The landlord, David Baker, left the pub within weeks of the incident.

The Prince of Wales was involved in an underage drinking episode when he was 14. During a school sailing trip, he led his four friends to the Crown Hotel on the Isle of Lewis. He asked for a cherry brandy, the first drink that came to his mind.

# LANGUAGE FOCUS
## Distancing the facts

Look at these sentences from the newspaper article.

*These incidents **are reported to have happened** last June . . .*
***It is believed** that Prince Charles was alerted to the problem . . .*
***It is expected** there will be widespread praise . . .*
***It would seem** the problem has been nipped in the bud.*

These are all ways of giving information without stating categorically that you know it to be true. The writer is putting distance between himself and the facts.

**1 Passive constructions**
Look at these sentences.

*They say he works in the City.*
*People assume he's earning a lot of money.*
*Everyone thought he had made his fortune in oil.*

These sentences can be expressed in the passive in two ways, beginning with *It* or *He*:

1 ***It is said that** he works in the City.*
***It is assumed that** he's earning a lot of money.*
***It was thought that** he had made his fortune in oil.*

2 *He **is said to** work in the City.*
*He **is assumed to be** earning a lot of money.*
*He **was thought to have** made his fortune in oil.*

What differences in form do you notice?

**2 *seem* and *appear***
*He **appears to have** learned his lesson.*
*The Sun **seems to have** found its information from a variety of sources.*
*The Independent **seems to be** more factual.*
*It **appears that** the Prince took the incident seriously.*

▶▶ **Grammar Reference p152**

## Passive constructions

**1** Rewrite these sentences, beginning with the words in *italics*.

1 It is reported that *the international criminal Jimmy Rosendale* is living in Ireland.
2 People believe that *he* is the head of a gang of bank robbers.
3 Everyone knows that *the gang* has carried out a series of robberies.
4 It is supposed that *they* have escaped with over €1 million.
5 It is thought that *they* are targeting banks in small provincial towns.
6 They say *Jimmy Rosendale* is wanted for questioning by police in five countries.
7 We understand *he* escaped from police custody by bribing a warder.
8 It is assumed that *he* has been involved in criminal activities all his life.
9 People presume that *he* learned his trade from his father.
10 It is alleged that *his father* was the mastermind behind the 2001 gold bullion robbery.

## *seem* and *appear*

**2** Change these sentences, beginning with the words in italics.

1 It seems *the weather* is changing.
2 It appears that *we* have missed the train.
3 Peter appeared to have been attacked by a bull. (*It*)
4 He seemed to have survived the ordeal. (*It*)
5 It would seem that *the Government* has changed its policy.
6 It appears that *they* are worried about losing the next election.

## Reporting the news

**3** In groups, write a short newspaper article for one of these headlines. Include some of the constructions you have practised.

### Athlete fails drugs test and loses medal

### PM lied to Parliament over donations from businessman

### PRICELESS PAINTING LOST IN FIRE TRAGEDY

### TV SOAP STAR RICKY GOES INTO REHAB

### ACTRESS CARRIE MOORE TO WED FOR NINTH TIME

### CITY TRADER EMBEZZLES £25 MILLION

### 'DANGEROUS' PRISONER ESCAPES BY HELICOPTER

### 12-year-old maths genius wins place at Oxford

**4** **T 6.2** Listen to the news broadcast and use it as a dictation. Elect one student to write on the board while the rest of the class helps.

I think you've spelt that word wrong.
I don't think it was 'would'. I think it was 'had'.

# VOCABULARY
## Nouns formed from phrasal verbs

> **1** There are many compound nouns formed with a verb + preposition, or preposition + verb combination.
>
> Here is an **update** on the news.
> At the **outbreak** of war I was just three years old.
> The health service is suffering from budget **cutbacks**.
> The town has a **bypass**, which keeps traffic out of the centre.
>
> Where is the stress on these words?
>
> **2** Some of these nouns operate as phrasal verbs, and some don't.
>
> Rioting **broke out** in the middle of the night.
> Funds allocated to research have been severely **cut back**.
>
> There is no verb ~~to date up~~. **To pass by** is used literally.
>
> We **passed by** the park on the way to the station.

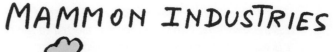

'He says his name is Billy and he's here to update our software.'

**1** Complete the sentences with a compound noun starting with the word given. Use the definitions to help you.

> out

1 *the final result of an election, or negotiations, when no one knows what to expect*
We are all waiting for the __outcome__ of the meeting.

2 *a set of clothes worn together*
She bought a new _____ for the wedding.

3 *what is expected to happen in the future*
The _____ for tomorrow's weather is bleak, I'm afraid.

4 *a shop or company through which products are sold*
The Body Shop has retail _____ in major cities throughout the world.

> take

5 *a meal you buy in a restaurant to eat at home*
Shall we eat out or get a _____?

6 *getting control of a company by buying most of its shares*
Business sections of newspapers are full of company mergers and _____.

> down

7 *failure or ruin following success*
She had a great career, but hard drugs were her _____.

8 *a lot of rain that falls fast and heavily*
I got soaked in yesterday's _____.

9 *information obtained from the Internet, usually free*
For free _____, click here.

> break

10 *new and successful development*
There have been great _____ in organ transplants in the last 20 years.

11 *a serious mental illness*
After his mother died, Paul suffered a complete nervous _____.

Use │ up │ at the end of these four words.

12 *ending a marriage*
Sarah was very depressed after the _____ of her marriage to Tony.

13 *something used for support if the main one fails*
At the end of a day's writing, I make a copy of my work on disk as a _____.

14 *a situation in which a lot of changes are made*
There's been a big _____ at work. They've fired six managers and introduced new working practices.

15 *a way of organizing or arranging something*
I don't understand the political _____ in the States. Their elections seem to last for years.

**2** Work with a partner. Choose some of the words from the box. Write a definition and a sample sentence with a gap. Use a dictionary if necessary. Test the other students.

| | | | | |
|---|---|---|---|---|
| lookout | setback | outbreak | backlash | upkeep |
| slip-up | offshoot | comeback | showdown | upturn |
| write-off | drawback | hold-up | outburst | knock-out |

# LISTENING AND SPEAKING
## A foreign correspondent

**1** Look at the photos. Who are the different people? Where are they? What's happening?

**2** *'News is always bad news. We listen for a couple of days, then we lose interest.'*

What recent news stories illustrate this or contradict it?

**3** Check you know these words.

- do somebody justice
- a pack (of wild animals)
- inconspicuous
- off-beat places
- a patch (of land)
- a skirmish
- to shrink (*pp* shrunk)
- subtlety
- focused

**4** **T 6.3** Listen to an interview with Simon Winchester, a foreign correspondent, and answer the questions.

### Part one
1 What is the interviewer's first question? How does Simon Winchester answer it?
2 What kind of journalist is he? What kind of journalist *isn't* he?
3 What big news story of the 1970s does he mention?
4 What kind of places does he like?

### Part two
5 What is the first reason he gives for the change in the foreign correspondent's role?
6 Why did the British press use to have a much better coverage of foreign affairs?
7 What does he say about *The New York Times*?
8 What is his attitude to television news reporting?
9 What sort of news reporting does he like?
10 How has an increased awareness of budgets affected foreign news coverage?

## Language work

**5** What do you understand by these lines from the interview?

- I was very much in the thick of things.
- a more fulfilling time personally
- I've never made a virtue out of danger.
- the echoes of Empire
- the little essay which illuminates brilliantly the inner workings of some distant place
- newspapers have become more market-driven, and less of a public service
- their hands are tied

**6** Simon Winchester often understates his points. For example, he refers to some dangerous situations as *skirmishes*. Find other examples of understatement in the tapescript on p138.

## What do you think?

- Do you agree that people aren't so interested in what is happening outside their own country any more? Has television numbed our curiosity? How much foreign news coverage is there in your newspapers?

- *'We go in … the blazing TV lights … for a short time, and then we go on to the next story.'*

  How much does TV report the news and how much does it create it nowadays? Think of recent big world stories that exemplify this.

- *'As soon as there's a disaster, reporters ask three questions. How many dead? Where were they from? How did you feel when it happened?'*

  Do you agree?

# THE LAST WORD
## Responding to news

**1** Match the statements and responses. Sometimes there is more than one possible answer.

| A | B |
|---|---|
| 1  Guess what! I won £5 million on the lottery! | a  So what? I don't care. |
| 2  My grandfather died last week. | b  In your dreams. |
| 3  One of my students told me I was a lousy teacher. | c  Over my dead body. |
| 4  Here we are! Home at last. | d  Now you're talking! |
| 5  I'm broke since I bought all those designer clothes. | e  Nice one! |
| 6  Have you heard that Jim's leaving to go to another job? | f  Where's the surprise? |
|  | g  Thank goodness for that! |
| 7  I missed the last bus and had to walk home. | h  Tough. |
| 8  When I get a job, I'm going to be a millionaire. | i  You're kidding! |
| 9  I'm going on holiday to Barbados for two weeks. | j  What a drag! |
| 10  My six-year-old daughter painted me a picture for Father's Day. | k  What a cheek! |
|  | l  Oh no! I'm so sorry to hear that. |
| 11  I'm fed up with revising. Let's go out for a beer. | m  Good riddance. |
| 12  Susan says she never wants to see you again. | n  Bless her! |
| 13  My team lost again last weekend. |  |
| 14  *(12-year-old girl)* Dad, I'm going to an all-night party. Is that OK? |  |

**T 6.4** Listen and check. What additional comments do you hear?

**2** What ideas do the responses in column B express?

- ☐ surprise at someone's lack of respect
- ☐ sympathy
- ☐ no sympathy
- ☐ pleasure that someone is leaving
- ☐ no surprise
- ☐ no concern
- ☐ relief
- ☐ I like what you're saying.
- ☐ Isn't she cute?
- ☐ How boring!
- ☐ I'm impressed!
- ☐ I don't believe you.
- ☐ What you're saying won't happen.
- ☐ I won't allow this to happen.

**3** Work with a partner. Cover the responses and try to remember the complete conversations.

**4** **T 6.5** Listen to these lines of conversation. Reply using a response from column B in exercise 1, then continue the conversations.

**5** **T 6.6** Listen to the conversations. What is the second speaker's attitude?

Look at the tapescript on p138 and practise the conversations with a partner. **B** should try to sound sarcastic.

**6** In pairs, make conversations from the chart. **B** needs to decide how to sound – sincere or sarcastic.

| A | B |
|---|---|
| I've done all the washing-up. | You've been a great help. |
| I've spilt paint all over your carpet. | Thank you so much. |
| I've burnt the meal. | That's just brilliant. |
| I've hoovered everywhere. | I don't know what I'd have done without you. |

"That's just brilliant!!"

▶▶ **Writing** A letter to a newspaper **p124**

# 7 Words of wisdom

**Modal auxiliary verbs  ·  Rhyme and reason  ·  Breaking the rules of English**

**STARTER**

1 Work with a partner. Which of these people have you heard of? Why are they famous?

2 What do their quotations mean? Which do you agree with? Do you have any favourites?

1 ❝A journey of one thousand miles begins with a single step.❞
**Confucius** 551–479 BC

2 ❝Health is the greatest gift, contentment the greatest wealth, faithfulness the best relationship.❞
**Buddha** 563–483 BC

3 ❝Our youth now love luxury. They have bad manners, contempt for authority; they show disrespect for their elders; they contradict their parents and tyrannize their teachers.❞
**Socrates** 469–399 BC

4 ❝The very atmosphere of firearms anywhere and everywhere restrains evil interference – they deserve a place of honor with all that is good.❞
**George Washington** 1732–1799

5 ❝One half of the world cannot understand the pleasures of the other.❞
**Jane Austen** 1775–1817

6 ❝When I was fourteen years old, I was amazed at how unintelligent my father was. By the time I turned twenty-one, I was astounded by how much he had learned in the last seven years.❞
**Mark Twain** 1835–1910

7 ❝I do not know with what weapons World War 3 will be fought, but World War 4 will be fought with sticks and stones.❞
**Albert Einstein** 1879–1955

8 ❝Love is like quicksilver in the hand. Leave the fingers open and it stays. Clutch and it darts away.❞
**Dorothy Parker** 1893–1967

9 ❝The old law about 'an eye for an eye' leaves everybody blind.❞
**Martin Luther King** 1929–1968

10 ❝Life is full of misery, loneliness and suffering – and it's over much too soon.❞
**Woody Allen** b.1935

3 Which quotations do you find relevant to today's world or your own life? In what ways? Discuss with your partner, then the class.

## READING AND LISTENING
### Letter to a newborn son

**Fergal Keane** is a BBC foreign correspondent. He recorded this letter to his newborn son for a programme called *From Our Own Correspondent* while he was working in Hong Kong. Following the broadcast, hundreds of people jammed the BBC switchboard in tears because they were so moved by his words.

**1** Read these lines from the letter and answer the questions below.

- You are asleep cradled in my left arm and I am learning the art of one-handed typing.
- One man said you were the first baby to be born in the block in the year of the Pig.
- Your coming has turned me upside down and inside out.
- Like many foreign correspondents I know, I have lived a life that, on occasion, has veered close to the edge: war zones, natural disasters, darkness in all its shapes and forms.
- And it's also true that I am pained, perhaps haunted is a better word, by the memory, suddenly so vivid now, of each suffering child I have come across on my journeys.
- But there is something more, a story from long ago that I will tell you face to face, father and son, when you are older. It's a very personal story . . .

1 What do the lines tell you about Fergal's feelings on the birth of his son?
2 What is *the year of the Pig*?
3 What do you learn of his job as a foreign correspondent?
4 What do you think the *personal story* from long ago might be?

**2** **T 7.1** Read and listen to the first part of the letter. Answer the questions.

1 What has Fergal learned about the practicalities of looking after a newborn baby?
2 What do you understand by *the new grammar* of their daily lives?
3 Why are the Chinese people in their apartment block so pleased?
4 Is fatherhood as he expected it would be?

# Letter to a newborn son

**PART ONE**

## My dear son,

It is six o'clock in the morning on the island of Hong Kong. You are asleep cradled in my left arm and I am learning the art of one-handed typing. Your mother, more tired yet more happy than I've ever known her, is sound asleep in the room next door and there is a soft quiet in our apartment. Since you've arrived, days have melted into night and back again and we are learning a new grammar, a long sentence whose punctuation marks are feeding and winding and nappy changing and these occasional moments of quiet.

When you're older we'll tell you that you were born in Britain's last Asian colony in the lunar year of the Pig and that when we brought you home, the staff of our apartment block gathered to wish you well. 'It's a boy, so lucky, so lucky. We Chinese love boys,' they told us. One man said you were the first baby to be born in the block in the year of the Pig. This, he told us, was good Feng Shui, in other words a positive sign for the building and everyone who lived there. Naturally your mother and I were only too happy to believe that. We had wanted you and waited for you, imagined you and dreamed about you and now that you are here no dream can do justice to you.

**3** **T 7.2** Listen only to part two. Are these statements true or false? Correct the false ones.

1 His Chinese friends say that his son has to be given a Chinese name.
2 He might call him *Son of the Eastern Star* after the beautiful sunrise.
3 He used to be very ambitious in his work.
4 These children he mentions were all hurt in floods.

- Andi Mikail from Eritrea
- Domingo and Juste from southern Angola
- Sharja from Afghanistan
- Three young children from Rwanda

**4** **T 7.3** Read and listen to part three. Answer the questions.

1 Who are these people? How are they connected to the places?

| | | |
|---|---|---|
| a young woman | – | a snowbound big city |
| a taxi driver | – | a shop doorway |
| an alcoholic man | – | a one-roomed flat |
| a baby boy | – | the Adventist Hospital |

2 What indications are there that Fergal's parents loved him and each other?
3 Describe his father. What is Fergal's attitude to him and his problems?
4 What regrets does he have about his father?

---

**PART THREE**

**Daniel,** these memories explain some of the fierce protectiveness I feel for you, the tenderness and the occasional moments of blind terror when I imagine anything happening to you. But there is something more, a story from long ago that I will tell you face to face, father and son, when you are older. It's a very personal story but it's part of the picture. It has to do with the long lines of blood and family, about our lives and how we can get lost in them and, if we're lucky, find our way out again into the sunlight.

It begins thirty-five years ago in a big city on a January morning with snow on the ground and a woman walking to the hospital to have her first baby. She is in her early twenties and the city is still strange to her, bigger and noisier than the easy streets and gentle hills of her distant home. She's walking because there is no money and everything of value has been pawned to pay for the alcohol to which her husband has become addicted. On the way, a taxi driver notices her sitting, exhausted and cold, in the doorway of a shop and he takes her to hospital for free. Later that day, she gives birth to a baby boy and, just as you are to me, he is the best thing she has ever seen. Her husband comes that night and weeps with joy when he sees his son. He is truly happy. Hungover, broke, but in his own way happy, for they were both young and in love with each other and their son.

But, Daniel, time had some bad surprises in store for them. The cancer of alcoholism ate away at the man and he lost his family. This was not something he meant to do or wanted to do, it just was. When you are older, my son, you will learn about how complicated life becomes, how we can lose our way and how people get hurt inside and out. By the time his son had grown up, the man lived away from his family, on his own in a one-roomed flat, living and dying for the bottle. He died on the fifth of January, one day before the anniversary of his son's birth, all those years before in that snowbound city. But his son was too far away to hear his last words, his final breath, and all the things they might have wished to say to one another were left unspoken.

Yet now, Daniel, I must tell you that when you let out your first powerful cry in the delivery room of the Adventist Hospital and I became a father, I thought of your grandfather and, foolish though it may seem, hoped that in some way he could hear, across the infinity between the living and the dead, your proud statement of arrival. For if he could hear, he would recognize the distinct voice of family, the sound of hope and new beginnings that you and all your innocence and freshness have brought to the world.

---

**5** **T 7.1–3** Listen again to the whole letter. Summarize each part in one or two lines.

## Vocabulary work

**6** Work with a partner. Who or what do the pronouns in *italics* refer to? What is the meaning of the words underlined? Use a dictionary if necessary.

1 *He* was <u>winded</u>, fed and <u>cradled</u>.
2 *He* <u>gambled</u> with death, <u>veering</u> close to the edge of danger.
3 *He* cried out when the wind blew <u>dust</u> onto *his* <u>wounds</u>.
4 *He* was dying from <u>malnutrition</u>.
5 *It* was <u>ransacked</u> and in ruins.
6 *They* <u>huddled</u> and <u>clung</u> together.
7 *She* <u>pawned</u> her possessions to pay for *his* addiction.
8 *He* was <u>hungover</u> and <u>broke</u>.
9 The <u>cancer of alcoholism</u> ate away at *their* lives.

## What do you think?

- What does Fergal Keane mean when he says:
  *'So much that seemed essential to me has, in the past few days, taken on a different colour.'*
- How will his relationship with his son differ from the one with his own father?
- What lessons about life does Fergal Keane want his son to learn from this letter?
- Which parts of the letter do you think particularly moved the listeners to the BBC?
- What lessons have you learned from your upbringing that you would like to pass on to your children?

**DPK**

Daniel Patrick Keane
was born on
Thursday, February 4th
in Hong Kong

# LANGUAGE FOCUS
## Modal auxiliary verbs

## Modal verbs in the present and future

1 All modal verbs can be used to express varying degrees of likelihood or probability. Match a sentence on the left with an explanation on the right.

| It | **will**<br>**must**<br>**could**<br>**may**<br>**might**<br>**can**<br>**can't**<br>**shouldn't** | be difficult. | I'm not sure but it's possible. (x3)<br>All evidence points to this. I predict this strongly.<br>I have a lot of evidence that it is.<br>I have a lot of evidence that it isn't.<br>There are times when it is difficult.<br>If everything goes according to plan. |
| --- | --- | --- | --- |

2 Certain modals can also be used to express *obligation* (mild and strong), *permission*, *ability*, *willingness*, and *habit*.

> You **should see** a doctor. (mild obligation/advice)
> You **may go** in now. (permission)
> She **will bite** her nails. (habit)

Give some more examples.

▶▶ **Grammar Reference p153**

1 Which sentences express a degree of probability?

1 He always looks so stressed. He *must* have a very demanding job.
2 You *must* come with us next time. You'd love it.
3 I *can't* hear you – the line's bad.
4 They *can't* be coming. They'd have been here by now.
5 She *might* change her mind if we keep on at her.
6 You *could* be right.
7 You *can* borrow the car. I don't need it.
8 We *may* stay over at Claire's if the party finishes late.
9 No, you *may* not go out on a school night just before your exams.
10 You *should* have no trouble passing. You're good at exams.
11 You *should* be studying three hours a night.
12 *Will* you give me a hand with this?
13 It's half past ten. She*'ll* be at the airport by now.
14 It's so annoying. He *won't* admit when he's in the wrong.
15 He *can* read and he's only three.
16 Learning English *can* be difficult.

What are the uses in the other sentences?

## Modal verbs in the past

1 Modals expressing probability all form their past in the same way.

| Verb + Perfect Infinitive | | |
| --- | --- | --- |
| She<br>It<br>They | will<br>must<br>may | have arrived. |

Give some more examples.

2 Modals expressing other meanings can have different forms in the past.

> We **must stop** to get petrol.
> (present obligation)
>
> We **had to stop** to get petrol.
> (past obligation)

3 What are the meanings of the modals in these sentences?

> She **could/was able to** read at three.
> He **wouldn't** admit that he was wrong.
> You **should have** seen the doctor.
> He **would** always argue the point.
> I **needn't have** brought my umbrella.

▶▶ **Grammar Reference p153**

*'I've got the bowl, the bone, the big yard,*
*I know I <u>should</u> be happy.'*

**2** Put the modal in the first sentence into the past to complete the second sentence.

1 It must be raining. Everyone's putting up their umbrellas.

It **must have been raining**. The ground is still wet.

2 I must stop smoking.

I _____ smoking because I became breathless just walking upstairs.

3 He should stop smoking before it's too late.

He _____ before it was too late.

4 We can go to Bob's party on Saturday.

We _____ to Bob's party last Saturday.

5 There's the phone. It'll be Paul.

Did he have a deep voice? It _____ Paul.

6 You needn't give me a lift, but if you're going my way that's great.

She _____ me a lift, but she did.

7 You needn't give me a lift because I've got my car with me.

She _____ me a lift, so she didn't.

8 My niece can't read very well because she's dyslexic.

My niece _____ until she was twelve.

9 Let's take a map. We'll get lost if we don't.

I'm glad we took the map. We _____ if we hadn't.

10 What's wrong with him? He'll just sit for hours staring into space.

Something was wrong. He _____ staring into space.

**3** Look at these pairs of sentences and discuss possible differences in meaning with a partner.

1 He must be on his way.
I must be on my way.

2 I must stop smoking.
I have to stop smoking.

3 They must share a flat together.
We must share a flat together.

4 You don't have to buy her chocolates.
You mustn't buy her chocolates.

5 The exam will have started.
The exam will be starting.

6 He can't be married.
We can't be married.

**4** Extend each sentence in exercise 3 to illustrate its meaning.

He must be on his way **because he said he was leaving at ten o'clock.**

I must be on my way. **I'm meeting John in half an hour.**

# SPEAKING
## Dilemma!

**1** Work in groups. In this game you have to predict how one of your classmates would behave in a certain situation. Your teacher will give each group cards like this.

> ## SITUATION
> **You are a taxi driver.**
> You find a bag in your cab with €20,000 in it. The name of the owner is on the bag, but not the address.
>
> ### WHAT WOULD YOU DO?

**2** Choose a card. Then choose someone in the room and discuss with your group how you think he or she would react in that situation. Write down their prediction.

**3** When it is your turn, read out the situation card to the person you chose. Ask him or her how he/she would react. If your prediction is right, your group scores a point. If it is wrong, challenge them and explain why you are right. The whole class votes to make a final decision.

**4** The secret is to match a person and a situation, and then it is a question of how well you know your classmates. Be prepared for some surprises!

## LISTENING AND SPEAKING
### Words of wisdom

**1** **T 7.4** Listen to some people talking about advice they have been given in their lives. Take notes after each person to complete the chart.

| Name | Words of wisdom | Given by whom? |
|------|-----------------|----------------|
| 1 Elaine | | |
| 2 Lizzie | | |
| 3 Justin | | |
| 4 Claire | | |
| 5 Henry | | |
| 6 Simon | | |
| 7 Fiona | | |
| 8 Chris | | |
| 9 Sue | | |
| 10 Martyn | | |

**2** Work with a partner and use your notes to talk to each other about the people in the chart.

Which pieces of advice do you find most interesting or relevant to you?

**3** Have you ever been given any particularly memorable words of wisdom that have helped you in your life? Tell the class.

## VOCABULARY AND PRONUNCIATION
### Rhyme and reason

**1** Work with a partner. Read the poem on p69 and discuss which is the best word to complete the lines. Use a dictionary if necessary. Compare your version with others in the class. Justify your choice of words.

**2** **T 7.5** Listen and compare with the actual poem. Whose was closest to the original?

**3** Listen again and mark the stresses in the first two verses. Read the poem aloud to each other, concentrating on the rhythm.

**4** **T 7.6** Read and listen to one of the poems some school children wrote, modelled on Lewis Carroll's verses.

> ## You are old, Uncle John
>
> 'You are old, Uncle John,' the young girl did say,
>
> 'Yet you spend six hours a day at the gym,
>
> And you jog down the road before break of day
>
> Pray, why keep yourself so very trim?'
>
> 'In my youth,' Uncle John replied to his niece
>
> 'I was hugely enormously fat,
>
> But now that I've met a young lady from Greece
>
> Motivation has got rid of that!'

**5** Work with your partner to write some similar verses. Read them to the class.

# You are old, Father William

BY LEWIS CARROLL

'You are old, Father William,' the young man said,
'And your hair has become very white;
And yet you incessantly stand on your _____ .   head/hands/bed
Do you think, at your age, it is _____?'   smart/right/bright

'In my youth,' Father William replied to his son,
'I feared it might _____ the brain;   injure/hurt/destroy
But, now that I'm perfectly sure I have _____,   none/one/gone
Why, I do it again and again.'

'You are old,' said the youth, 'as I _____ before,   stated/mentioned/suggested
And have grown most _____ fat,   hugely/uncommonly/unnaturally
Yet you turned a back somersault in at the door,
Pray what is the reason of that?'

'In my youth,' said the sage, as he shook his grey _____,   curls/beard/locks
'I kept all my limbs very _____   supple/fit/nimble
By the use of this ointment – one shilling the box –
Allow me to sell you a couple?'

'You are old,' said the youth, 'and your jaws are too weak
For anything tougher than _____;   cake/suet/jelly
Yet you finished the goose, with the _____ and the beak   body/feathers/bones
Pray, how did you manage to do it?'

'In my youth,' said his father, 'I took to the law,
And argued each _____ with my wife;   case/day/night
And the muscular strength which it gave to my _____,   tongue/jaw/chin
Has lasted the rest of my life.'

'You are old,' said the youth, 'one would hardly suppose
That your eye was as _____ as ever;   steady/true/focused
Yet you balanced an eel on the end of your nose –
What made you so _____ clever?'   really/awfully/very

'I have answered three questions, and that is enough,'
Said his father. 'Don't give yourself _____!   airs/manners/away
Do you think I can listen all day to such _____?   rubbish/stuff/nonsense
Be off, or I'll kick you downstairs!'

# THE LAST WORD
## Breaking the rules of English

1  Look at two quotations on the subject of English grammar rules.
What point is being made by both writers?

> ❛Ending a sentence with a preposition is something up with which I will not put.❜
>
> WINSTON CHURCHILL

> ❛There is a busybody on your staff who devotes a lot of his time to chasing split infinitives. Every good literary craftsman splits his infinitives when the sense demands it. I call for the immediate dismissal of this pedant. It is of no consequence whether he decides to go quickly or quickly to go or to quickly go. The important thing is that he should go at once.❜
>
> GEORGE BERNARD SHAW in a letter to *The Times* newspaper

2  There are many 'rules' in English which linguistic pedants insist should be
taught to children. Work with a partner. Read these tips and say how the 'rule'
in each one is broken. Correct them according to the rule where possible.

## 20 TIPS FOR PROPER ENGLISH

1  A preposition is a terrible word to end a sentence with. Never do it.
2  Remember to never split an infinitive.
3  Don't use no double negatives.
4  Don't ever use contractions.
5  And never start a sentence with a conjunction.
6  Write i before e except after c. I'm relieved to receive this anciently weird rule.
7  Foreign words and phrases are not 'chic'.
8  The passive voice is to be avoided wherever possible.
9  Who needs rhetorical questions?
10  Reserve the apostrophe for it's proper use and omit it when its not necessary.
11  Use fewer with number and less with quantity. Less and less people do.
12  Proof read carefully to see if you any words out.
13  Me and John are careful to use subject pronouns correctly.
14  Verbs has to agree with their subjects.
15  You've done good to use adverbs correctly.
16  If any word is incorrect at the end of a sentence, an auxiliary verb is.
17  Steer clear of incorrect verb forms that have snuck into the language.
18  Take the bull by the hand and avoid mixing your idioms.
19  Tell the rule about 'whom' to who you like.
20  At the end of the day avoid clichés like the plague.

3  Which rules above do you think are 'good' rules and which are not? Why?

4  Which rules in your language do you think are unnecessary or silly?

▶▶▶ **Writing** Describing a personal experience **p126**

# 8 Altered images

**Metaphors and idioms • Real and unreal tense usage • Softening the message**

**STARTER**

1 Are these all examples of art? Are some more 'arty' than others?
   What is the purpose of art? Or does it, by definition, have no point?

2 Work with a partner and try to describe each one. Discuss your reactions to them.

*For artwork references see p6*

3 **T 8.1** Listen to different people describing the works of art. Which picture are they talking about? Make notes about what they say and discuss with your partner. Which picture is not described?

4 Compare the reactions of you and your partner with those of the people you listened to. Discuss them with the class.

## LISTENING AND SPEAKING
### At home with an artist

1 Look at the photographs. How would you describe Joe Downing's style of painting and sculpting? What's your opinion of it?

2 Read the biodata. Work with a partner and write some questions you would like to ask Joe Downing if you met him.

3 **T 8.2** These statements about Joe are *all* false. Listen to the first part of an interview with him and correct them. Check any unknown vocabulary in your dictionary.

**Part one    The early years**

1 Joe wanted to be an artist from childhood.

2 He grew up surrounded by beautiful paintings.

3 He helped at home with the domestic chores, such as making quilts and shelling beans.

4 His mother showed no appreciation of beautiful things.

5 His childhood was idyllic until he had to go to war when he was 16.

6 He had his nineteenth birthday in Germany.

7 After the war he wanted to study optometry in Chicago.

8 As a country bumpkin he found it very difficult to be plunged into city life.

9 He says he would never have become an artist if he hadn't seen Georges Seurat's painting, *La Grande Jatte*.

## Joe Downing Ménerbes

Joe Dudley Downing is a painter and sculptor who holds the distinction of being one of only three Americans ever to have had their work exhibited at the Louvre Museum in Paris.

Born in Kentucky, he grew up on a tobacco farm in the village of Horse Cave, but has lived in France since 1950, dividing his time between Paris and the southern village of Ménerbes.

Picasso visited his first exhibition in Paris in 1968 and offered him advice. His work can now be found in the permanent collections of museums in France, Belgium, Luxembourg, Israel, Canada, Australia, and the United States of America.

**4** **T 8.3** Before you listen to the second part of the interview, check that you understand the words in *italics*.

**Part two  On being a painter**

1  Has Joe always been an abstract painter? What was his development as an artist? In what way did he *follow his bent*?
2  How did he *keep the pot boiling* when he moved to Paris?
3  What does he mean when he talks about *a very strong thread, what the French call a 'fil conducteur'*, in his work?
4  What does he say is *fragile* for all artists?
5  What is the connection between *velvety-looking lasagne* and *green leather gardening gloves*? Tell Joe's ridiculous story in your own words.

**5** **T 8.4** Listen to the final part of the interview and answer the questions.

**Part three  On living in the South of France**

1  What does Joe believe happens anywhere there's sunshine, olives, and Roman tiles?
2  What do you learn about the village of Ménerbes?
3  Why does Joe feel selfish and mean?
4  Who said: 'I'm tired of lugging you two around'? Why?
5  How did he discover his house in Ménerbes?
6  Why was it so inexpensive? What was written on the shoebox?
7  In what way has Joe's life come full circle?
8  Does he have any regrets about his life?

## What do you think?

• Which of the questions you wrote with your partner in exercise 2 were answered?
• In what ways has fate played a part in Joe's life? How might his life have been different?
• What overall impression do you get of Joe as a man? Would his lifestyle appeal to you?

## Talking about a work of art

Do you have a favourite work of art? A painting? A sculpture? A piece of music? A building? Where and when did you see/hear it? Make notes describing it and saying why you like it. If you can, bring a picture to the class.

# VOCABULARY AND LISTENING
## Metaphors and idioms

**1** **T 8.5** Read conversation **A** and listen to conversation **B**. What are the differences?

**2** Look at the tapescript on p140 and find the metaphors in conversation **B**. Match the metaphors to their meanings in conversation **A**. What are their literal meanings?

**Time flies.**
*It means to go through the air.*
*Usually, birds, planes, and insects fly.*

**3** Work with a partner. Here are some more sentences that contain metaphors. What is the literal meaning? What is the metaphorical meaning?

### Conversation A

**A** Hi, Annie! I haven't seen you for ages.

**B** I know. Time goes so fast, doesn't it?

**A** It's true. Work as busy as ever, is it?

**B** Yes, I'm working very hard as usual, but we have an awful lot of work at the moment. We're just about coping, but it isn't easy. How about you?

**A** OK. Business was bad this time last year, and we really had to make a lot of economies, but things have improved since then. You've moved, haven't you? Where are you living now?

**B** We've bought an old house in a little village where not much happens. You must come and visit us.

**A** I'd love to, but we're very busy at the moment. Does it need much doing to it?

**B** Everything. I hope we haven't given ourselves more work than we can manage.

**A** You'll be fine. Anyway, I must go. Lovely to see you again.

**B** And you. Bye!

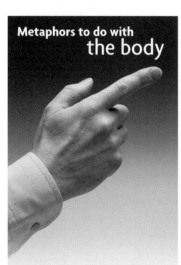

**Metaphors to do with the body**

1 I don't want to point the finger at anyone for this defeat. I think we're all to blame.

2 When we set up the business, we had a few hiccups, but nothing we couldn't get round.

3 It broke his heart when she left him for another man.

4 The view over the snow-capped mountains takes your breath away.

5 Her terrible childhood experiences scarred her for life.

**Metaphors to do with light**

6 I couldn't solve the problem at all, and then the answer came to me in a flash.

7 When my daughter got her prize, she was glowing with pride.

8 It was going to an exhibition that sparked my interest in photography.

9 James has lived his whole life being overshadowed by his famous brother.

10 I didn't know why she was being so nice. Then it suddenly dawned on me. She wanted my money.

**Metaphors to do with nature**

11 Joe and Helen have a stormy relationship. They have some blazing rows.

12 His career blossomed after he was nominated for an Oscar.

13 She was in floods of tears when she was told she'd been made redundant.

14 The root of all my problems is lack of money.

15 Sorry. I haven't the foggiest idea what you're talking about.

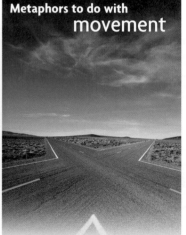

**Metaphors to do with movement**

16 Help! I've reached a crossroads in life. What should I do next?

17 He followed in his father's footsteps and became a doctor.

18 The politician gave a long, rambling speech on the subject of monetarism.

19 We aren't getting any nearer to solving our problem. We're going round in circles.

20 There have been great strides in medical technology over the past fifty years.

**4** **T 8.6** Listen to the conversation. Who and what is being talked about? The speakers use a lot of idioms. Which can you remember?

**5** **T 8.6** These sentences are similar to some of those in the conversation. Replace the words in *italics* with the idioms you heard. Listen again and check.

1 *It was a complete surprise when* he inherited a fortune.

2 When he heard about it, he was *thrilled*.

3 He's *in real trouble* because he spent the whole lot in a month.

4 He was going to ask her to marry him, but then he *lost the courage.*

5 He'll have to *change his attitude*, *try harder* and get a job.

6 Marilyn – no, that's not it. *I can almost remember* her name.

7 She told him he was *useless*.

8 I'm glad you told me, otherwise I might have *said something really insensitive.*

**6** Replace the words in *italics* with a metaphor or idiom from exercises 3, 4, and 5. Make any necessary changes.

1 I *did what my mother did* and became a teacher.

2 The actors had a few *small problems* at the beginning of the play, but then it went smoothly.

3 My neighbours *row a lot*.

4 When I heard I'd got the job, I was *very, very happy*.

5 When Jane's marriage ended, she knew she *had to make an important decision that would affect the rest of her life.*

6 This argument is stupid. We're *making no progress at all.*

7 When she showed him the finished statue, it *left him stunned and he couldn't speak.*

8 The business *developed successfully* when they won an order worth £1 million.

9 I was going to ask the film star for his autograph, but then I *lost the courage* and couldn't do it.

10 I went to the lecture on nuclear physics, but I didn't have *a clue* what it was about.

11 The book got a *review with a lot of praise*, so I went out and bought it.

12 You're *in real trouble*. I saw you steal that book.

## READING AND SPEAKING
### The man behind the mouse

**1** What Disney films can you name? Have you ever been to a Disneyland® Theme Park? What do you know about them?

**2** Which of these words or expressions would you relate to the world of Disney?

| | | |
|---|---|---|
| airbrushed reality | harmonious | romanticized |
| cruel | harsh | troubled |
| a dream factory | imaginative | a tormented childhood |
| fantasy land | idealized | violent |
| happy endings | magical | |

**3** Read the opening lines of the article. What first impression do you get of Walt Disney's childhood?

**4** Read the rest of the article. Which of the words in exercise 2 on p75 relate to the life of the man, Walt Disney?

**5** Imagine that Walt Disney lied about his life, and said these things. What in fact was the truth?

1 I had an idyllic childhood with everything I could have wanted.
2 We were a tight family unit, and we all got on well together.
3 I wasn't particularly close to my brother.
4 I put all of my childhood experiences into my work.
5 Success came to me easily. I didn't have to work hard.
6 I was a self-made man. Nobody helped me.
7 I always put my family before my work, and I was always blessed with good health.
8 The idea for Mickey Mouse was mine. I created every aspect of the character.
9 There were never any hiccups in my career.
10 I wasn't particularly involved in the creation of Disneyland.

## Language work

**6** Who might have said these things? About what?

1 He'd beat us regularly for no reason.
2 You'd better not do that again or I'll run away.
3 I'd have been able to do more drawing if we'd been less poverty-stricken.
4 If he'd asked our permission, we'd never have allowed him to go.
5 Supposing we'd kept the name Mortimer?
6 I know he'd rather we'd had a son.
7 I'd have slept at home if she'd been quieter.
8 If only you'd given up smoking years ago!

Are the *'d* contractions short forms of *would* or *had*?

**7** Work with a partner. Discuss the meaning of the words highlighted in the article.

## What do you think?

- In what ways was Walt Disney a workaholic? What drove him?
- Successful people often have unhappy childhoods. Why is this? Do you know any examples?
- Are there features that all creative geniuses have in common?
- Compare the lives of Walt Disney and Joe Downing.

# Walt
## The man

It was 3.30 in the morning and 8-year-old Walt Disney was doing what he did at that time every morning – rolling hundreds of copies of the *Kansas City Morning Times* that he would soon place behind the screen door of subscribers along his route.

It was hard work for a little kid who also had to go to school, then deliver another round in the evening. Sometimes he had to traipse through three feet of snow. Other times he got so tired he'd sneak into an alley for a catnap. But the paper round beat picking apples for a living. That's what he'd been doing before, on his family's failing farm in Marceline, Missouri. The problem was that his boss – his stern father, Elias – had the nasty habit of delivering daily beatings both to Walt and his brother Roy, eight years Walt's senior. After a disgusted Roy left home, the brunt of the work, and the beatings, fell on Elias' youngest son.

Walt Disney, born on December 5, 1901, never had time for a childhood. As a result, he spent all of his adult life attempting to invent one for himself. In the process – almost by accident – he created wonderful childhood memories for generation after generation of children worldwide.

### An airbrushed boyhood

Later, Walt would paint a nostalgic picture of life in Missouri, carefully airbrushing away the difficult times. He'd talk about sketching the farm animals, which he did when he could find pencil and paper – rare commodities in the dirt-poor Disney home. Once he was punished for painting a cartoon on the wall of the house. As always, it was his teenage brother, Roy, who comforted him, rocking him to sleep.

When the Disneys moved to Chicago, Walt signed up for cartooning classes at the Chicago Academy of Fine Arts, working three part-time jobs to pay for them. But all these were abandoned during World War I, when, at the age of 16, he forged his parents' signatures and became an ambulance driver for the Red Cross in France.

Home again, Walt joined Roy in Kansas City and found work as a commercial artist. Here he met another artist, Ub Iwerks, and together they developed a series of short films called *Alice in Cartoonland*. Walt moved to Los Angeles, where Roy was in hospital with tuberculosis. He searched desperately for a distributor. The night he got a telegram offering him $1,500

# Disney behind the mouse

### by Melissa Burdick Harmon

apiece for six *Alice* shorts, Walt raced to the hospital where Roy was a patient, and persuaded him to leave hospital and come to work for him the next day.

Roy Disney would devote the rest of his life to helping his baby brother, skilfully handling the business end of the Disney empire. Walt also employed Ub Iwerks as chief animator.

## Of mice, marriage and men

When he was 24, he married one of his employees, Lillian Bounds. It was a union that would last – although not always happily – until his death 41 years later. At 24, Walt was already married to his work. He created a cartoon character called *Oswald the Lucky Rabbit*, who was a great success. He then shifted his attention to mice, or one particular mouse called Mortimer. Lillian dismissed the name Mortimer as 'too sissy', so Mortimer became Mickey. Surprisingly, it was Ub Iwerks, not Walt, who first drew him. Walt, however, provided Mickey's voice. They made a talkie, *Steamboat Willie*, which premiered on November 18, 1928, to rave reviews, and Mickey Mouse became an overnight sensation.

Success followed success, but Walt pushed himself ever harder. In 1930 he suffered a nervous breakdown due to overwork, and when Lillian surprised him with the news that she was pregnant, he became severely depressed. How could a man whose whole life was dedicated to giving *himself* a childhood take on the burden of becoming a parent?

He produced his first feature-length cartoon, *Snow White and the Seven Dwarfs*, for which he won a special Oscar. Then came the birth of a second daughter, Sharon, who took to crying all night. Walt, who had wanted a son, took to sleeping at the studio.

In many ways Walt was a benevolent employer, but, like his father he was subject to terrible fits of rage. Feeling totally betrayed when his animators went on strike because they wanted to join a union, he started working for the 'House of Un-American Activities Committee', which investigated 'communists' in Hollywood, and informed on the strike leader.

## The last, best times

Post second World War, Walt continued to work prolifically. In 1950 he produced his first live-action film, *Treasure Island*. Then came Disneyland®. Everyone tried to dissuade him, saying it was too costly a dream, but he wouldn't listen. He oversaw every nut and bolt of its creation. His great world of fantasy opened on July 17, 1955. In the next seven weeks, more than one million people walked down Disneyland®'s Main Street USA, an idealized version of Main Street, Marceline, Missouri, circa 1900. The man who had spent his painful childhood in the real-life version of that town now stood in the window of an apartment decorated exactly like his boyhood home, tears streaming down his face, watching other people enjoy the perfect childhood world that he had created.

In November 1966 he was diagnosed with lung cancer. He was given six months to two years to live, but two weeks later, after spending the evening with Roy working on a new Florida theme park, Walt Disney died. He had just turned 65.

Walt Disney used to say jokingly, 'I hope we never lose sight of one thing ... none of this would have happened if it hadn't been for a mouse.' But in truth, it was started by a tormented childhood and became reality through Walt's irrepressible drive and imagination and the tireless help of a devoted brother.

# LANGUAGE FOCUS
## Real and unreal tense usage

### would

> **1** *Would* has several different uses. Look at these examples from the text.
>
> a *Roy Disney* **would** *devote the rest of his life . . .*
> *It was a union that* **would** *last . . . until his death . . .*
>
> b *. . . he'd sneak into an alley for a catnap.*
> *He'd talk about sketching the farm animals . . .*
>
> c *. . . but Walt* **wouldn't** *listen.*
>
> **2** Which sentences, a, b, or c, express . . .?
> - past habits
> - refusal on a past occasion
> - the future in the past
>
> ▶▶ **Grammar Reference p154**

**1** Which use of *would* is expressed in these sentences?

1 My car wouldn't start this morning. I had to get the bus.

2 When I was a kid, I'd get up at 7.00 and take the dog for a walk.

3 In Paris Charles met Penny, who he would marry five years later.

4 Whenever we had time, we'd go windsurfing. Those were the days!

5 When he was first going out with Jacky, he'd buy her presents all the time.

6 So he took the job, did he? I knew he'd change his mind.

7 I asked him why he'd lied, but he wouldn't tell me.

8 Sorry about the noise. I didn't think you'd hear it.

**2** Complete these sentences in a suitable way.

1 I could have smashed my computer this morning.
### It just wouldn't ...

2 My grandad was such a kind man.
### He'd ...

3 I don't know why she left me.
### I told her a thousand times I'd ...

4 My mother used to drive me mad.
### She'd always ...

5 I don't believe Manchester United lost 2–0!
### I thought they'd ...

6 Why did you tidy the flat?
### I said I'd ...

### Past tenses to express unreality

> **1** The examples of *would* in exercises 1 and 2 express real time. *Would* is also used in conditional sentences to express a situation which is contrary to reality.
>
> *I* **would** *sleep at home if the baby didn't make so much noise.*
> *. . . none of this (success)* **would** *have happened if it hadn't been for a mouse.*
>
> Which is a second and which is a third conditional? What are the rules of form and use?
>
> **2** There are other ways of expressing a situation which is contrary to reality. Identify the tenses in the examples below. What is the reality in each one? Complete the sentences.
>
> I wish I didn't smoke so much. (But . . .)
> She wished she hadn't opened her big mouth. (But . . .)
> I wish you'd think before you speak. (But . . .)
> I wish I could drive. (But . . .)
> If only we'd set off earlier! (But . . .)
>
> ▶▶ **Grammar Reference p154**

**3** These sentences all have verbs in the Past Simple. Which ones refer to real past time?

1 Suppose we called him Mickey?

2 He would become nostalgic when he told stories about his upbringing.

3 I couldn't swim until I was fourteen.

4 If I could afford it, I'd buy it.

5 Isn't it time we had a break?

6 My childhood was poor. If we had any money, it went to pay debts.

7 He behaves as if he owned the place.

8 I wish you didn't have to go.

**4** These sentences all have verbs in the Past Perfect. Which ones refer to real past time?

1 I wish you hadn't said that. It was cruel.

2 I knew I'd seen her before.

3 Had he known the truth, he would have acted more cautiously.

4 She apologized, saying she hadn't had time to phone me.

5 I'd rather you'd kept the news to yourself, but it's too late now.

6 They looked as though they'd had a good time.

**5** Put the verbs in brackets in the correct tense or verb form. Where there is no verb given, use an auxiliary verb.

**Seth and Amy are having a row in a hotel. They're on their way to London.**

**Amy** Ugh! This hotel is horrible. I wish we (1)_____ (not come) here. I (2)_____ never _____ (see) such a dirty hotel in my life! It (3)_____ (not be) so bad if the bathroom (4)_____ (be) clean, but it (5)_____ (be) filthy. I (6)_____ even _____ (not wash) my socks in it.

**Seth** I know, but it (7)_____ (get) late, and we (8)_____ (drive) all day, and I (9)_____ (want) to stop. If we (10)_____, we might not have found a hotel and we (11)_____ still _____ (drive). That (12)_____ (be) awful. At least this is better than nothing.

**Amy** Well, I wish we (13)_____ (set off) earlier. Then we (14)_____ (can arrive) in London today, and we (15)_____ (have) a whole day to go round the galleries and museums. As it is, we (16)_____ (not get) there till tomorrow lunchtime, and we (17)_____ only _____ (have) a few hours.

**Seth** I (18)_____ (like) (19)_____ (spend) more time in London, too, but I (20)_____ (have) to go to work this morning. If I (21)_____, we (22)_____ (stay) in a top London hotel now instead of this dump.

**Amy** I (23)_____ (love) (24)_____ (see) a show, but we can't, so that's all there is to it. Anyway, it's time we (25)_____ (think) about getting something to eat. If it (26)_____ (not be) so late, I (27)_____ (suggest) going into town, but if we (28)_____ we might not find anywhere. It's quite late already.

**Seth** I wish you (29)_____ (not moan) about everything. I (30)_____ (not mind), but you're so indecisive. If it (31)_____ (leave) up to you, we (32)_____ never _____ (do) anything or go anywhere.

**Amy** OK, OK. I'm sorry. Let's go.

**T 8.7** Listen and check. Practise the conversation with a partner. Pay attention to short forms and contractions.

# THE LAST WORD
## Softening the message

**1** Sometimes we want to express ourselves in a tactful, polite way. We don't want to be too direct or confrontational.

*Could you possibly lend me some money?* is less direct than *Lend me some money.*

Read the lines and number them in order, 1 being most direct. What makes each message less direct?

**T 8.8** Listen and check. Practise the stress and intonation.

▶▶ **Grammar Reference p156**

a ☐ I wonder if you could help me?
  ☐ Could you help me?
  ☐ Can you help me?
  ☐ I was wondering if you could possibly help me? I'd be very grateful.

b ☐ Do you mind if I open the window?
  ☐ Would you mind if I opened the window? It's so stuffy in here.

c ☐ I want to speak to you.
  ☐ I wanted to have a word with you, if that's all right.

d ☐ If I were you, I'd dye it black.
  ☐ I'd have thought the best idea would have been to dye it black, but it's up to you.
  ☐ You could dye it black.
  ☐ Dye it black.

**2** **T 8.9** Listen to some conversations. How is the message softened in each one?

Look at the tapescript on p141 and practise with a partner.

**3** Rephrase these sentences so that they sound softer. Use the words in brackets.

1 I want to use your phone. (*mind*)
2 Don't paint the wall red. (*If I … you*)
3 We should go in my car. (*better*)
4 Ring back later. (*possible/possibly*)
5 We should phone to say we'll be late. (*Don't …?*)
6 Give me a lift to the station. (*hoping*)
7 She's French. (*think/thought*)
8 Would you like to come to the cinema with me? (*wondering*)
9 Fill in this form, please. (*mind*)
10 It'll rain this afternoon. (*surprised*)
11 I'm going for a walk. Anyone interested? (*thinking*)
12 I've popped in to see if you need anything. (*thought*)
13 It's a bad idea. (*say/said*)
14 Apologize to her. (*'d have said … best idea*)
15 I gave her a present. She didn't say thank you. (*You'd have thought*)

**T 8.10** Listen and check. Practise saying the sentences, paying attention to short forms and rhythm.

**4** With a partner, write some conversations for these situations, using tactful, polite language. Choose one and act it out in front of the class.

• You want to invite someone to go out with you. Meal? Cinema? Dance? Picnic?

• You phone a hotel. You want to stay three nights, and you'd like a quiet room.

• Your friend has just moved into a new flat. He/She wants some ideas about what to do with it.

• Someone rings to speak to your flatmate. She's out. What time will she be back? (*I'd have thought …*)

**T 8.11** Listen and compare.

▶▶ **Writing** Reviewing a film or book **p127**

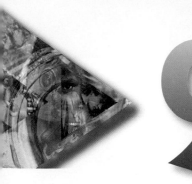

# 9 History lessons

**Verb patterns · Homonyms, homophones, and homographs · Telling jokes**

**STARTER**

1 Work in groups. Which historical events do the pictures illustrate? Match them to the events.

2 Put the twelve events in chronological order. In which century did they happen? Give any precise dates that you know.

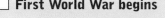

- ☐ First World War begins
- ☐ Great Wall of China built
- ☐ Charles Darwin publishes *On the Origin of Species*
- ☐ Storming of the Bastille – start of French Revolution

- ☐ Terrorist attack demolishes World Trade Center in New York
- ☐ Gottlieb Daimler and Karl Benz produce the first automobiles
- ☐ Leonardo da Vinci paints the *Mona Lisa*
- ☐ First Olympic Games held in Greece

- ☐ US drops first atomic bombs on Hiroshima and Nagasaki
- ☐ American War of Independence begins
- ☐ AIDS becomes a major health threat throughout the world
- ☐ Berlin Wall demolished

3 Write down the three events which you feel are most important. Add any others that you feel have been omitted from the list. Compare and justify your ideas in your groups and then with the whole class.

4 Which recent news events do you feel will go down in history?

## READING AND SPEAKING
### I was there

**1** Where do these historical events fit chronologically with those on p81?

- The destruction of Pompeii by Mount Vesuvius
- The first transatlantic radio message
- The sinking of the *Titanic*
- The first aeroplane flight across the Channel
- The first men on the moon

**2** Match the events in exercise 1 with these extracts from eyewitness accounts.

1 It stood upright in the water for four full minutes, then it began to slide gently downwards.
2 There is nothing to be seen – neither the destroyer, nor France, nor England. I am alone. I am lost.
3 It had been awaiting its first visitors for a long time.
4 We saw the sea sucked away and apparently forced back by the earthquake.
5 The result meant much more to me than the mere successful realization of an experiment, it was an epoch in history.

Quickly scan all the texts to check your ideas.

**3** Work in groups. Look at the historical events on pp82–5 and divide them among you, choosing two or three that interest you. Read them and answer the questions.

1 What was the exact date of the event?
2 Who is describing it? Is the person a protagonist or an observer? In what way?
3 What kind of event is it? Natural or man-made? Good or bad? Describe it.
4 Who were the people involved? How did they react?
5 Why was it so important? What repercussions have there been since it took place?

Compare the answers with your group and share information about all the events.

### Vocabulary work

**4** Which of these words are from the texts you chose? Divide them into nouns, verbs, and adjectives. Use a dictionary if necessary.

| | | | |
|---|---|---|---|
| amplifiers | crude | shriek | toss |
| ashes | deploy | slant | trunk |
| blaze | jettison | slide | unimpeded |
| blot out | lunar | snowdrift | valves |
| bow | mob | stern | violent |
| cart | overwhelmed | stranded | wailing |
| coils | panic-stricken | swarm | whirl |
| condensers | pungent | sway | |

**5** Explain the words from your texts to your group.

**6** Which words are technical words? Which texts are they from?

## I was there...

### 24 August, AD79

# The eruption of Vesuv

BY PLINY THE YOUNGER

This was the eruption that destroyed and buried the towns of Pompeii and Herculaneum.

On 24 August, in the early afternoon, my mother drew attention to a cloud of unusual size and appearance. It was not clear at that distance from which mountain the cloud was rising. (It was afterwards known to be Vesuvius.) Its general appearance can best be expressed as being like an umbrella pine, for it rose to a great height on a sort of trunk and then split off into branches. Broad sheets of fire and leaping flames blazed at several points. By this time the courtyard was full of ashes so that its level had risen. The buildings were now shaking with violent shocks and seemed to be swaying to and fro.

My mother and I finally decided to leave the town. We were followed by a panic-stricken mob of people. Once beyond the buildings we stopped, and there we had some extraordinary experiences which thoroughly

## 12 December, 1901

## The first radio signal
### across the Atlantic

### BY GUGLIELMO MARCONI

The signal was sent from Poldhu in Cornwall to Guglielmo Marconi, waiting on a cliff in Newfoundland.

Shortly before mid-day I placed the single earphone to my ear and started listening. The receiver on the table before me was very crude – a few coils and condensers – no valves, no amplifiers, not even a crystal. But I was at last on the point of putting the correctness of all my beliefs to the test. The answer came at 12.30 when I heard, faintly but distinctly, pip-pip-pip. I handed the phone to Kemp: 'Can you hear anything?' I asked. 'Yes,' he said, 'the letter S' – he could hear it. I knew then that all my anticipations had been justified. The electric waves sent out into space from Poldhu had traversed the Atlantic – the enormous distance of 1,700 miles – unimpeded by the curvature of the earth. The result meant much more to me than the mere successful realization of an experiment, it was an epoch in history. I now felt for the first time absolutely certain that the day would come when mankind would be able to send messages without wires not only across the Atlantic but also between the furthermost ends of the earth.

---

## us

alarmed us. We saw the sea sucked away and apparently forced back by the earthquake: it receded from the shore so that quantities of sea creatures were left stranded on dry sand. On the landward side a fearful black cloud parted to reveal great tongues of fire, like flashes of lightning magnified in size. Soon afterwards the cloud sank down to earth and covered the sea; it had already blotted out Capri. You could hear the shrieks of women, the wailing of infants, the shouts of men. Many besought the aid of gods, but still more imagined there were no gods left, and that the universe was plunged into darkness for evermore.

At last the darkness thinned. Then there was genuine daylight, and the sun actually shone out. We were terrified to see everything changed, buried deep in ashes like snowdrifts.

## 25 July, 1909

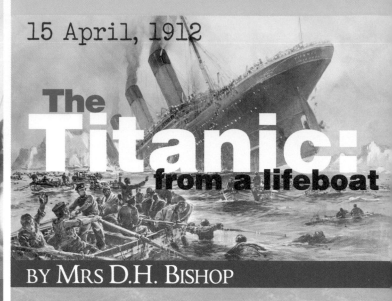

# The first flight
## across the Channel

### BY LOUIS BLÉRIOT

Blériot's monoplane averaged 46 mph and made the crossing in 40 minutes.

In the early morning of Sunday, 25 July 1909, I left my hotel at Calais and drove out to a field where my airplane was garaged. I had ordered the destroyer Escopette, placed at my disposal by the French government, to go to sea. I examined my aeroplane. I started the engine, and found it worked well.

At half past four daylight had come. Four thirty-five. Tout est prêt! In an instant I am in the air, my engine making 1,200 revolutions – almost its highest speed. I begin my flight steady and sure, towards the coast of England. The Escopette has seen me. She is driving ahead across the Channel at full speed. She makes perhaps 26 miles per hour. I am making over 40 mph. Rapidly I overtake her, travelling at a height of 250 feet. The moment is supreme, yet I surprised myself by feeling no exultation. Ten minutes go. I turn my head to see whether I am proceeding in the right direction. I am amazed. There is nothing to be seen – neither the destroyer, nor France, nor England. I am alone. I am lost.

Then I saw the cliffs of Dover! The wind had taken me out of my course. I turned and now I was in difficulties, for the wind here by the cliffs was much stronger, and my speed was reduced as I fought against it. My beautiful aeroplane responded and I found myself over dry land. I attempted to land, but the wind caught me and whirled me round two or three times. At once I stopped my motor, and instantly my machine fell on the ground. I was safe on your shore. Soldiers in khaki ran up, and also a policeman. Two of my compatriots were on the spot. They kissed my cheeks. I was overwhelmed.

## 15 April, 1912

# The Titanic:
## from a lifeboat

### BY MRS D.H. BISHOP

The 'unsinkable' Titanic had only 1,178 lifeboat spaces for 2,224 people on board. A total of 1,513 lives were lost.

We did not begin to understand the situation till we were perhaps a mile or more away from the Titanic. Then we could see the rows of lights along the decks begin to slant gradually upward from the bow. Very slowly these lines of light began to point downward at a greater and greater angle. The slant seemed to be greater about every quarter of an hour.

In a couple of hours, though, she began to go down more rapidly. Then the fearful sight began. The people in the ship were just beginning to realize how great their danger was. When the forward part of the ship dropped suddenly, there was a sudden rush of passengers on all the decks towards the stern. It was like a wave. We could see the great black mass of people in the steerage sweeping to the rear part of the boat. We could make out the increasing excitement on board as the people, rushing to and fro, caused the deck lights to disappear and reappear as they passed in front of them.

This panic went on for an hour. Then suddenly the ship seemed to shoot up out of the water and stand there perpendicularly. It stood upright in the water for four full minutes, then it began to slide gently downwards. Its speed increased as it went down head first, so that the stern shot down with a rush. The lights continued to burn until it sank. We could see the people packed densely in the stern till it was gone and we could hear their screaming a mile away. Gradually this became fainter and fainter and died away. Some of the lifeboats that had room for more might have gone to their rescue, but it would have meant that those who were in the water would have swarmed aboard and sunk her.

# I was there...

## 21 July, 1969

## The first men on the Moon

### BY NEIL ARMSTRONG & BUZZ ALDRIN

Apollo 11, carrying Neil Armstrong, Edwin (Buzz) Aldrin and Michael Collins, was launched on 16 July. Five days later they stepped down onto the moon.

### NEIL ARMSTRONG

*On the way there* Of all the spectacular views we had, the most impressive to me was on the way to the Moon when we flew through its shadow. We were still thousands of miles away, but close enough so that the Moon almost filled our circular window. It was illuminated only by earthshine. It made the Moon appear blue-grey, and the entire scene looked decidedly three-dimensional. It seemed almost as if it were showing us its roundness, its similarity in shape to our Earth, in a sort of welcome. I was sure it would be a hospitable host. It had been awaiting its first visitors for a long time.

*After touch down* The sky is black, you know. It's a very dark sky. But it still seemed more like daylight than darkness as we looked out the window. It's a peculiar thing but the surface looked very warm and inviting. From the cockpit it seemed to be tan. It's hard to account for that, because later when I held the material in my hand, it wasn't tan at all. It was black, grey and so on.

### BUZZ ALDRIN

*On the Moon* The blue colour of my boot has completely disappeared now into this – still don't know what colour to describe this other than greyish-cocoa.

*Back on board* The Moon was a very natural and pleasant environment in which to work. On the Moon, in one-sixth gravity, you have a distinct feeling of being somewhere. As we deployed our experiments we had to jettison things, some objects we tossed away and they would go in a slow, lazy motion.

Odour is very subjective, but to me there was a distinct smell to the lunar material – pungent, like gunpowder. We carted a fair amount of lunar dust back inside the vehicle, on our suits and boots, and we did notice the odours right away.

## Listening

7 **T 9.1** Listen to Justin Baines' eyewitness account. Which historical event did he witness? Where was he at the beginning of his story? From where did he watch events unfold?

Describe what he saw in your own words.

Do you remember where you were on that day? How did you hear about what happened? What were the repercussions of this event?

## Personal history

- Close your eyes and select an important event in your own life.
- Write brief notes on what, where, and when.
- Discuss its significance with your group. Ask and answer questions.

# VOCABULARY AND PRONUNCIATION
## Homonyms, homophones, and homographs

> **1** The word *bow* is both a homonym (same pronunciation, same spelling but different meanings) and a homograph (same spelling, but two pronunciations with different meanings).
>
> | **bow** /baʊ/ | |
> |---|---|
> | noun | 1 The front of a ship is called the **bow**.<br>2 The cast took their **bows** after the performance. |
> | verb | The Japanese **bow** when they greet each other. |
>
> | **bow** /bəʊ/ | |
> |---|---|
> | noun | 1 The ribbon made a beautiful **bow** in her hair.<br>2 Robin Hood used a **bow** and arrow to fight.<br>3 You play the violin with a **bow**. |
>
> 1 Read aloud all the sentences in the boxes.
> 2 Which meaning is both a noun and a verb?
> 3 Choose sentences to illustrate *bow* as a homonym.
> 4 Choose sentences to illustrate it as a homograph.
>
> **2** *bow* /baʊ/ is also a homophone. *bough* /baʊ/ has the same pronunciation, a different spelling and a different meaning. What is the meaning?

## Homonyms

**1** These sentences all contain words which have homonyms in the texts on pp82–5. Use your dictionary to check meanings and find the homonyms in the texts.

1 Our company has branches in New York, Frankfurt, and Singapore.
2 It's time I replaced my battered old trunk with a new suitcase.
3 Don't pine for him, Clarissa. Cheer up! He isn't worth it!
4 We were given a stern warning about the dangers of drink-driving.
5 This deck of cards has both the jokers missing.

**2** Identify the homonyms in these sentences. Make sentences for the other meanings.

1 One swallow doesn't make a summer.
2 We spotted a really rare bird in the forest.
3 Don't go making any rash promises that you can't keep!
4 Lessons were interrupted for a fire drill.
5 I think we should scrap that idea. It's rubbish.
6 Stop rambling and get to the point!

## Homophones

**3** Read these words aloud. Think of a homophone for each one.

| wail | whirled | fort | heir | site | hire | caught | soar |
|---|---|---|---|---|---|---|---|

**4** Complete the sentences with the correct homophone.

1 They tied their boat to a small _____ in the harbour. | a buoy<br>b boy
2 His _____ remarks upset all those present. | a coarse<br>b course
3 Public speaking makes my voice go _____. | a horse<br>b hoarse
4 They say it was a _____ gunman that shot the president. | a loan<br>b lone
5 The thieves got away with a large _____ of old bank notes. | a hall<br>b haul
6 Squirrels _____ nuts in woods and gardens. | a berry<br>b bury
7 She lifted her _____ and smiled at her new husband. | a vale<br>b veil
8 This is only a _____ contract. You don't have to sign it. | a draft<br>b draught

## Homographs

**5** **T 9.2** Listen and write the homograph you hear in each pair of sentences. What are the different pronunciations?

**We're sitting at the back in row 102.**
**We've had another row about our finances.**

**6** Divide into two groups. Use your dictionaries to find the two pronunciations and the meanings of the words in your box. Make sentences to illustrate the meanings to the other group.

| **GROUP A** | | | **GROUP B** | | |
|---|---|---|---|---|---|
| wind | refuse | defect | wound | minute | object |

# LISTENING AND SPEAKING
## Peace and goodwill

**1** Many historical events are concerned with war. Which major wars have there been over the last hundred years? What conflicts are in the news at the moment?

**2** **T 9.3** Listen to an extract from a musical called *Oh, What a Lovely War!*

1 Which war is it? Who is fighting who?
2 What nicknames do the two sides have for each other?
3 Where are they standing?
4 What is surprising about this enemy interaction?
5 The scene depicts the beginning of the so-called Christmas Truce, which took place on Christmas Eve in the first year of the war. What do you think happened next?

**3** **T 9.4** Listen to an interview with Graham Williams and Harold Startin, who were on sentry duty that night. Complete the sentences with the exact words you hear.

1 … lights began to appear all along the _____.
2 They sang this _____ right through.
3 … when I woke up I found everyone was walking out into _____.
4 They were giving us _____ about as big as your arm.
5 … we'd got no _____ against them, they'd got no _____ against us.
6 We were the best of _____, although we were there to kill one other.
7 They helped us _____ our dead, and we _____ our dead with their dead.
8 … they'd come and help you _____ your defences against them.

**4** Answer the questions.

1 How is Graham Williams' account similar to the scene in the play?
2 In what ways did the two sides communicate at first?
3 What is 'no-man's land'?
4 In what ways did they show goodwill towards each other?
5 How long did the truce last?
6 Who was Otto?

## What do you think?

• Do you find the story depressing or uplifting? Why?
• How is it possible that enemies become friends in the middle of a war?
• Do you think that commanding officers could become friends in the same way?
• Could such an incident happen in modern warfare? If so, where? If not, why not?

# LANGUAGE FOCUS
## Verb patterns

**1** Complete these common verb patterns from this unit with a verb on the right.

| verb + infinitive | The buildings **seemed** _____ to and fro.<br>We finally **decided** _____ the town.<br>The lights **continued** _____ until it sank.<br>I **attempted** _____ my plane.<br>I placed the earphone to my ear and **started** _____ . | appear<br>burn<br>bury<br>go<br>hate<br>land<br>leave<br>listen<br>make<br>see<br>sing<br>sway |
|---|---|---|
| verb + object + infinitive | They had **trained us** _____ the Germans.<br>I had **ordered the destroyer** _____ to sea.<br>They **helped us** _____ our dead.<br>It **made the Moon** _____ blue-grey. | |
| verb + preposition + -*ing* | The Germans **joined in** _____ with the British.<br>Not speaking German **didn't stop him from** _____ friends. | |
| verb + adjective + infinitive | We **were terrified** _____ everything changed. | |

▶▶ **Grammar Reference p156**

**2** Read the *Oxford Advanced Learner's Dictionary* entry on verb patterns with the verb *agree*. Use it to help you decide which of the sentences below are correct. Correct the others.

> **agree** /əˈgriː/ *verb*
> SHARE OPINION | **1** ~ **(with sb) (about/on sth)** | ~ **(with sth)**; to have the same opinion as sb; to say that you have the same opinion: [V] *When he said that, I had to agree.* ◇ *He agreed with them about the need for change.* ◇ *I agree with her analysis of the situation.* ◇ *'He's a lousy cook.' 'I couldn't agree more* (= I completely agree).*'* ◇ [V **(that)**] *We agreed (that) the proposal was a good one.* ◇ [V **speech**] *'That's true', she agreed.* OPP DISAGREE **2 be agreed (on/about sth)** | **be agreed (that ...)**; if people **are agreed** or sth **is agreed**, everyone has the same opinion about sth: [VN] *Are we all agreed on this?* ◇ [VN **(that)**] *It was agreed (that) we should hold another meeting.*
> SAY YES | **3** ~ **(to sth)** to say 'yes'; to say that you will do what sb wants or that you will allow sth to happen SYN CONSENT: [V] *I asked for a pay rise and she agreed.* ◇ *Do you think he'll agree to their proposal?* ◇ [V **(that)**] *She agreed (that) we could finish early.* ◇ [V **to** inf] *He agreed to let me go early.*

1 She thinks the war ended in 1918 and I am agree.
2 He agreed that they should spend some time apart.
3 They agreed on fighting the proposal was a bad idea.
4 He agreed to give us more time to finish the project.
5 They always agree to each other with the major decisions in life.
6 We agree to differ about politics.
7 Is this plan agreed with everyone?
8 They agreed to me with the time we should start the meeting.

**3** Do the same with this entry.

> **persuade** /pəˈsweɪd; *AmE* pərˈs-/ *verb* **1** ~ sb **(into sth/into doing sth)** to make sb do sth by giving them good reasons for doing it: [VN **to** inf] *Try to persuade him to come.* ◇ [VN] *Please try and persuade her.* ◇ *She's always easily persuaded.* ◇ *I allowed myself to be persuaded into entering the competition.* ◇ *I'm sure he'll come with a bit of persuading.* **2** to make sb believe that sth is true SYN CONVINCE: [VN **that**] *It will be difficult to persuade them that there's no other choice.* ◇ *She had persuaded herself that life was not worth living.* ◇ [VN] *No one was persuaded by his arguments.* ◇ *(formal) I am still not fully* **persuaded** *of the plan's merits.*

1 He persuaded his mother into lend him the money.
2 We were persuaded that it was the best course of action.
3 What do I have to do to persuade you that I love you?
4 You'll never persuade me of taking up mountaineering.
5 Eventually I was persuaded of all their arguments.

*'Rugged romantic seeks elegant lady. Must like hunting and gathering.'*

**4** Choose the verb which completes each sentence correctly. Change the verb patterns to make correct sentences with the other verbs.

| 1 | He | enjoys<br>used<br>is used<br>would rather | to be a soldier. |
|---|---|---|---|
| 2 | We | are trying<br>have decided<br>are thinking of<br>had better | selling our flat. |
| 3 | They | stopped<br>wanted<br>hoped<br>let | us to go. |
| 4 | I | am looking forward to<br>happened<br>avoided<br>suggested that he | meet her. |
| 5 | Did you | mind<br>see him<br>remind him<br>manage | do it? |
| 6 | She | didn't feel like<br>made me<br>couldn't help<br>promised not | to laugh. |
| 7 | Why | didn't you dare<br>were you made<br>are you threatening<br>were you forced into | resigning? |
| 8 | He | is keen<br>helped me<br>encouraged me<br>can't stand | learn English. |

*'"Society for the preservation of dragons" –*
*You don't want them to become extinct, do you ?!!'*

**5** **T 9.5** Listen and report the conversations using different verb patterns.

1 She was delighted _____ .
  He congratulated _____ .

2 She was concerned _____ .
  He urged _____ .

3 She was annoyed _____ .
  They offered _____ .

4 She complained _____ .
  They denied _____ .

5 She promised _____ .
  He threatened _____ .

6 She accused _____ .
  He apologized _____ .

7 He's really scared _____ .
  She advised _____ .

8 He boasted _____ .
  He challenged _____ .

**6** Complete these sentences in your own words, using the correct verb pattern. Compare with a partner.

1 I remember _____ when I was young.
2 I'll never forget _____ for the first time.
3 I like _____ when it's raining.
4 I'm thinking of _____ next year.
5 I find it difficult _____ .
6 I mustn't forget _____ .
7 I've always tried _____ .
8 I'm looking forward to _____ .
9 I try to avoid _____ .
10 Our teacher always makes us _____ .

# THE LAST WORD
## Telling jokes

**1** Work with a partner. Match the questions and answers to make jokes.

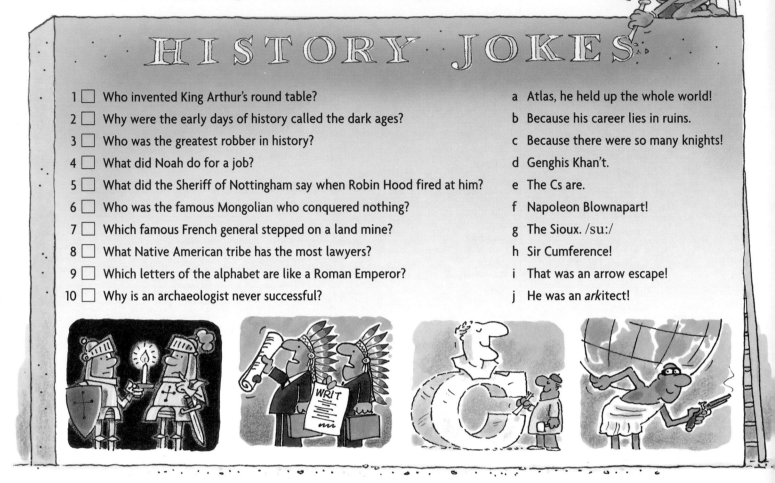

### HISTORY JOKES

1 ☐ Who invented King Arthur's round table?
2 ☐ Why were the early days of history called the dark ages?
3 ☐ Who was the greatest robber in history?
4 ☐ What did Noah do for a job?
5 ☐ What did the Sheriff of Nottingham say when Robin Hood fired at him?
6 ☐ Who was the famous Mongolian who conquered nothing?
7 ☐ Which famous French general stepped on a land mine?
8 ☐ What Native American tribe has the most lawyers?
9 ☐ Which letters of the alphabet are like a Roman Emperor?
10 ☐ Why is an archaeologist never successful?

a  Atlas, he held up the whole world!
b  Because his career lies in ruins.
c  Because there were so many knights!
d  Genghis Khan't.
e  The Cs are.
f  Napoleon Blownapart!
g  The Sioux. /suː/
h  Sir Cumference!
i  That was an arrow escape!
j  He was an *ark*itect!

**2** **T 9.6** Listen and check. Each joke depends on a play on words. Explain how. Which jokes rely on homophones and homonyms for their humour?

**3** **T 9.7** Notice which words are stressed in the way the jokes are told.

> *Who invented King Arthur's round table?*

> *I don't know. Who **did** invent King Arthur's round table?*

> *Sir Cumference! D'you get it?*

> *Aaargh! Of course I get it! How corny is that!*

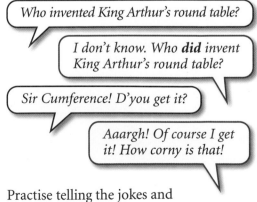

Practise telling the jokes and responding with your partner.

**4** **T 9.8** Mark the main stresses in B's replies in these conversations. Listen and check.

1 **A** Have you heard the one about the old man and his dog?
  **B** I told you it!
2 **A** I invited Anna but she isn't coming.
  **B** I told you she wouldn't.
3 **A** Peter hasn't told anybody.
  **B** He told me.
4 **A** I hope you didn't tell Clara.
  **B** I didn't tell anyone.
5 **A** Who told Clara?
  **B** I didn't tell her.
6 **A** John won't like it when you tell him.
  **B** If I tell him.
7 **A** It's the worst film I've ever seen.
  **B** Tell me about it!
8 **A** He dumped me.
  **B** I don't want to say 'I told you so'!

Practise them with your partner.

**5** Do you know any jokes in English? Tell the class.

▶▶ **Writing** Personal profile **p128**

# 10 The body beautiful

Sports · Intensifying adverbs · The body · Clichés

**STARTER**

**1** Think of ten sports where you have to compete against an opponent, and ten sporting activities which you can do as an individual.

| Competitive |
| --- |
| squash |
| wrestling |
| netball |

| Individual |
| --- |
| yoga |
| aerobics |
| skateboarding |

Compare your ideas with the class.

**2** **T 10.1** Listen to radio commentaries of six different sports. Can you identify each one? What were the clues that helped you?

**3** Which sports do you like to take part in? Which sports do you like to watch? What do you do to keep fit?

# READING AND SPEAKING
## The age of sport

**1** What sports are these people renowned for?
Why, do you think?

- Australians
- African-Americans
- Kenyans
- Brazilians
- Chinese
- Russians

**2** Who is the most highly-paid sportsperson in your country?
In the world?

Is he/she in … ?

- motor-racing
- golf
- boxing
- football
- athletics
- baseball

**3** What are the biggest sporting events in your country?
In the world?

**4** Look at the paragraph headings in the article and make
some notes on what the text might be about. Compare your
ideas with the class before reading the article.

**5** Read the article and answer the questions.

1 What is the correlation between sport and strawberries?
2 The first paragraph describes various aspects of the
current 'Age of Sport'. What, by implication, were these
aspects like before this era?
3 'Sport knew its place.' What does this mean? Why doesn't
it know its place any more?
4 How has TV changed sport? Has this change been
beneficial or not?
5 Why is the London Marathon mentioned?
6 In what ways are most sports stars like everyone else?
7 What is the correlation between modern sports stars and
ancient gladiators?
8 What can sport offer that a rock concert can't?
9 What is special about the Olympics and the World Cup?
10 Why is the besotted fan in a minority?

### Vocabulary work

**6** Work out the meanings of the highlighted words in the
article.

### What do you think?

- Do you agree that our culture is obsessed by sport?

- Which sporting events are taking place now? Do you think
there is too much sport in the world? Too much sport on
television?

- 'As individuals become rich, sport becomes impoverished.'
Can you think of any examples that support this opinion?

- Who are the sports icons of the moment? Why are they
famous?

- Who do you think is more interested in sport, men or
women? Why?

**'It's not just a pastime**

**S**port used to be like fresh fruit and
vegetables. Football had its season,
then it ended, and you had to wait a
while to get some more. Tennis was
an explosion of Wimbledon at the
end of June, Flushing Meadow in September
and the Australian Open in January, and that
was that. Now, just as you can get fresh
strawberries all year round, there are major
championships for every sport taking place
somewhere in the world all of the time.

### Sport is everywhere

Sport is ubiquitous. Sky TV has at least thirteen sports
channels. Throughout the world there is a proliferation
of newspapers and magazines totally dedicated to
sport. Sports personalities have become cultural icons,
worshipped like movie-stars and sought after by
sponsors and advertisers alike. Where sport was once
for fun and amateurs, it is now the stuff of serious
investment.

Of course, sport has always mattered. But the point is
that in the past sport knew its place. Now it invades
areas of life where previously it had no presence:
fashion, showbiz, business. It is a worldwide
obsession.

### Why this obsession with sport?

What is it that makes sport so enjoyable for so many?

First, we seriously believe that sport is something we
can all do, however badly or however well. Tens of
thousands set off on the London and New York
Marathons. Amateur football matches take place all
over the world every weekend. Sport is a democratic
activity.

Second, sports stars are self-made people. Sport is
dominated by athletes from ordinary backgrounds.
This is why it is a classic means by which those from
the poorest backgrounds can seek fame and fortune.

Third, we enjoy watching sport because we like to see
the supreme skill of those who act like gladiators in

# age of sport

the modern arena. There is the excitement of not knowing who is going to win. No rock concert, no movie, no play can offer that kind of spontaneous uncertainty. This gut-wrenching experience can be shared with a crowd of fifty round a widescreen TV in a pub, or a thronging mass of 100,000 live in a stadium.

## The role of television

Television has been absolutely crucial to the growing obsession with sport. It gives increased numbers of people access to sporting events around the globe. With this, certain sports have accumulated untold riches via advertising, sponsorship and fees. Television changes sport completely, nearly always for the worse. We are saturated with football nearly every night of the week with the same top clubs playing each other again and again. TV companies dictate tennis players' schedules. The most important matches must take place at a time when most people are at home, even if this is late at night. Only in this way are the highest advertising fees commanded.

## Sport as big business

The growing importance of sport is reflected in the money that surrounds it. Sky TV's sports channels are worth over £8bn. Manchester United football club is a public limited company worth around £1bn. It has even formed a superclub with baseball's New York Yankees, so that they can package themselves collectively.

The rise of sport has been accompanied by the growing prominence of sports stars. They have become public figures, hence in great demand for TV commercials. For advertisers, they convey glamour, success, credibility and authenticity. The rise of the sports star is mirrored by the rise of sports companies such as *Nike* and *Adidas*. Along with pop music, the Internet, and multinational companies, sport is one of the key agents of globalization.

## Sport the global unifier

'Sport probably does more to unify nations than any politician has ever been capable of.' So said Nelson Mandela. The only truly global occasions are the Olympics and the World Cup, watched by thousands of millions across the world. These great sporting events bring together players and athletes from different races like no other. Not only that, but sport provides just about the only example of global democracy where the rich do not dominate: on the contrary, Brazilians have long been supreme at football, the Kenyans at middle-distance running, and black Americans at boxing.

## The ultimate risk

However, there are signs of disquiet in this vast, global industry. The sheer volume of sport is reaching bursting point for all but the most besotted fan. In football, the president of FIFA has suggested staging the World Cup every two years instead of four, and overpaid tennis players and golfers fly endlessly in personal jets from one meaningless tournament to the next. Sport risks killing itself through greed and over-exposure. The danger is that we will all become satiated and ultimately disillusioned.

# LANGUAGE FOCUS
## Intensifying adverbs

> Intensifying adverbs often go together with certain verbs and adjectives. Look at these examples from the article on pp92–3.
>
> **totally** dedicated    change **completely**
> **seriously** believe    **absolutely** crucial
>
> ▶▶ **Grammar Reference p157**

**1** Choose the *two* correct adverbs in these sentences.
  1 I *totally / perfectly / quite* agree with you.
  2 She *totally / quite / strongly* disagrees with me.
  3 Some people *sincerely / seriously / entirely* believe there's life in space.
  4 I *perfectly / strongly / completely* understand what you're trying to say.
  5 I *totally / really / quite* like spicy food.

**2** Choose the *one* correct adverb in these sentences.
  1 I *absolutely / completely / sincerely* adore ice-cream.
  2 I *perfectly / strongly / totally* forgot about her birthday.
  3 What you believe depends *entirely / seriously / sincerely* on your point of view.
  4 I *really / quite / completely* can't stand getting up in the morning.
  5 I have *absolutely / entirely / thoroughly* enjoyed the evening with you.

**3** Match a gradable adjective with an extreme adjective.

| Gradable adjective | Extreme adjective |
| --- | --- |
| stupid | delightful |
| expensive | brilliant |
| pleasant | exorbitant |
| unusual | devastated |
| upset | extraordinary |
| clever | ridiculous |

With which group or groups of adjectives can we use these intensifying adverbs?

| very | absolutely | really | quite |
| --- | --- | --- | --- |

**T 10.2** Listen and check. Practise the sentences.

**4** **T 10.3** Listen to the sentences. When does *quite* mean …?

• *up to the top* with an extreme adjective
• *up a bit* with a gradable adjective
• *down a bit* with a gradable adjective

Practise the sentences, paying attention to stress and intonation.

**5** Choose the *two* correct adverbs in these sentences.
  1 Kate thinks maths is hard, and she's *absolutely / very / quite* right.
  2 Personally I find maths *extremely / totally / quite* impossible.
  3 She's *absolutely / completely / extremely* terrified of dogs.
  4 I was *absolutely / very / terribly* pleased to hear you're getting married.
  5 I'm sure you'll be *totally / extremely / really* happy together.

**T 10.4** Listen and check. Practise the sentences, paying attention to stress and intonation.

**6** Choose the *one* correct adverb in these sentences.
  1 This wine is *absolutely / totally / rather* pleasant. You must try it.
  2 I'm *absolutely / terribly / very* determined to lose weight.
  3 The film was *totally / utterly / quite* interesting. You should see it.
  4 The restaurant was *quite / utterly / absolutely* nice, but I wouldn't recommend it.
  5 If you ask her, I'm *terribly / pretty / completely* sure she'll say yes.

**T 10.5** Listen and check. Practise the sentences, paying attention to stress and intonation.

**7** Work with a partner. Write questions to prompt responses which use some of the adverb collocations you have practised. Ask and answer questions with another partner.

A  **Are you going to take the exams?**
B  **Yes, I'm absolutely determined to pass.**

*'He's not totally lacking in ambition.
He dreams of one day owning a bigger TV set.'*

# VOCABULARY AND SPEAKING
## Words to do with the body

**1** Label the numbered parts of the body, using the words in the box. The numbers in black boxes are inside the body.

| | | | | |
|---|---|---|---|---|
| ankle | earlobe | jaw | neck | throat |
| armpit | eyebrow | knee | rib | thumb |
| bone | forehead | kidney | shin | toe |
| brain | groin | knuckle | shoulder | vein |
| calf | heart | lip | spine | waist |
| cheek | heel | liver | stomach | wrist |
| chest | hip | lung | temple | |
| chin | intestines | muscle | thigh | |

What other body parts can you name?

**2** Complete the sentences with a part of the body used as a verb in the correct form.

1 In the final seconds of the match, Martin _____ the ball into the back of the net.

2 After his father's death, Tom had to _____ the responsibility for the family business.

3 When a couple gets married, it's usually the bride's family who _____ the bill.

4 The boys stood on one side of the room, _____ up the girls on the other side.

5 You've got to _____ facts, Jack. You're in debt, and you have no income.

6 Old ladies are the worst people in queues. They just _____ everyone else out of the way.

7 I ran out of petrol, so I had to _____ a lift to the nearest petrol station.

8 Maria, could you help me by _____ out these books to the other students?

9 My friend Pat loves _____ around other people's houses, looking in cupboards and reading their letters.

10 When a mugger tried to attack Jane, she _____ him in the groin and left him collapsed on the ground.

**3** What part of your body do you use to do these things?

| | | | | | | |
|---|---|---|---|---|---|---|
| tickle | stroke | nudge | thumb | sniff | slap | munch |
| smack | pinch | squeeze | grin | rub | clap | pat |
| hug | frisk | shove | spit | wink | scratch | |

Why might you do these things?

**You tickle someone to make them laugh.**

**4** Close your books and work with a partner. Take turns to mime a verb for your partner to guess.

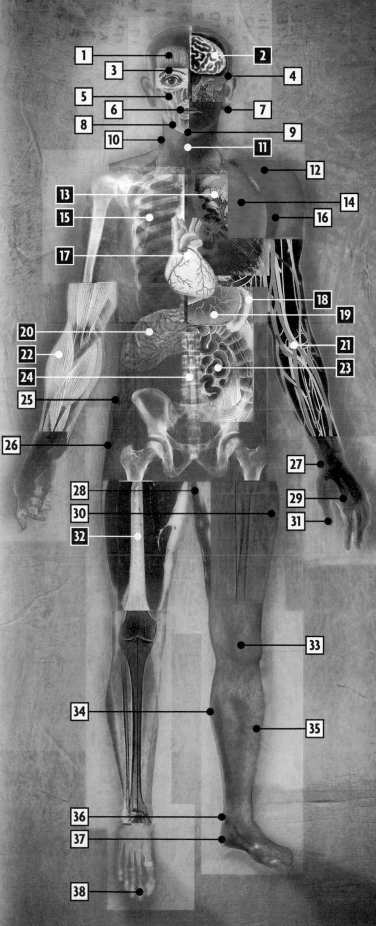

# LISTENING AND SPEAKING
## Sporting heroes and heroines

### The rower and the ballet dancer

1 Do you have a particular sports person that you admire? Who? Why? Discuss as a class.

2 What do you think the life of a professional sportsperson is like? What are the highs and lows?

3 Look at the photos and read the quotations on the right. Who do you think says what?

> 66 When you get tired, you can't slow the pace. You have to go through the pain barrier. You can't stop. 99

> 66 Of course the worst thing that happens to you is your feet. I haven't had toenails for years. 99

**STEVE REDGRAVE** – the only sportsperson to have won gold medals at five consecutive Olympic games. His dedication to rowing has brought him a knighthood, and turned him into a national hero.

**DARCEY BUSSELL** – dancing queen and OBE, has been at the top of her profession for ten years. She is adored by the general public, and utterly obsessed with ballet.

4 Work in two groups.

Group A **T 10.6** Listen to Mick and Jez talking about Steve Redgrave, the Olympic rower.

Group B **T 10.7** Listen to Adelhaide and Kate talking about Darcey Bussell, the ballerina.

Answer the questions.

1 Why are the speakers interested in Steve/Darcey?
2 What have been the best moments of Darcey's/Steve's career?
3 What health problems has he/she had?
4 What is her/his training programme?
5 What does his/her diet consist of?
6 How does she feel during a performance? How does he feel during a race?
7 What sacrifices has he/she had to make?
8 Who are the significant people in her/his life?
9 What are his/her ambitions for the future?
10 What kind of a relationship do the two speakers have? What do you learn about them?

5 Work with a partner from the other group. Compare and exchange information.

### What do you think?

1 Whose training programme is harder, Darcey Bussell's or Steve Redgrave's? Who has suffered more?
2 What sort of person do you have to be to succeed in sport? Why do you think they do it?
3 Do you know any examples of sports people burning out? What were the pressures on them?

## SPEAKING

### How healthy and fit are you?

**1** *'If you're fit, you don't need to exercise. If you aren't fit, exercise is dangerous.'*
Do you agree with this logic or not? How can you injure yourself taking exercise?

**2** Work with a partner and ask each other the questions in the quiz. Work out and compare your scores, and decide on your priorities for action.

### What do you think?

• How effective and useful are these quizzes?

• Will you pay attention to the results and alter your lifestyle?

*'My doctor wants me to walk a mile after every meal.
but, frankly, ten miles a day is killing me.'*

# HEALTH & FITNESS QUIZ

## How healthy & fit are you? How healthy & fit could you be?

### How **true** are these statements for you?

**5** Always   **4** Often   **3** Sometimes   **2** Rarely   **1** Never

**1** I start the day with a sensible breakfast. ☐

**2** I tend to have 4 or 5 smaller meals a day. ☐

**3** On an average day, my diet would include 5 portions of fruit and vegetables. ☐

**4** Less than 30% of my daily calorific intake is fat. ☐

**5** I regularly take food supplements of vitamins and minerals. ☐

**6** Fried foods don't feature in my diet. ☐

**7** I don't eat red meat. ☐

**8** I make sure I drink 6–8 glasses of water a day. ☐

**9** My sugar consumption is generally low. ☐

**10** I don't have more than 2 alcoholic drinks (for men, 1 for women) a day. ☐

**11** I exercise aerobically at least 3 times a week. ☐

**12** I work out with weights or exercise machines twice a week. ☐

**13** As well as a proper lunch break, I take a couple of breaks during the working day. ☐

**14** I get about 7–8 hours of sleep a night. ☐

**15** I actively cultivate relationships and interests outside of work. ☐

**16** I probably break into laughter about 20 times a day. ☐

**17** I allow myself adequate time off for holidays. ☐

**18** I meditate, pray, or practise some form of relaxation technique daily. ☐

**19** I feel in charge of my health and take full responsibility for it. ☐

**20** I generally have a positive mental attitude. ☐

**Check your answers to each question.** To score your profile, add up the numbers.

My total score is: ☐

**If your total score is:**

**100–80** you have **excellent** health habits (great job, keep up the good work!)

**79–70** you have **good** health habits (good, but let's work on it a little)

**69–60** you need **special** attention (let's go to work on it now)

**59–0** is a **red alert**! (do something about it now!)

Decide on your top three priorities for action from your lowest scores in the quiz:

1 _____
_____

2 _____
_____

3 _____
_____

# THE LAST WORD
## Clichés

**1** **T 10.8** A cliché is a phrase which has been used so often that it has lost much of its force. Read and listen to the conversations and identify the clichés. What do they mean?

**1 A** You should get a new job, stop smoking, and have a healthier lifestyle.
   **B** Easier said than done.

**2 A** I don't know whether to apply for that job or not. What do you think?
   **B** Well, I'm not sure. At the end of the day, it's your decision.

**3 A** Jamie and I are off out for the evening.
   **B** Have a great time! Don't do anything I wouldn't do.

**2** Match a line in **A** with a line in **B**. Where are the clichés? What do they mean?

| A | B |
|---|---|
| 1 Mum! Tommy's broken the vase! | a Oh, well. A change is as good as a rest. |
| 2 I just need to go back in the house and make sure I've turned off the iron. | b Never mind. Accidents will happen. |
| 3 It's been raining non-stop for weeks! Do we need some sunshine! | c Well, you know what they say. No pain, no gain. |
| 4 Work's awful at the moment, and I have to go away on business this weekend! | d Good idea. Better safe than sorry. |
| 5 I got a card from Jerry a week after my birthday. | e Oh dear! They say these things come in threes, you know. |
| 6 We're having a complete break for a fortnight. | f You can say that again. |
| 7 Took me ten years to build up my business. Nearly killed me. | g It takes all sorts. |
| 8 Larry's failed his exams, Amy's got chicken pox. Whatever next? | h The mind boggles. It doesn't bear thinking about. |
| 9 They've got ten kids. Goodness knows what their house is like. | i Oh, well. Better late than never. |
| 10 Bob's a weird bloke. Have you heard he's going to walk across Europe? | j Sounds like just what the doctor ordered. |

**T 10.9** Listen and check. Do you have any similar clichés in your language?

**3** **T 10.10** Listen and respond to the statements, using a suitable cliché.

▶▶ **Writing** Entering a competition **p129**

# 11 The ends of the earth

**Relatives and participles · Compound nouns and adjectives · Idiomatic expressions**

**STARTER**

**1** Work in groups and answer the questions.

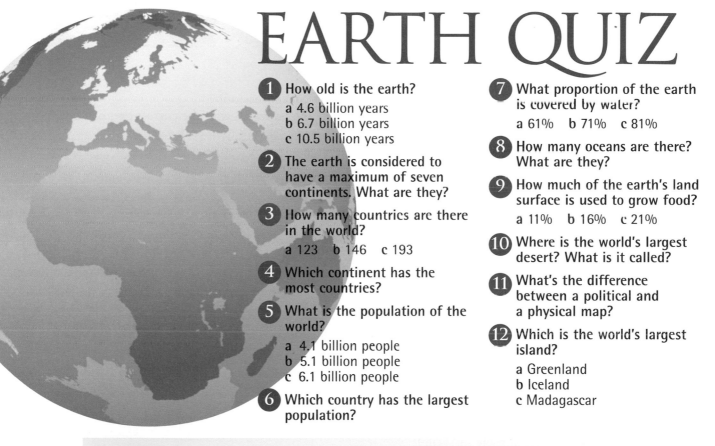

# EARTH QUIZ

**1** How old is the earth?
a 4.6 billion years
b 6.7 billion years
c 10.5 billion years

**2** The earth is considered to have a maximum of seven continents. What are they?

**3** How many countries are there in the world?
a 123    b 146    c 193

**4** Which continent has the most countries?

**5** What is the population of the world?
a 4.1 billion people
b 5.1 billion people
c 6.1 billion people

**6** Which country has the largest population?

**7** What proportion of the earth is covered by water?
a 61%    b 71%    c 81%

**8** How many oceans are there? What are they?

**9** How much of the earth's land surface is used to grow food?
a 11%    b 16%    c 21%

**10** Where is the world's largest desert? What is it called?

**11** What's the difference between a political and a physical map?

**12** Which is the world's largest island?
a Greenland
b Iceland
c Madagascar

**2** **T 11.1** Listen and check. What extra information do you learn about each?

**3** Read these 'howlers' (funny mistakes) from some students' geography exams. Explain them.

| 1 | The chief animals of Australia are the kangaroo and the boomerang. |

| 2 | Floods from the Mississippi may be prevented by putting big dames in the river. |

| 3 | The inhabitants of Moscow are called Mosquitoes. |

| 4 | The Mediterranean and the Red Sea are connected by the Sewage Canal. |

| 5 | The Pyramids are a range of mountains between France and Spain. |

| 6 | In the West, farming is done mostly by irritating the land. |

# READING AND SPEAKING
## Three island stories

1  Did you know that one in ten people in the world live on an island? Which islands have you visited? When? What were they like?

2  Match the photos above to the islands of **Greenland**, **Tristan da Cunha**, and **Zanzibar**. Which island do you know most/least about? Compare ideas with the class.

3  Work in groups of three.

   **Student A**  Read about Greenland on p101.
   **Student B**  Read about Tristan da Cunha on p102.
   **Student C**  Read about Zanzibar on p103.

   As you read, underline at least three things that you find interesting or surprising. Tell your group about them.

4  Answer the questions by comparing information about the islands.

   1  What do you learn about the islands' names?
   2  Which island lies furthest west?
   3  Which has the smallest population?
   4  Which is the most economically successful?
   5  Which has the most varied history?
   6  Do any of the islands share the same native tongue?
   7  Which imports the most goods?
   8  Which is the most self-sufficient?
   9  Which is the most colourful? Which the least? Why?
   10  Which attracts the most tourists?

   Discuss these questions in your groups.

   11  In what ways does the location influence life on the islands?
   12  In what ways has its history influenced present island life?

## Language work

5  **Geographical expressions**
   Complete the sentences with the correct prepositions. Which island is being referred to in each sentence?

   1  It is situated _____ the South Atlantic, 2,800 km _____ the nearest mainland and south _____ the island of St Helena.
   2  Temperatures range _____ 0°C _____ 15°C in summer.
   3  Its landscape is made _____ _____ grey granite rock.
   4  It lies just _____ the coast of East Africa.
   5  It is equal _____ size _____ half of Western Europe.
   6  If all this ice were to melt the world's oceans might rise _____ six _____ seven metres.
   7  He didn't settle _____ the island but, nevertheless, he named it _____ himself.
   8  The history of the island is _____ _____ all proportion _____ its size.
   9  It is divided _____ three areas.
   10  It is an island burgeoning _____ spices and subject _____ favourable trade winds.
   11  The population now numbers just _____ 300.
   12  The population is estimated _____ _____ 800,000.
   13  It lacks the abundance _____ wildlife found _____ the mainland.

## What do you think?

• Which of these islands would you like to visit? Which not? Why?

• People often dream of living on a desert island. Decide in your groups what kind of island the three of you would most like to inhabit. What climate would you want? What would you want the island to provide? What and who would you like to take with you?

# GREENLAND

## The largest island in the world

## Geography

Greenland is the largest island in the world, measuring 2,670 km from north to south, but with a population of only about 56,000, one-quarter of which lives in the capital, Nuuk. It lies just south of the Arctic Circle, so its summer temperatures range from just 0°C to 15°C. Eighty-five percent of its 2,175,600 km² area is covered with a massive ice cap, which holds 9% of the world's fresh water. If all this ice were to melt, the world's oceans would rise by six to seven metres. Despite its name, Greenland is anything but green. Its bare haunting landscape is made up of grey granite rock and massive icebergs, with only tiny pockets of greenery.

## History

The Inuit people (previously known as Eskimos) were the first people of this island. Then, around 980 AD, Eric the Red, a bloodthirsty Norwegian Viking, fled to the island and founded a colony. Despite the desolate greyness, Eric cunningly named the island 'Greenland', so as to attract settlers. His trick worked and the colony grew but then died out suddenly and mysteriously in the 1400s. In 1721, the Danish established a settlement there, and ruled for over 200 years, until 1979, when Greenland was declared an autonomous nation within the Kingdom of Denmark.

## Greenland today

Regional boundaries divide the country into three areas: North, East, and West Greenland. East Greenland, known as Tunu, is the most isolated, blocked by ice for 9 months out of 12. Only 4,000 people live here, despite it being equal in size to half of Western Europe. In the harbour there are corpses of hunted seals, sunk in the cold water which acts as a natural refrigerator. The presence of polar bears is always a possibility. These dangerous, man-eating creatures are feared but also loved as the embodiment of the human spirit in a harsh land.

This is also the region of the semi-permafrost. Tombs are shallow and the dead are often stored for months before being buried in warmer months, when the soil can be dug. There are serious social problems, such as alcoholism and suicides, as a result of unemployment and seasonal depression. The latter is a common syndrome in places where winter lasts more than half the year, where there is no light at all.

Nowadays Greenlandic, or East Inuit language, has become the first language, and Danish the second. The Civil Service is largely Greenlandic as well and there are more Inuit signs than Danish ones. However, like most small remote nations, economic independence is non-existent. Most of the national budget is funded by Denmark. Everything in the supermarket is Danish. Job prospects remain poor and most services, from air transport to seal hunting, are subsidised by the Danish taxpayer.

# TRISTAN DA CUNHA

## The remotest island in the world

## Geography

Tristan da Cunha is the remotest island in the world. Situated in the South Atlantic, it is 2,800 km from the nearest mainland, South Africa, and 2,575 km south of the island of St Helena. The island is roughly circular with an average diameter of 10 km. It rises out of the ocean, its volcanic peak crowned with an almost permanent cap of white cloud, and its 40 km of wild, storm-tossed coastline comprising magnificent, massive basalt cliffs. The surrounding seas are rich in fish, providing Tristan da Cunha with its main export.

## History

The island was discovered in 1506 by a Portuguese explorer, Tristao da Cunha, who, despite being unable to land there, named the island after himself. The first actual settler was an American, Captain Jonathan Lambert, in 1811. Unfortunately he drowned a year later.

In 1816, the British annexed the island as a defence against the French, who, it was thought, were planning to rescue Napoleon from exile on the island of St Helena.

The British left, leaving the founder of the present community — a Scot, Corporal William Glass, who settled on the island with his family, two companions, and a mulatto woman from St Helena, making

a total of six inhabitants. The community comprised still no more than eleven thatched cottages when, in 1867, Alfred, Duke of Edinburgh and second son of Queen Victoria, visited the island and gave his name to the capital, which is called the Edinburgh of the South Seas. Throughout the nineteenth century the population slowly increased but Tristan da Cunha passed into obscurity. Then, in October 1961 a dramatic volcanic eruption forced the evacuation of the entire island. Its people were taken to what was glibly referred to as 'civilization' in South Africa and England. By August 1962 the eruptions had died down and in November 1963 the islanders chose to return home.

## Tristan today

To visit Tristan da Cunha is to visit another world, another life, another time. The settlement of Edinburgh has a distinct air of yesteryear about it, although it has all modern conveniences. There is a small museum, a large supermarket, a swimming pool, and a radio station but no television.

The population now numbers just under 300 — a proud and hospitable people with only seven surnames between them: Hagan, Rogers, Glass, Lavarello, Swain, Green, and Repetto. Through their veins flows the blood of English sailors from Nelson's fleet, Americans, Italians, two Irish girls, Dutch, and mulattos from St Helena and South Africa. English is the native tongue, albeit a slightly strange, old-fashioned dialect, laced with a few early Americanisms.

The island is self-supporting with a thriving economy. Income tax is low (although imported goods are very expensive). Serious crime is unknown, unemployment is virtually non-existent.

As well as the fishing industry, a main source of income on the island is the sale of postage stamps, which are prized by philatelists worldwide.

# 3

# ZANZIBAR
## The most exotic island in the world

## Geography

A large proportion of the world's population have heard of Zanzibar. The name conjures up all sorts of exotic images: sultans, slaves, spices, ebony, ivory, gold, and explorers – words that start to tell the story of Zanzibar. However, only a small proportion of the world's population know exactly where Zanzibar is. It is located in the Indian Ocean, just off the Tanzanian coast of East Africa, immediately south of the equator. Zanzibar Island is 83 km long and 38 km wide with magnificent, golden, sandy beaches fringed by coconut palms and coral reefs. Zanzibar lacks the abundance of wildlife that is found on mainland Africa. No giraffes, elephants, or lions here today, just a few monkeys and small antelopes. However, in 1295, when visiting the island, Marco Polo recorded that Zanzibar had 'elephants in plenty'.

## History

The history of Zanzibar is one out of all proportion to its size. It was the richest place in Africa for centuries, an island burgeoning with spices and subject to such favourable winds that it has served as the centre of trade between Africa, Arabia, and India for over five thousand years. The islands have always been highly prized by empire builders: Egyptians, Arabs, Portuguese, Chinese, Dutch, and British have all taken possession, valuing it not only for its strategic trading position, but also because of its fertile soils and temperate climate. Zanzibar used to be the world's largest producer of cloves, grown on plantations, established in the early 1800s by Sultan Said of Oman.

In 1964, the islands joined with the country of Tanganyika on the East African mainland, to become the United Republic of Tanzania. 'Zanzibar' forms half the name of 'Tanzania.'

## Zanzibar today

The population is estimated at about 800,000, an incredible mixture of ethnic backgrounds, indicative of the island's colourful history. Zanzibaris speak Swahili, a language which is spoken extensively in East Africa. Many believe that the purest form is spoken in Zanzibar as it is the birthplace of the language. Fishing and agriculture are the main economic activities of the local people. Although cloves are still a major export along with coconut products and spices, tourism has been earmarked as the primary foreign exchange earner, with more visitors coming to Zanzibar each year. Some of these come to visit the birth place of the late Freddie Mercury, lead singer of the band Queen, who was born Farouk Bulsara in Zanzibar City on 5 September 1946. However, the numbers of tourists are still relatively low (less than 100,000 annually) and the potential for tourism is still largely untapped. The island is trying hard to develop sensitive tourism that benefits both visitors and community, without losing the magic that is Zanzibar.

# VOCABULARY AND LISTENING
## Compound nouns and adjectives

### Weather words

**1** How many compound nouns and adjectives can you make using the 'weather' words on the left?

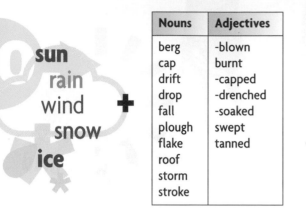

sun
rain
wind
snow
ice

**+**

| Nouns | Adjectives |
|-------|------------|
| berg  | -blown     |
| cap   | burnt      |
| drift | -capped    |
| drop  | -drenched  |
| fall  | -soaked    |
| plough| swept      |
| flake | tanned     |
| roof  |            |
| storm |            |
| stroke|            |

**2** Complete these sentences with compounds from exercise 1.

1 The annual _____ in London is 610 mm.
2 My sister stayed out in the sun for too long and she was ill for two days with _____.
3 One winter's night there was a terrible _____. In the morning the _____ were so deep that even the _____ couldn't get through to our village.
4 I'd love a convertible on warm days like these. My car doesn't even have a _____.
5 The *Titanic* sank because it hit a huge _____.
6 Did you know that Kilimanjaro is a _____ mountain even though it's on the Equator?
7 After a hot day's sailing my face was _____ and my hair was _____.
8 Did you know that the pattern of every single tiny _____ is different?
9 I love the sight of _____ on rose petals after a shower.
10 I love both the hot _____ beaches of the Caribbean and the wet _____ hills of Scotland for my holidays.

### Adjective order

**3** Look at these examples of adjectives before nouns. Which adjectives are more factual? Which are more opinion? What is their position? Try to work out some rules.

1 Beautiful, old, thatched cottages
2 Glorious, golden Mediterranean beaches
3 Amazing, huge, grey, granite rocks
4 Strange, old-fashioned English dialect
5 Wild, storm-tossed Atlantic coast
6 Dangerous, man-eating polar bears

▶▶ **Grammar Reference p157**

**4** Put the adjectives in brackets into a natural-sounding order.

1 He gave us some bread. (wholemeal; delicious; home-made)
2 A lady arrived. (Irish; little; funny; old)
3 I bought a shirt. (silk; red and white; gorgeous; striped)
4 She's just had a boy. (baby; lovely; bouncing; fat)
5 He showed me into a room. (airy; light; high-ceilinged; delightful; living)
6 I met a student. (young; trendy; art; Venezuelan)
7 She's wearing trousers. (leather; black; shiny; tight-fitting)
8 It's a rose. (sweet-smelling; exquisite; apricot-coloured)

**5** Add some extra information for each sentence in exercise 4.

It's a beautiful, old thatched cottage **with a beautiful garden./ hidden from the road.**

**T 11.2** Listen and compare your answers.

### Farflung spots

**6** **T 11.3** Listen to some people describing the most farflung place they have visited and write down the adjectives they use. Then answer these questions about each person, using the adjectives you wrote down to help you.

1 Where did they go?
2 What did they do and see?
3 Why was it unusual and memorable?

**7** Which of the places would you like to visit and why? What is the most unusual place you've been to?

**8** Write a short description of a place you have visited, using both factual and opinion adjectives.

# LISTENING AND SPEAKING
## A meeting in the desert

**Simon Winchester** is a foreign correspondent who travels widely, often to the more remote parts of the world.

**1** Look at the illustrations which tell Simon's unusual story about a railway journey in the far west of China. Work with a partner to try and predict what happens.

**2** **T 11.4** Listen to the first part of the story. Are these statements true or false? Correct the false ones.

1 Simon made the journey alone.
2 He was attracted to the idea of travelling on a new railway line in such a remote area.
3 They stopped in a desert town called Urunchi.
4 The engine driver spoke impeccable English.
5 He met an exquisitely lovely, rather serious Chinese lady.

What do you think happens next?

**3** **T 11.5** Listen to the second part. Were any of your predictions correct? Answer the questions.

1 Why did the lady check her watch?
2 How do Anthony Trollope and his book *The Eustace Diamonds* figure in the story?
3 Who struggled and scribbled? Why?
4 Who scrabbled? Why?
5 Why did the lady say 'Don't be silly!'?
6 Complete these extracts with the next three words.
   a I could just about remember _____ ...
   b The last vision I have of her was her scrabbling on her _____ ...

How do you think the story ends? What do you think was in the letter? The pictures may help you predict.

**4** **T 11.6** Listen to the last part. How close were your predictions? Are these statements true or false? Correct the false ones.

1 The lady wrote to Simon to ask if she could meet him again soon.
2 She and her husband had to move to Kwi Tun as a punishment.
3 She called Kwi Tun 'this lovely little town.'
4 She regularly cycles thirteen miles across the desert to meet the train.
5 Her main motivation is to find somebody to talk to in English.
6 She once had a conversation with a migrant worker about Trollope.
7 She talked to Simon about religion.
8 Simon and the lady have unfortunately lost touch with each other.

**5** Work with your partner to retell the story in your own words, using the pictures to help.

*Simon and his friend decided to . . .*
*After about 150 miles . . .*

# LANGUAGE FOCUS
## Relatives and participles

### Defining and non-defining relative clauses

> Underline the relative clauses in these sentences. Then answer the questions.
> a  Here's somebody who speaks English.
> b  The Chinese lady, who speaks impeccable English, lives in the desert.
> c  She works for a company which organizes adventure holidays.
> d  They made a railway journey across the desert to Kazakhstan, which sounded fascinating.
> e  The friend who he travelled with is a doctor.
> f  The islanders were taken to what was referred to as 'civilization'.
>
> 1  Which sentences still make complete sense if the relative clauses are removed? Which are defining relative clauses? Which are non-defining?
> 2  In which sentences can *who* and *which* be replaced by *that*? Why?
> 3  In which sentence can the relative pronoun (*who* or *which*) be omitted? Why?
> 4  In which sentence can *whom* replace *who*? Transform this sentence. What effect does this have?
> 5  Read the sentences aloud. What is the role of the commas?
>
> ▶▶ **Grammar Reference p158**

**1** Work with a partner and discuss any differences in meaning and/or form between the sentences in each pair.

1  The sailors whose cabins were below deck all drowned.
   The sailors, whose cabins were below deck, all drowned.
2  My sister, who's a travel agent, is terrified of flying.
   My sister who's a travel agent is terrified of flying.
3  The explorer Tristao da Cunha, after whom the island was named, never actually landed there.
   The explorer Tristao da Cunha, who they named the island after, never actually landed there.
4  I'm appalled at everything that happened.
   I'm appalled at what happened.
5  The map showed the place in which the treasure was buried.
   The map showed where the treasure was buried.
6  People seeking adventure meet all kinds of danger.
   People who seek adventure meet all kinds of danger.
7  There are white coral sands fringed by coconut palms.
   There are white coral sands which are fringed by coconut palms.

**2** Read these incomplete sentences and discuss whether they should be completed with a defining or non-defining relative clause, or whether both are possible.

1  I don't like children …
2  The journey from work to home … took over two hours yesterday.
3  Politicians … aren't worth listening to.
4  The Taj Mahal … is built from exquisitely carved white marble.
5  These are the photographs …
6  We docked at the small port on the coast of East Africa …
7  My cousin … went hang-gliding at the weekend.
8  We went on a cycling holiday in Wales …

**T 11.7** Complete them with your ideas, then listen and compare.

**1** The part of Britain _____ I most like to visit is _____ I was born in the north-east of England.

**2** I was born in Sunderland _____ is on the coast and _____ there used to be a large ship-building industry.

**3** My sister _____ husband is an artist still lives in the town _____ is the reason I often return there.

**3** Complete the text above with relative pronouns and commas where necessary. If it is possible to omit the pronoun, add nothing.

## where I was born

4  My grandfather _____ worked in the shipyards went to London only once in his life and that was _____ the Sunderland football team won the FA cup in 1973.

5  The Wear Bridge_____ outline you can see from miles around spans the estuary of the River Wear and _____ once dockyards and warehouses stood there are now trendy restaurants and yacht clubs.

6  My brother-in-law _____ has travelled widely and _____ paintings depict many exotic places, still prefers to paint _____ is most familiar to him – the grey, stormy North Sea.

7  _____ I like most _____ I visit my home town are all the memories _____ come flooding back.

4  Write some notes about the town where you were born. Give it to a partner to read and ask questions.

### Participles

> Participle clauses can express these ideas.
> • at the same time   • so that/with the result that
> • because   • if   • after
> ▶▶ **Grammar Reference p159**

5  Which ideas do the participles in these sentences express?
1  Living in London, I appreciate the pros and cons of city life.
2  I cut myself opening a tin.
3  Having read the minutes of the meeting, I wrote a report.
4  Having read the minutes of the meeting, I understood the problems.
5  Cooked in a red wine sauce, ostrich meat can be delicious.
6  Knowing my love of chocolate, she hid it away in her drawer.
7  Taken from his mother as a child, he's always had difficulty establishing relationships.
8  Browsing in our local bookshop, I came across this great book on computing skills.

6  Complete the pairs of sentences with the same verb, once as a present participle and once as a past participle.
1  Tomatoes _grown_ under polythene ripen more quickly.
   _Growing_ up in the countryside is really healthy for young kids.

2  We took a short-cut, _____ an hour on our journey time.
   With the money _____ from not smoking we've bought a new computer.

3  _____ all things into account, we've decided to offer you the job.
   _____ three times a day these tablets can really help hayfever.

4  Flights _____ one month in advance have a 10% discount.
   _____ your flight in advance gives you a better deal.

5  I fell on the ice, _____ my wrist.
   The two boys _____ in the car accident are doing well in hospital.

6  _____ promises leads to lack of trust.
   _____ promises lead to lack of trust.

7  _____ away secrets won't win you any friends.
   I don't believe a word he says, _____ that he never tells the truth.

8  The new uniforms _____ by the flight attendants looked very smart.
   Students _____ studs in their noses will be asked to remove them immediately.

# THE LAST WORD
## What on earth!

**1** Complete the sentences with a suitable noun from the box.

| earth   ground   floor   land   soil   world |

1 The sailors didn't see _____ again until the ship reached Australia.
2 Communication satellites orbit the _____ once every 24 hours.
3 This rich, black _____ looks extremely fertile.
4 He fell off the wall and hit his head on the _____.
5 We are all striving for _____ peace.
6 In American English they say 'the first _____', but in British English we say 'the ground _____'.
7 What on _____ are you doing down there on your hands and knees?
8 He lives in a _____ of his own, you just can't get through to him.
9 I like her because she's such a down-to-_____ kind of person.

**2** Here are some idiomatic expressions using the words in exercise 1. Match a line in **A** with a line in **B**. Use a dictionary if necessary.

| A | B |
|---|---|
| 1 I'm cleaned out! This new jacket cost the earth. | a I nearly wasn't. I had to move heaven and earth to get here. |
| 2 Believe me, that guy's really going places. | b I can't. My dad caught me smoking and I've been grounded for two weeks. |
| 3 The holiday's over. It's back to the real world. | c Come on! It's good to spoil yourself every now and then. |
| 4 What? You're not coming out on Saturday night! | d Don't I know it! He landed that consultancy job that we all applied for. |
| 5 Hey! Great to see you! I thought you weren't going to be able to make it. | e In your dreams. Not if you were the last man on earth! |
| 6 We're throwing caution to the wind and emigrating to Oz. | f Don't ask me. I was totally floored by the last lot I read. |
| 7 Come on, you know you want to go out with me really. | g Great! That suits me down to the ground. |
| 8 Can you follow these instructions? Where on earth do all these screws go? | h You can say that again. Back to earth with a bump! |
| 9 I don't want to drink, so I'll do the driving tonight. | i Don't your folks already live down under? |

**3** **T 11.8** Listen and check. Practise the conversations with a partner.

**4** Write some similar conversations with your partner, using some of the expressions from exercise 2. Read them to another pair.

▶▶ **Writing** Describing a journey **p130**

# 12 Life goes on

Linking devices · Synonyms and antonyms 2 · Euphemisms

**1** Describe Pieter Bruegel's picture, *Landscape with the Fall of Icarus*. Where is Icarus?

**2** Ask your teacher questions.

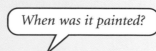

*When was it painted?*

*Who was Icarus?*

*Which one is he in the picture?*

**3** **T 12.1** Listen to a description of the picture by an art historian. What does she say about . . . ?

- the three men
- the central event
- direction and movement
- an interpretation of the picture

**4** Do you agree with Bruegel's message on life? Isn't it good to be ambitious?
Is it true that 'life goes on'?

## READING AND SPEAKING
### A sideways look at time

**1** What activities do you do at exactly the same time each day? Are you the kind of person who arrives early, exactly on time, or fashionably late? Are you annoyed by people who are unpunctual?

**2** Why do people often say that the older you are, the faster time seems to go by? When does time seem to fly by? When does it drag?

**3** Check these action verbs. Demonstrate some of them.

| | |
|---|---|
| look sideways | blink |
| winkle sth out | spin |
| sigh | slip |

**4** What do you think these mean?

- clock-time
- chronological time
- universal time
- kairological time

Read the article to find out. Explain the title.

**5** Answer the questions.

1 What is meant by 'Urban modernity lives under an assault of clocks'? Give some examples of the way our lives are governed by the clock.

2 Give examples of fast food. What is fast knowledge?

3 What is UT?

4 In what way is the earth inaccurate?

5 How is the forest a clock for the Karen tribe?

6 Explain how 'sunset' can be described as 'three kilometres away'.

7 What is a 'scent calendar'? What would you name the 'scent months' where you live?

8 How are adults and children different in their attitudes to time?

9 What is the difference between the two Greek gods of time?

10 How is the passage of time different in the town and in the country?

Of course you know what the time is. You can look at your brand new DIGITAL watch, can't you? **But do you really know?** JAY GRIFFITHS invites you to think again and take:

# A *sideways* look at TIME

## MEASURING TIME

Time's measurement is everywhere. Leaving London, Berlin, New York, Washington or Paris: at the airport every transaction, each ticket and money exchange is timed. Around Heathrow, as at any other major airport, there are clocks, blinking the date and time, down to tenths of seconds. Urban modernity lives under an assault of clocks. Alarm clocks put the frighteners on sleep: the first thought in so many people's minds, every single waking day is 'What's the time? Am I late?' Digital clocks with their digital seconds seem to speed time, relentlessly tightening deadlines. People speak of the frenetic pace of modern society, everything is speeded up, from fast food to fast clothes and fast knowledge.

There are 86,400 seconds in a day and every one is artificially pipped off, day in, day out, by the MSF service of broadcast standard frequency and time on wavelength 60kHz in the LF band. This is the time, since on the first of January 1972 the second was defined as the atomic second, and Co-ordinated Universal Time (abbreviated to UT) was set by international agreement. Roughly every year a leap-second is added to realign the time with that of the earth – it is added to 'accommodate' the earth's unreliable time. For the earth, you see, is too inaccurate for modernity's time measurement, because its spin changes by up to a thousandth of a second in some years. A thousandth of a second, indeed, tut tut, how unpunctual the earth is!

So the timekeepers of today must tell the time from outside the earth itself, insisting that there is one time, abstract and universal, mono-time: the time. There is no such thing.

## NOT JUST ONE TIME

The Karen, a hill-tribe in the forests of Northern Thailand, always know the time. Living with them for six months it became clear to me that the only person with a watch and the only person who could never tell the time was, well, myself. To the Karen, the whole forest was a clock. The morning held simplicity in its damp air, unlike the evening's denser wet when steam and smoke thickened the air. The Karen always know where they are and when they are, how far they are from sunset or home: for time and distance are connected in the Karen language: díyi ba – soon – means, literally, 'not far

## What do you think?

1 'There is no such thing as a time-saving device. They should be renamed time-slaving devices.'

Do you agree? Think of some devices that are supposed to save us time. Do they, in fact? In what ways are our lives obsessed with speed?

2 Think of some examples of nature's clocks at work.

sunrise    hibernation

3 Rename the months of the year according to where you are and what nature is doing in that month.

4 **T 12.2** Read and listen to the poem. What does it say about how time can appear to go quickly or slowly?

away'. Sunset, therefore, could be expressed as 'three kilometres away', because the only way of travelling is to walk, which takes a known length of time.

Across the world the nature of each moon-month is characterized and, through each people's names for the months, you can see the specific landscape they inhabit. The Natchez tribes of the lower Mississippi river valley have months which include the Deer month and the Strawberries month, the Turkey, Bison, Bear and Chestnut months. In India's Andaman forests, people have a scent-calendar, using the smells of flowers and trees to describe the time of the year. Other peoples characterize time by starscapes. So, see how false is the ideology of Western imperialist time, declaring itself *the* time. There are thousands of times, not one.

## CHILDREN AND TIME

Adults, generally, have learned clock-time. While old people sigh over how fast it goes, children are incapable of patience. How long is an hour to a child? Far, far longer than to an adult; asking a small child to wait a few hours for ice cream is like asking yourself to wait till Wednesday week for a whisky. Children live in the heart of the ocean of time, in an everlasting now. A child's eternal present is present-absorbed, present-spontaneous, present-elastic. Children have a dogged, delicious disrespect for punctuality.

## GODS OF TIME

The ancient Greeks had different gods for time's different aspects. One of the most important was Chronos, who gives his name to absolute time, linear, chronological and quantifiable. But the Greeks had another, far more slippery and colourful, god of time, Kairos. Kairos was the god of timing, of opportunity, of chance and mischance, of different aspects of time. Time qualitative. If you sleep because the clock tells you it's way past your bedtime, that is chronological time: whereas if you sleep because you're tired, that is kairological time. If you eat biscuits when you're hungry, that is kairological: whereas if you eat by the clock, that is chronological time. Children, needless to say, live kairologically until winkled out of it.

## KAIROLOGICAL TIME

Kairological time has a different sense of movement compared to chronological time. For a rough comparison, contrast an urban with a rural day. In cities, where time is most chronological, your progress through the day is like an arrow, while the day of itself 'stays still', for time is not given by the day but is man-made, and defined by the working day or rush-hours. In a rural place, time moves towards you and is nature-given, defined by sun or stars or rainstorms. In this more kairological time, the future comes towards you and recedes behind you while you may well stay still, standing in the present, the only place which is ever really anyone's to stand in.

Time is too slow
for those who wait,
too swift for those
who fear,
too long for those
who grieve,
too short for those
who rejoice,
but for those who
love, time is eternity.

# LANGUAGE FOCUS
## Linking devices

There are many ways of making links between parts of a sentence or between sentences.

1 With conjunctions:
... the future comes towards you **and** recedes behind you
This is *the* time, **since** on the first of January 1972 the second was defined as the atomic second ...

2 With adverbs:
**However**, roughly every year a leap second is added...
**So** the timekeepers of today must tell the time ...

3 With infinitives:
... it is added to **accommodate** the earth's unreliable time ...

4 With relative pronouns:
In cities, **where** time is most chronological ...

5 With participles:
... there are clocks on corporate buildings and hotels, **blinking** the date and time ...

Find more examples in the article on p110.

▶▶ **Grammar Reference p159**

**1** Choose the correct linker. Sometimes two are possible.

### A day in the life of
# Benjamin Ellis

" I always wake up on the dot of six o'clock in the morning, (1) *unless/wherever/no matter where* I am in the world. I'm a morning person, (2) *so/therefore/since* I like to make the best of my creative period. (3) *As soon as/Whenever/After* I've had a shower, I take the dog out, and (4) *then/at last/finally* it's time for tea and emails. (5) *Since/As/Even though* I work at home, I get a lot of emails, and (6) *providing/if/unless* I clear them daily, they build up and up.

I work downstairs (7) *to not/in order not to/so as not to* wake up the rest of the family.

(8) *Since/In case/Once* everyone is up, we have breakfast, and (9) *after/afterwards/after that* it's the mad rush for school. (10) *Even though/Even so/Although* we ask the children every evening if they have everything for school the next day, there is always something they have forgotten. 'Where's my ...?' is the cry in our house (11) *however/as long as/whenever* a child has lost something. This is followed by the fatuous question from a parent, usually me, 'Where did you last have it?' (12) *Provided/Supposing/If* the child knew that, there wouldn't be a problem.

(13) *When/While/Whenever* everyone's ready, we all pile into the car. I like to leave early (14) *in case/unless/although* the traffic is bad. We go on country lanes (15) *to avoid/so as to avoid /because we avoid* the rush-hour, but (16) *even so/all the same/yet* the journey takes half an hour.

(17) *Immediately/Since/As soon as* I get home, it's back to the computer. (18) *Working/As I work/So that I work* at home, I know how easy it is to be distracted. (19) *As long as/Provided/Except when* I do about eight hours' work a day, I manage to keep on top. In the evening we all eat together (20) *so that/in order to/since* we can catch up with each other's news from the day.

**2** Write a paragraph about a typical day in your life, using linking devices.

**3** Rewrite each sentence in different ways, using the words in the box.

1 The bank robber wore a mask.
   No one recognized him.

   | so that | so as not to |
   |---------|--------------|

   **The bank robber wore a mask so that no one recognized him.**

   **The bank robber wore a mask so as not to be recognized.**

2 I saw the film. Then I read the book.

   | having | after |
   |--------|-------|

3 Look after this carefully. It will last a lifetime.

   | as long as | provided |
   |------------|----------|

4 The curry was hot. We couldn't eat it.

   | so | such | too |
   |----|------|-----|

5 It doesn't matter what you do, but don't touch this switch.

   | no matter | whatever |
   |-----------|----------|

6 Do I like her or not? I'm not sure.

   | whether |
   |---------|

7 I'm on a strict diet. I still haven't lost any weight.

   | even though | however | even so |
   |-------------|---------|---------|

8 I took an umbrella. I thought it might rain.

   | in case | as |
   |---------|----|

9 He was penniless and starving, but he still shouldn't have stolen the food.

   | nevertheless | although | despite |
   |--------------|----------|---------|

10 I went to the party. I met Jenny. We got married and had three children.

   | Supposing I hadn't . . . |
   |--------------------------|

**4** Rewrite the biography of Salvador Dalí, using linkers to change each group of sentences into one sentence.

> Salvador Dalí was born in 1904.
> He was born in a small town, Figueres, in Catalunya, north-east Spain.
> His father was a prestigious notary in the town.

**Salvador Dalí was born in 1904 in a small town, Figueres, in Catalunya, north-east Spain, where his father was a prestigious notary.**

> Dalí wanted to study art.
> He went to the Royal Academy of Art in Madrid.
> He was expelled from the Academy twice.
> He never took his final examinations.

> In 1928 he went to Paris.
> He met the Spanish painters Pablo Picasso and Joan Miró in Paris.
> He established himself as the principal figure of a group of surrealist artists.
> The leader of the group was André Breton.

> By 1929 Dalí found his style.
> This style would make him famous.
> It consisted of the world of the unconscious.
> This world is recalled during our dreams.

> In 1927 he met Gala.
> She was a Russian immigrant.
> She was ten years older than Dalí.

> She was married to a French poet at the time.
> She decided to leave her husband.
> She wanted to stay with Dalí.

> In 1940 he went to the United States.
> He stayed there for eight years.
> In 1948 Dalí and Gala returned to Europe.
> They spent most of their time in Spain or Paris.

> Gala died in 1982.
> Dalí became deeply depressed.
> He moved to Púbol.
> Púbol was a castle.
> He had bought it for Gala.

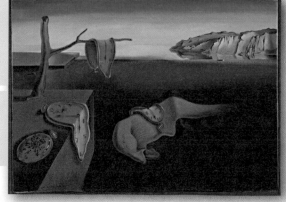

> He lived in his castle for the rest of his life.
> He died there in 1989.
> He died of heart failure.

 **T 12.3** Listen and compare your answers.

# LISTENING AND SPEAKING
## Do you believe in miracles?

1 What stories of miracles do you know? Do you believe miracles can happen? Are there any rational explanations for these phenomena?

2 Look at the pictures of pilgrims. Where are they? Which religion do they belong to?

3 Dr Raj Persaud, a consultant psychiatrist at a London hospital, visited Lourdes to make a radio programme.

- Where is Lourdes?
- What is it famous for?
- Who goes there? Why?
- Why do you think the doctor wanted to go there?

4 These words are in the programme. What do you think they refer to?

- reverential
- introspective atmosphere
- in wheelchairs or borne on stretchers
- sanctuary
- 1858
- six million people every year
- paralysed
- multiple sclerosis

**T 12.4** Listen and check your ideas.

5 **T 12.4** Listen again and answer the questions.

**Part one**

1 What strikes Dr Persaud most? Why is this surprising?
2 What are some of the statistics he quotes?
3 What does the sanctuary consist of?
4 What did Bernadette see?

**Part two**

5 What is special about the spring that Bernadette discovered?
6 Why is Dr Persaud puzzled?
7 Why, according to Andrew Walker, are Christians divided?
8 What is the miracle that he quotes?

**Part three**

9 What were Jean-Pierre's early symptoms?
10 What happened in 1984? What were the stages of his cure?

**Part four**

11 What, for Dr Persaud, is the danger of modern medicine?
12 What is his explanation of the attraction of Lourdes?

## What do you think?

- The programme began with the question 'Can miracles exist in the age of science?' What is your opinion?
  Can miracles only have existed in the past?

- Is there a conflict between science and religion? What different theories of the creation of the universe do you know?

# VOCABULARY
## Synonyms and antonyms 2

**1** We often use synonyms for reasons of style. Look at these sentences from the article.

> … the earth's **unreliable** time …
> … how **unpunctual** the earth is …

Complete the sentences with a word that has a similar meaning to the words in *italics*. Sometimes the word class changes.

1 It was an *immense* task, but its _____ only became apparent when we started working on it.

2 Progress will be *slow*, but if we persist, things will _____ improve.

3 You *can't count* on her. She's totally _____ .

4 You want an *approximate* figure? At a _____ guess, I'd say there were about fifty.

5 'Did he *say* how his job's going?'
   'No. He didn't _____ it.'

6 Massage *eased* the pain in my back, and _____ the tension I've felt for so long.

7 He's a very *cunning* opponent. He plays some _____ tricks.

8 He made a *miraculous* recovery, due to his _____ strength.

9 Soldiers *attacked* the enemy headquarters. The _____ took place before dawn.

10 Drugs can treat most *illnesses*, but there are some _____ that are incurable.

**IMPENDING DOOM…**
annihilation, calamity, catastrophe, condemnation, danger, disaster, downfall, end, fore ordination, Judgment Day, predestination, ruin, tragedy.

*Ironically, a well developed brain actually contributed to the early extinction of the Thesaurus Rex.*

**2** Divide the adjectives in the box into four groups, with three synonyms and three antonyms for each head word.

| ancient | essential | impeccable | petty |
|---------|-----------|------------|-------|
| antiquated | faultless | irrelevant | prejudiced |
| antique | faulty | liberal | second-rate |
| biased | flawed | novel | up-to-date |
| bigoted | immaculate | trivial | urgent |
| current | impartial | open-minded | vital |

| | synonyms | antonyms |
|---|----------|----------|
| **old** | ancient | novel |
| **fair** | | |
| **perfect** | | |
| **unimportant** | | |

**3** Match adjectives from exercise 2 with nouns from the box that they collocate with.

| machinery | crime | organs | Greece |
|-----------|-------|--------|--------|
| idea | Press | vase | manners |
| racist | performance | mail | affairs |

# THE LAST WORD
## Euphemisms

**1** A euphemism is a polite way of expressing something thought to have negative connotations.

For example, a blind person is *visually challenged*, a fat person is *full-figured*, and politicians don't lie, they are *economical with the truth*.

**2** Complete the newspaper article with euphemisms from the box.

| | | |
|---|---|---|
| pass away | low IQ | Ministry of Defence |
| companion animal | disadvantaged senior citizen | working to rule |
| leisure garden | disabled | under the weather |
| retirement pension | job seeker's allowance | lower income bracket |
| taking industrial action | have a dialogue | |

'I've never been fired, but I've been dehired a few times.'

## Letters

# Stop being coy

### I will die – not pass away

I AM an old cripple, drawing an old-age pension, working hard to raise vast quantities of vegetables on an allotment, and well aware that, one of these days, I shall die. All this is fact.

If, however, I listen to the voice of officialdom, it turns out that I am a (1)_____, registered as (2)_____, drawing a (3)_____, renting a (4)_____, and presumably immortal, because I shall never die – I shall merely (5)_____.

The euphemisms which pour from the lips of politicians and trade union leaders are endless. (6)_____ equals going on strike, and (7)_____ equals being bloody minded.

And let us please do away with the following:
(8)_____ (poor)
(9)_____ (ill)
(10)_____ (stupid)
(11)_____ (unemployment benefit)
(12)_____ (Ministry of War)
(13)_____ (talk)
(14)_____ (pet)

All this effort to avoid unpleasantness is certain to fail, because the euphemism quickly acquires the stigma of the word it replaced. I, and probably others, do not feel younger because I am called a senior citizen.

**Bryan Heath**
*Retired vet*

'I need some short-term economic stimulus.'

**3** What do you think these political euphemisms mean?
1 The rebel fighters were *neutralized*.
2 With all due respect, I think your figures are *misleading*.
3 Could you please *regularize* your bank account?
4 We had a *frank, open exchange of views*.
5 This is not a *non-risk policy*.
6 The company is in a *non-profit situation*.

**4** Can you translate any euphemisms from your language?

▶▶ **Writing** Bringing a biography to life **p131**

# Writing

## UNIT 1 FORMAL AND INFORMAL LETTERS

**1** You are going to write a formal and an informal letter. Before you begin, think about these things.

- Layout: where to put the address/date.
- Register and style: who are you writing to? Should you use formal or informal language?
- Greeting/Opening: do you know the person's name? Do you know them well?
- Planning: are you asking for/giving information, thanking, or complaining? Always include your reason for writing in the first paragraph.

**2** You are planning to work in the USA this summer, and wrote to your friends asking them about jobs for students. Read their reply and write back to your friends thanking them, explaining what you have decided to do, and asking them for more information on Florida about these things:

- possible to stay with them for a couple of weeks?
- Orlando expensive?
- travel cheap to other states?

Great news that you're thinking of coming over this summer. Orlando is a fantastic place to live. The weather is wonderful, the beaches are great, and people are really friendly. It's only been four months since we arrived, but we've made lots of new friends. I already feel at home and Jon does too.

I'm not sure exactly how you can get a work permit, but I do know that there are organizations, like Go America!, which help foreign students find summer work. There are certainly lots of jobs in the amusement parks and restaurants, so I'm sure you'd have no trouble getting something. Anyway, let us know what you decide.

Lots of love

Sally

**3** Now read this advert and write a letter to the employment agency giving them details of your qualifications and asking for further information about these things:

- type of jobs in Florida?
- accommodation?
- cost of flight included?
- work permit?

**Go America!**

offers students exciting summer jobs in the world's most exciting continent

Work anywhere in the USA – the choice of location is yours! Experience the wide open spaces 'out west', the bright lights of the city or beach life on east coast resorts. Then take time out and travel.

*For more information contact:*

**Go America!**
65 Renard Square
London SE6 WH9

**1** Read these opening paragraphs from three different stories and answer the questions below.

**A**

Christmas again. Joyce looked out of the frosted window at the bare, winter garden. A pair of sparrows were hopping through the frozen grass, searching for food. It'd been three long years and she still hadn't got over it. She sighed and pushed a wisp of white hair back behind her ear. The pictures on the mantlepiece were her only companions now, and she treasured them like nothing else. A few Christmas cards kept them company, but as the years went by they were fewer and fewer. No, she'd never get used to it … but she didn't want to go into a retirement home, not yet. This house was her home, she thought fiercely as she walked unsteadily towards an old threadbare armchair and sat down next to the fire.

**B**

Hannah glanced anxiously at her watch. It was 11.54 p.m. and the night train for Bangalore was leaving in 6 minutes. She peered along the dimly-lit platform, searching for a familiar figure in faded jeans, carrying a well-worn rucksack. But the station was deserted, apart from a tired-looking porter shuffling around aimlessly and smoking a cigarette. She thought back to their conversation earlier that day, perhaps he'd been serious after all? They'd argued many times during their 3-month trip and he'd often gone off on his own to 'cool off'. But then he'd always turn up later and they'd sort out their differences. Hannah fingered her ticket nervously. She didn't want to leave without Peter …

**C**

'What was that!' whispered Jes, his eyes wide with fear. 'Shhh', said Luis, slowly edging his way up the creaking stairs. 'Probably just a rat.' It had been Luis's great idea to explore 'Fletcher's place' as it was known, named after the eccentric old man who last lived there. It was the archetypal haunted house and had been deserted for years – nobody brave enough to buy it, or even break into it Luis had said. They'd been laughing about it just that afternoon, and had speculated wildly about the supposed murder that happened years before. School was out and they were both in high spirits so when Luis suggested a midnight raid, he'd readily agreed. Now, faced with the grim reality of a creepy, damp house, Jes was having second thoughts. 'Was there really a murder here?' he thought desperately.

1   How do the opening sentences attract the reader's attention?
    What atmosphere do they create? How do the characters feel?

2   Which tenses are used in the story? Is direct speech used?
    What effect does it have?

3   Who are the main characters in the story? What is their relationship?

4   How old are the main characters? How do you know this?

## Brainstorming ideas

**2** Discuss what happens next in the stories. Ask yourself these questions:

- In each story, someone is facing a choice. What is that choice and what decision do you think each person will make?
- What could be the consequences of that decision? How will it affect other people?
- What do you think will happen in the end?

**3** Now read the rest of story A. Make it more interesting by adding the adverbs below. There may be more than one possible answer.

> carefully   softly   instinctively   gently   strangely   encouragingly   slowly

It was his favourite chair and as she sat there (1) _carefully_ warming her hands, she smiled to herself. She could almost see him at the table, browsing through the Sunday papers. After a while she fell into a deep sleep.

'Joyce, Joyce,' a voice whispered (2)_____ in her ear. Joyce opened her eyes. At first she didn't know him – he looked younger and slightly different than she remembered – but she recognized his voice. 'What's the matter, dear?' she asked almost (3)_____ . 'Come on old girl,' he said. 'Let's go for a walk.' He helped her up and (4)_____ took her arm. She felt calm and (5)_____ light as they walked (6)_____ out of the room. 'Almost there,' he said (7)_____ , as he pulled at the latch on the front door. The door creaked open and warm sunlight streamed into the hall. Joyce smiled and stepped outside – it was a beautiful spring day.

**4** In what ways were your ideas for story A similar or different? What happens in the end? Which ending do you prefer and why?

**5** Choose extract B or C on p118 and complete the story in 200–300 words. Use the ideas you brainstormed in exercise 2, and follow the advice below.

- Plan your story carefully. Decide what happens next, the order of events, and how the story ends.
- Decide how the main characters will react to the events in your story, and which verbs, adjectives, and adverbs will best describe their feelings and actions.

- Use linking words to order the events in your story.
- Use direct speech to vary the pace and focus.
- When you have finished check your grammar carefully – make sure you have used past tenses and time adverbials correctly.

**1** What features are typical of report writing? Choose from these alternatives.

1  a  state your aims in the introduction
   b  state your recommendations in the introduction

2  a  use headings for each section
   b  have one general heading

3  a  give mostly opinions rather than facts
   b  give mostly facts rather than opinions

4  a  use mostly active tenses
   b  use mostly passive tenses

5  a  give recommendations based on your personal experience
   b  give recommendations based on the facts

**2** Read the report and check your answers.

**3** Read the report again. Underline words or expressions the writer uses to introduce recommendations.
e.g. *should introduce*

**4** Circle six different ways that customers' opinions are reported.
e.g. *commented that*

**WORLDNET**
**24HR INTERNET CAFÉ**

---

# WORLDNET REPORT

## INTRODUCTION

The purpose of this report is to evaluate Internet services provided by *Worldnet*, a chain of 24-hour Internet cafés in London. There has been a steady decrease in the number of customers over the past six months. This report will attempt to analyse and explain this trend based on findings from a series of customer questionnaires. It will evaluate the current services in relation to client needs, and will conclude with recommendations for improvements.

## MAIN AREAS FOR IMPROVEMENT

*Worldnet* caters for a wide range of customers with different backgrounds and ages. However nearly all customers (65%) commented that the cost of the Internet service at £2 per hour was too high and suggested half-hourly rates. The speed of the Internet connection was also criticized. At peak times the service was said to be extremely slow and unstable.

## OTHER AREAS FOR IMPROVEMENT

In terms of the hardware, the computer terminals were generally thought to be out of date and badly maintained. The screens were felt to be too small and the seating uncomfortable. On a more positive note, the café was considered to be good value. The prices compared favourably with other cafés, and customers were satisfied with the quality of the food provided. However, although the café was popular, there were some complaints about the lack of variety.

## RECOMMENDATIONS

In order to become more competitive, *Worldnet* should introduce new half-hourly rates immediately. Special student rates should also be considered as this would attract 16–25-year-old customers, who represent the majority of Internet users. In addition I would strongly recommend a faster and more reliable Internet service provider. The computer terminals and chairs also need upgrading and maintaining more regularly. Finally, the café could be improved by introducing a wider variety of food and drinks. If these recommendations are put into practice, the number of *Worldnet* customers should start to increase substantially.

**5** Report these opinions about a new mobile phone, using the prompts in brackets.

*'I've used the built-in digital camera – the photos are really good.'*
(considered /good quality)

**The built-in digital camera was considered very good quality.**

1 *'It makes no difference to me if the display screen is in colour.'*
(commented /made no difference)

2 *'I don't use the voice recorder – to be honest I don't know how to!'*
(said / too complicated)

3 *'I prefer sending text messages to making a call. They're a lot cheaper.'*
(thought / better value for money)

4 *'I don't care about the gadgets. I just want a phone that's reliable.'*
(felt / unimportant)

5 *'The battery doesn't last very long. It's a real pain having to recharge it all the time!'*
(complaints / recharging inconvenient)

6 *'I never use the WAP service. There's nothing worth accessing apart from the football results.'*
(commented / limited value)

**6** Read this introduction to a report on mobile phones. Rewrite it in a more suitable way.

Trident wanted me to write a report telling them what I thought about their new range of hi-tech mobile phones. People haven't been buying the phones, although they have lots of great new gadgets. Trident gave me about 50 questionnaires, asked me to have a look at them, explain why sales were dropping, and give a bit of advice on how to improve things.

**The aim of this report is to ...**

**7** Look at the table containing the results of Trident's survey.

**Trident 550–750 mobile phones**
survey overview

| | Good | Satisfactory | Poor | General comments |
|---|---|---|---|---|
| Price / quality ratio | | | ✓ | *too expensive* |
| WAP service | | | ✓ | |
| Voice mail service | ✓ | | | *clear and reliable* |
| Battery life | | | ✓ | |
| Colour display screen | | ✓ | | *not important* |
| Digital camera | ✓ | | | *good quality* |
| Voice recorder | | | ✓ | |
| Text messages | ✓ | | | *cheap and effective* |

Write a report evaluating Trident's new generation of mobile phones, based on the survey and the opinions in exercise 5. Use the paragraph plan below to help you.

Paragraph 1: Introduction. State the aims of the report.

Paragraph 2: Summarize the problems and report customer opinions. Select three or four main points you want to address.

Paragraph 3: Summarize areas that are satisfactory and report customer opinions.

Paragraph 4: Conclusion. Give your recommendations for improving the service and/or ways of lowering the cost of the phone.

**1** Read the essay title and the essay below. Tick the ideas a–g which appear in the essay. Are any of the ideas not relevant to the question?

a We're intrigued by people who do anything to become famous.
b Personally, I'd say that the conversations are quite boring.
c I think that many people would love to be on television.
d Unlike soap operas, I don't think they're based on interesting stories.
e I think they are totally unpredictable which is very exciting.
f Generally speaking, I'd say detective series are quite boring.
g I can't imagine life without soap operas.

> ### 'TV reality shows are third-rate entertainment and not worth watching.' What do you think?
>
> There is nothing new about reality TV. Confessional shows, where ordinary people make their private life public, have been around for a long time. However, over the last five years TV reality shows such as *Big Brother* and *Survivor* have become more and more popular. (1) *In fact / Obviously* some of these programmes have been the most successful shows in television history. (2) *After all / Surely* it's unfair to say they are third-rate entertainment?
>
> In order to evaluate reality TV, we need to define (3) *ideally / exactly* what a TV reality show is. Reality shows have several things in common with soap operas. (4) *Generally speaking / Actually*, they both involve a group of people who have to live together and get on with each other whilst solving various problems. The difference is that reality shows aren't scripted, so the dialogues are often quite tedious. In addition, the problems contestants deal with are artificial and don't arise naturally from a 'story'. (5) *Apparently / Clearly*, in this sense, they could be seen as third-rate entertainment.
>
> Why then do people watch them? (6) *After all / Presumably*, what holds the audience's attention is the 'reality' or spontaneity of the shows. You never know what is going to happen next, and we are fascinated by people who will stop at nothing in their pursuit of fame. (7) *Naturally / At least* we're also fascinated by how the contestants cope in different situations, and to some extent measure their reactions against our own.
>
> To conclude, it's (8) *probably / exactly* true to say that reality shows are third-rate entertainment when compared with classic films or award-winning documentaries. However, as audience figures prove, they are strangely compelling because (9) *incidentally / basically*, we are able to empathize with ordinary people in extraordinary situations. This (10) *ultimately / ideally* is what makes TV reality shows worth watching.

## Adverbs and expressions of opinion

**2** Read the essay again. Choose the most appropriate adverb or expression of opinion.

**3** Writers often use adverbs to express or intensify their opinions. Match sentences 1–6 with follow-on sentences a–f, adding an adverb or phrase from the box below. There may be more than one possible answer.

| Admittedly | Presumably | Obviously |
|---|---|---|
| Naturally | Frankly | As a matter of fact |

1 ☑ f  Some people say that the price of fame is too high.
2 ☐  Famous people complain if there is a sensational story in the newspapers.
3 ☐  Celebrities claim it's difficult to make new friends.
4 ☐  People think celebrities have an easy life.
5 ☐  Stalkers pose a very real threat to many celebrities.
6 ☐  Why are we obsessed with fame?

a _____ they shouldn't because they exploit newspapers to get famous.
b _____ most celebrities have to work very hard.
c _____ it must be difficult to know why people are 'friends'.
d _____ it's because it's 'the new religion'.
e _____ they have to spend a lot of money on security.
f **Admittedly** life is difficult if your private life is public.

**4** Write a 250-word essay on the subject below. Use the ideas from exercise 3 and the paragraph plan to help you.

> ### 'Most people think that being famous is heaven, but in fact it's more like hell.' What do you think?

Paragraph 1: Summarize why people might want to be famous and paraphrase the question.
Paragraph 2: Why might people think being famous is 'heaven'? Do you agree?
Paragraph 3: Why might it be hell? What's your opinion?
Paragraph 4: Conclusion: summarize the main points and restate your opinion.

**1** Read this extract from a magazine article and the essay which follows. Put the paragraphs of the essay in the correct order.

> Up to the early twentieth century, marriage was considered a necessity. People chose partners who provided them with economic support and stability. Since then attitudes have changed and fewer people are tying the knot. Marriage is no longer necessary in modern society.
>
> Do you agree with this view of marriage? What are the arguments for and against marriage today? ***PBS Student*** magazine invites readers to write in with their opinions.

**A** Secondly, it has been suggested that marriage provides more stability for children. Certain surveys of children in single-parent families claim they are more likely to commit a serious crime than children from two-parent, married households. But in spite of this, having married parents isn't necessarily the best thing. It's obvious that a stable single-parent environment is a lot healthier for children than an unhappy marriage.

**B** First of all, it could be argued that marriage brings emotional and financial security to a relationship. This is partly true as married people are still legally bound to support their spouses. On the other hand, getting married and divorced is becoming increasingly easy. As a result, fewer people are prepared to work at their relationship, marriage vows are broken, and many couples are left emotionally scarred.

**C** Finally, some people claim that marriage is becoming more flexible, with personalised vows and contracts enabling couples to define their relationship themselves. Nevertheless, precisely because the ceremony is flexible and easy to adapt, many people are abusing it. In America there have been televised game shows, where people can win and marry spouses, and in Australia one man actually married his television set.

**D** To conclude, it's clear that marriage is no longer necessary to a successful, modern relationship. Nowadays a growing number of people simply prefer to live together. This continuing decline in marriage means there is greater freedom for individuals to choose their own partners and decide how they wish to live, which is ultimately a good thing.

**E** Marriage used to be considered a necessity for anyone wanting to live together and start a family. But over the past two decades fewer and fewer couples have felt the need to tie the knot. What then are the advantages and disadvantages of marriage?

**2** Read the essay again and look at the highlighted words. How does the writer introduce …

• arguments he agrees with?   • arguments he disagrees with?

What examples does the writer use to illustrate different arguments? Which arguments do you agree with?

**Linking words: contrast, reason, and result**

**3** Find phrases in the essay which introduce …
• a contrasting point of view
• a reason
• a result

**4** Rewrite these sentences, using the words in brackets.

1 It's common for young adults to live at home in some countries, but not in others. (whereas)
2 Many young adults live at home because of the money they save. (on account of)
3 Some people prefer to leave home, even if they don't have much money. (despite)
4 Some people stay at home because of economic circumstances. (due to)
5 Many young adults save money for their own flat by living at home. (so that)
6 Some people want more independence so they move out as soon as they can. (in order to)
7 One mother evicted her sons because of their selfish behaviour. (owing to)

**5** Choose a subject a–c and write a 250-word essay.

a What are the arguments for and against young adults living at home?
b What are the arguments for and against dating agencies?
c What are the arguments for and against living alone?

• First, brainstorm arguments for and against.
• Then organize your arguments into a plan:
   introduction
   first argument
   second argument
   third argument
   conclusion
• Make sure you write a general introduction to the issue and paraphrase the essay question.
• Use phrases you found in exercise 3 to introduce arguments, and the linking words in exercise 4.
• Try to illustrate your arguments with examples.
• State the arguments you agree with last.
• Make sure you summarize the main ideas and give a clear opinion in your conclusion.

1 Look at this extract from a newspaper editorial, and read the letter to the editor.

'CANNABIS IS NO different from cigarettes in terms of health risks. And unlike cigarettes, for certain conditions such as multiple sclerosis, it has proven medicinal qualities. In short, there is no real reason why cannabis shouldn't be legalized.'

**Legalize cannabis?** We want to hear from YOU. Write a letter to the editor with your opinions at: *In the News*, PO Box 33, Bristol BH2 7YH

Richard Pearson
15 Hessel Road
London N7 6PS

7th March

The Editor
In the News
PO Box 33
Bristol BH2 7YH

Dear Editor

A ——————————————————— There has been much debate about drugs in the papers recently, and I am very concerned about the arguments put forward in support of new, more liberal laws. I feel that legalization would not only be the wrong decision to make, but also a dangerous one.

B ——————————————————— According to your article, cannabis is no more harmful than cigarettes. You state that in some circumstances, such as the treatment of MS, it can actually be beneficial. It is also claimed that cannabis is not a gateway to harder drugs, and that there is no proof to support the argument that it is. Finally, the article insists that it is a waste of police time and money to bring a cannabis user to court, when this money could be better spent on preventing 'real' crime.

C ——————————————————— Tests have shown that the average joint contains more than twenty times the amount of cancer-causing agents than cigarettes. Moreover, it is a well-known fact that heavy users develop acute mental problems and dependency on the drug. This far outweighs any beneficial effects. Secondly, it is not true that cannabis use is unrelated to hard drugs. As rehabilitation centres have shown, there is a disturbing trend from cannabis use to cocaine, then heroin use. Essentially all these drugs feed the same addiction. Thirdly, I would argue that controlling the drug is not a waste of time and money. Preventing people from buying cannabis ultimately saves money for the health and social services, as well as saving lives.

D ——————————————————— Legalizing a drug which is addictive and encourages the use of other drugs is not only irresponsible but downright dangerous.

Yours faithfully

Richard Pearson

**2** Now match paragraphs A–D to the descriptions below.
Which paragraph …

- ☐ summarizes arguments in the article that the writer disagrees with?
- ☐ concludes and restates the writer's point of view?
- ☐ puts forward arguments the writer agrees with?
- ☐ introduces the reason for writing and states the writer's point of view?

How many arguments does the letter put forward? Which ones do you agree with?

**3** Choose the best introductory sentence for each paragraph.

**Paragraph A**
1 Here's my reply to your article about making cannabis legal.
2 I am writing in response to your article on the legalization of cannabis.

**Paragraph B**
1 One of the main arguments for legalization is related to health.
2 In your article you say that cannabis really isn't that bad for our health.

**Paragraph C**
1 Taking each of your arguments in turn, first of all it has been scientifically proven that cannabis is more of a health risk than cigarettes.
2 Looking at your arguments one by one, it really is true that smoking cannabis is a lot riskier than smoking cigarettes.

**Paragraph D**
1 To be honest, I can think of lots of reasons why cannabis users should be arrested.
2 To conclude, there are many reasons why cannabis should not be legalized.

**4** Rewrite these sentences in the passive, using phrases from the box. There may be more than one possible answer.

| | |
|---|---|
| It could be argued that … | It is believed that … |
| It is assumed that … | It would seem that … |
| It would appear that … | It has been proved that … |

1 If we ban cigarettes, we should ban hamburgers too.
   **It could be argued that if cigarettes were banned, hamburgers should be banned too.**
2 Young people's friends often encourage them to smoke.
3 Lack of exercise and an unhealthy diet causes most ill health.
4 Passive smoking kills people.
5 People know about the risks of smoking.
6 Companies have increased the nicotine content in cigarettes.
7 You can't frighten people into giving up smoking.

**5** Read the newspaper extract below and write a letter to the editor in 200–300 words. Make sure the layout is correct and that you use an appropriate register. Use the paragraph plan to help you.

EVERY YEAR MILLIONS of people die from cigarette-related illnesses. Despite awareness of the health risks, many people are unable to control their addiction. It's time we banned all cigarette advertisements, extended no – smoking policies to all public areas, and forced cigarette companies to contribute to a crippling healthcare bill.

**Do you agree with this editorial? We'd like to hear your point of view. Write a letter to** *the editor* **at:**

**YOU AND YOUR HEALTH**
**56 Hoole Place, Edinburgh EB3 9QT, Scotland.**

Paragraph 1: Introduction: state your reason for writing and your point of view.

Paragraph 2: Summarize the arguments you disagree with.

Paragraph 3: Discredit the arguments you disagree with and put forward the arguments you agree with.

Paragraph 4: Conclusion: restate your opinion.

**1** Read these two versions of the opening paragraph from a personal account, then answer the question below.

> **A** **Two years ago** I was in Wick, a small town in the North of Scotland. I'd just been to John O'Groats and had gone to Wick so I could catch a train there the next morning. I arrived at 11 at night and most places were closed. I suppose I should have booked somewhere before I arrived. I was walking around the streets looking for a place to stay, but everywhere was closed. Then I met an old man who offered me a room for the night.

> **B** **It was a** freezing November night and the stars shone coldly as I trudged through the deserted town of Wick with my heavy overnight bag. It was the third time I'd walked round the wintry streets looking for somewhere – anywhere – to stay. But there was no sign of life, even the pubs were shut. A bitter wind blew in from the North as the church clock struck midnight. I paused to wrap my scarf round my neck. 'Five more hours before the next train to Thurso,' I thought miserably, resigning myself to a bleak night on the streets. Then suddenly I heard a voice behind me: 'What's up, laddie? Need some help?'

Which opening paragraph …

- describes emotions, the surroundings and the weather?
- gives a mostly factual narrative?
- uses a variety of vocabulary?
- uses similar sentence structures throughout?
- has more impact on the reader?

**2** Choose the most suitable title.

 a   The weather in Scotland     c   An interesting journey
 b   The kindness of strangers

**3** Now read the rest of the account and answer the questions below.

> **The voice belonged** to a sprightly old man called Robert MacDougal. He was walking home after a meal at a friend's, when he noticed me huddled in the street. When I explained my predicament he immediately offered shelter for the night. At first I was suspicious. I'd learnt from experience not to trust strangers, having been robbed once in London. That incident had left its mark, but it soon became clear that what motivated Robert was a genuine desire to help. Wick was a small town and it was obvious I wasn't a local. It was also obvious that I needed a place to sleep.
>
>   I followed Robert back to a small cottage on the edge of town where he offered me a whisky. As we sat in front of a warm fire we talked for a while about Wick. Robert was a widower and had lived there all his life. He had three children and several grandchildren, although most of them had moved away. I began to understand why Robert was glad of some company.
>
>   After a peaceful night on an old sofa, I got up at 4.30 a.m. to catch my train, leaving behind a crumpled note of thanks. Today I sometimes think about Wick, and wonder if Robert is still there. I'll always remember with gratitude his simple act of kindness.

1 What was the writer's first reaction to Robert's offer?
2 Why did Robert offer to help?
3 Why was the writer suspicious at first?
4 What did he learn about Robert?
5 Why won't he forget him?

## Ways of creating emphasis

**4** Look at this example from the account.

Robert was motivated by a genuine desire to help. (*What* …)

**What motivated Robert was a genuine desire to help.**

Now rewrite these sentences in a more emphatic way.

1 People rarely help a stranger in trouble. (*Rarely* …)
2 The problem is mistrust. (*It's* …)
3 People worry about being robbed. (*What* …)
4 We should try to help in some way. (*The thing* …)
5 I won't forget the first time a stranger helped me. (*Never* …)

**5** Write about a small or great kindness that happened in your life. Write 200–300 words. Use the paragraph plan below to help you.

Paragraph 1:   Set the scene for the story. Remember to grab the reader's attention at the beginning. Describe the surroundings or the situation, but don't give them all the facts at once.

Paragraph 2–3:   Describe what happened. What were you doing? Were you alone? Why did you need help? How did you feel? Who did you meet? How did they help you?

Paragraph 4:   What happened in the end? Did you learn anything from the experience?

**1** Quickly read the film review.

- What's the purpose of the review?
- Who is likely to read it?
- Is the language mostly formal or informal?

**2** Divide the review into paragraphs, then match the paragraphs to these headings.

a Recommendation
b Positive points
c Negative points
d Subject of the review
e Summary of the plot

**3** Read the review again and answer the questions.

1 What type of film is it?
2 What does the writer compare the story to?
3 What does the writer compare some scenes to?
4 Which words are used to describe …

- the visual imagery?
- the atmosphere?
- the acting?
- the plot and the ending?

5 What tense does the writer use to describe the story?

**4** Complete the sentences with a verb from the box in the correct form.

| create strike adapt suspend reveal set tell see |
|---|

1 The story _____ in Washington, DC, in 2054.
2 It _____ from a book by Philip K Dick.
3 The film _____ the story of a man accused of a future crime.
4 When the truth _____ he goes on the run.
5 The soundtrack and special effects help _____ an atmosphere of suspense.
6 The plot is sometimes unconvincing. You have to _____ your disbelief.
7 What _____ you most is Tom Cruise's impressive performance.
8 I highly recommend it. I'd say it's well worth _____.

**5** Write a 250-word review of a film, play, or book. Follow this advice.

- Choose a film, play, or book that you know well.
- Brainstorm your opinions about the characters, the plot, the acting, and the special effects.
- Use intensifiers to reinforce your opinions.
- Summarize the story, but don't give too much away.
- Organize your review into logical paragraphs with logical linkers.
- End the review with a personal recommendation – try to give a balanced opinion.

## Reviews films

### Road to Perdition    rating ★★★

*Road to Perdition* is the latest film by Sam Mendes, director of the Oscar winning film *American Beauty*. Adapted from a novel by Max Allan Collins and Richard Piers Rayner, *Road to Perdition* is extremely dark and atmospheric. Like a Greek tragedy, it follows the predestined fates of the main characters on their road to perdition (or hell). The film is set in a wintry 1930s Chicago and tells the story of a hitman called Mike Sullivan (Tom Hanks) and his mafia boss John Rooney (Paul Newman). Sullivan looks up to Rooney as a 'father figure'. However, when Sullivan's son witnesses a gangland killing, Rooney turns against him, and both father and son are forced to go on the run. Visually, the film is quite stunning. There are some impressive special effects, but what strikes you most are the dark images of rain and shadow. These create a heavy atmosphere of bleakness and fear. In many scenes brown and black are the dominant colours, which often make the film look like a well-crafted oil painting. The acting too is first-rate, with both Hanks and Newman giving completely convincing performances. However, although it is wonderfully directed and acted, *Road to Perdition* is not a gripping film. The plot is quite slow and the ending is totally predictable. But what the film really lacks is human warmth – the characters ultimately fail to move us. To sum up, *Road to Perdition* is a beautifully-filmed gangster movie. It's well worth seeing, but it doesn't quite deliver the great film we expect.

**1** Many people need to write a personal profile as part of an application for a place at university or for a new job.

Quickly read this personal profile and match paragraphs A–D to the descriptions below.

- ☐ Summary of main skills and qualities
- ☐ Leisure activities
- ☐ Present responsibilities and skills
- ☐ Experience and achievements

**A** I am currently a student at Leeds University, completing a degree in History. As a member of the Student Union Executive Committee, I am actively involved in the day-to-day running of student life. The Committee takes responsibility for improvements to student facilities, coordinating student events such as concerts and sports days, as well as fund-raising activities such as Rag Week. I play a large part in organizing these events, my role specifically being to oversee publicity and manage the budgets. These responsibilities test my leadership as well as my organizational and negotiating skills.

**B** For many years I have been keenly interested in journalism. While I was at school, I helped to run the school magazine, and in my first year at university I often contributed articles to the Student Magazine, 'Juice'. Running and writing a magazine requires the ability to produce interesting, topical articles while working under pressure and meeting tight deadlines. The success of the school magazine shows that I managed to develop these abilities to a high standard.

**C** In my free time I enjoy watching films. I am a member of a local community film club and helped organize a short film festival last year. I contributed my own short video about student life to the festival, which was very well received. My involvement with this local community project has given me experience of organizing off-campus events as well as working with young people in the community.

**D** I believe I have made a positive contribution to both school and university life, as well as to the local community. I am confident and competitive, but also a good team worker. My natural enthusiasm has often helped me motivate others and achieve excellent results.

**2** Read the profile again and answer these questions.

1 How does the writer contribute to university life? What skills has he developed?
2 What did the writer do at school?
3 What type of challenges did he experience?
4 Which hobby does he mention? What experience has he gained from it?
5 What qualities help the writer do a good job?

**3** Complete the sentences with a verb from the box in the correct form.

| take | manage | work | play |
|------|--------|------|------|
| coordinate | meet | run | |

1 Matt didn't want to _____ responsibility for the project. It was too much work.
2 Your education and experience _____ a large part in the skills you have to offer.
3 It's not easy to _____ a newspaper. You often have to _____ very tight deadlines.
4 People are sometimes most creative when they _____ under pressure.
5 Holly had to _____ a lot of people for the fundraising event.
6 He's no good at _____ budgets. He's hopeless at maths!

**4** Write your own personal profile in 250–300 words. Use the plan below and the phrases in exercise 3 to help you.

Paragraph 1: Introduce yourself and what you do. Talk about your current responsibilities and skills.

Paragraph 2: Talk about your past experiences and achievements. Highlight the personal qualities you developed as a result of them.

Paragraph 3: Talk about your leisure activities. Think about how they contribute to the skills and experience you already have.

Paragraph 4: Point out the main contributions you have made to your school / university / work. Summarize your main skills and qualities.

**1** Read this advert for a competition. What do people have to do?

# Calling all sports people–

**NO** LIMITS magazine is offering a free weekend of skydiving. All you have to do is write and answer these questions about an adventure sport you enjoy: **1** How did you start? **2** Why do you enjoy it? **3** Why do you think adventure sports are popular? The winning entry will be published in next month's magazine.

Send in your article to:
NO LIMITS magazine, 67 Walford Road, London SW6 7TY.

**2** Now read the competition entry and answer the questions below.

There comes a time in everyone's life when you want to try something completely new. I'd been a wife and a mother for some years when I started climbing – I knew I was ready for a change. Most winters the family would go to Zermatt in Switzerland. We would rent a chalet there and go skiing. But three years ago it wasn't skiing that interested me. It was climbing. The idea of climbing had always appealed, but I'd never really tried it. That year was different and I decided to take a guided climb up Mount Matterhorn. It proved a difficult experience, but when I reached the top the feeling of excitement and achievement was overwhelming. I knew then that this was what I wanted to do.

When friends find out that I climb, they often want to know what motivates me. It's difficult to put into words because I'm not the stereotypical adrenaline addict and I'm not terribly competitive. For me climbing is more about personal achievement. It provides a challenge, a change of scene, and a bit of escapism. My friends might relax by watching a film or reading a book. Well, I prefer to climb. It transports me out of my everyday life and into a world where anything is possible.

1 Is the style of writing mostly formal or informal?
2 How does the opening paragraph engage the reader's interest?
3 How does the writer explain her hobby to her friends?

## Answering the question

**3** Look at these two versions of the final paragraph. Which do you think is the best at answering the question? Why?

**A** Some people argue that sports like climbing are dangerous and that the sportsmen and women who do them are totally irresponsible. Others say that adventure sports are no longer interesting as there's nothing new to do. But whatever people say, the fact remains that for many of us these sports satisfy a very real need – the need to explore, to push ourselves to the limits, or simply to feel 'alive'.

**B** Why are more and more people doing adventure sports? Firstly, it's probably a result of the whole modern-day obsession with sport. Adventure sports especially have a very positive image. They're seen as exciting, daring and different. Secondly, many people are attracted to the challenge or are curious to see what they are capable of achieving. But whatever the reason, the fact remains that for many of us adventure sports fill a very real need – the need to explore, to push ourselves to the limits, or simply to feel 'alive'.

**4** Read this advert for another competition.

## *free gym membership for one year

**SportingLife** is offering a free gym membership for one year for the best article about sport.

Simply write 200–300 words about what sport means today.
1 – Is it about teamwork or individual achievement?
2 – How are we influenced by sports and sports people?
3 – Why are sport and fitness centres so popular?

Send your article to:
Sporting Life, 56 Ryan Street, Chester CH6 9KJ.

Closing date: 30 August

**5** Write your competition entry in 200–300 words. Use the paragraph plan to help you.

Paragraph 1: Begin with a personal anecdote which illustrates what sport means today. It could describe an experience where you were watching a sport, or taking part in a sport.

Paragraphs 2–3: Answer the questions in the competition entry one by one. State your opinions clearly and give examples where relevant.

Paragraph 4: Sum up your ideas and give your opinion.

**1** Read three extracts from a travel diary and answer the questions.

1 Which countries did the writer visit?

2 How did he travel? Where did he sleep?

3 In which extracts does he …

- get on with the local people?
- experience bad weather?
- comment on the changing scenery?
- feel anxious about his journey?

**A** *After picking up the Honda in Buenos Aires, I carefully packed my camping equipment and left the city. I was soon making my way south along the storm-tossed Atlantic coast, passing glorious, golden beaches and small bustling resorts. I decided to stop off at Bahia Blanca and enjoy the hospitality of the friendly locals, before heading out west. A few days later I set off inland, and was soon riding through bleak wasteland. The days were getting shorter now and the night temperatures were definitely cooler. It was exciting, but also a little troubling to see the next stage of my journey loom ahead – the barren, snow-clad Andes.*

**B** *Chile's lush green vegetation was a welcome change after the desolate landscape of the Andes. But then it started raining. Unfortunately, this was no ordinary shower – it was a real downpour and it went on for days, which was pretty depressing. I passed several rain-drenched, dreary towns, which were about as welcoming as the gloomy-looking people. In fact the rain continued until I reached the capital, Santiago.*

**C** *After Santiago, the weather picked up. It was great riding along the wild Pacific coast in the bright sunshine. But as I approached the Atacama desert, the scenery started to change again. Instead of grassland, there was cactus, then sand. Soon I found myself on the edge of the driest desert in the world, where temperatures ranged from a sizzling 40°C in the day to a freezing –5°C at night.*

**Adding interest**

**2** Read another extract by the same writer. Add adjectives from the box to make it more interesting.

| windswept | desolate | spectacular | derelict | shimmering | blazing |
|---|---|---|---|---|---|

*In the Atacama desert, the road ahead was my only link with civilization. The sun beat down on the sand dunes and ghost towns which lined the route. In the distance I could see volcanoes which marked the edge of the desert and the border with Bolivia.*

**3** Find adjectives in extracts A–C which describe …

- beaches
- towns and cities
- the coastline
- people
- the mountains

**4** Match these sentence halves describing different journeys.

1 It was a beautiful sunny day when we headed
2 They crossed the swamp, then slowly made
3 After travelling for several hours on the motorway we stopped
4 The road was flooded so we had to turn
5 If you follow this road for 15 kilometres, you'll find
6 It was hard work hiking through the snow, but we soldiered
7 The express train sped
8 We were crossing a bridge when the bus broke

a off at a service station for lunch.
b their way to the crocodile farm.
c out towards the mountains.
d through the countryside without stopping. / towards the gloomy city.
e on until we got to the cabin.
f back and look for an alternative route.
g yourself on the coast.
h down and blocked the road.

**5** Write a 250-word description of a memorable journey you have taken. Use the paragraph plan and the questions to help you.

Paragraph 1: Describe the beginning of your journey. Where were you going? Who were you travelling with? How did you get there?

Paragraph 2–3: Describe what happened during the journey. What was the weather like? What were your impressions of people and places? How did you feel? Did anything unusual happen?

Paragraph 4: Describe the end of your journey. What was your final destination? When did you arrive? How did you feel about the journey? Was it a good or a bad experience?

**1** Look at these facts taken from a biography. Combine the sentences to make one sentence, using the words given.

1 Robert Capa was a famous photojournalist. **Robert Capa, the ...**
He was also the founder of Magnum Photos.
He was born in Budapest in 1913.

2 He was a very talented photographer. **A talented, ...**
He was self-taught.
He started working for a publishing house when he was just 18.
At the same time he studied journalism at a Berlin university.

3 There was much political upheaval in the 1930s. **During the 1930s ...**
Many of his student companions became involved.
Capa was also very much involved.

4 Capa had to leave Hungary as a result. **Consequently ...**
Later he had to leave Berlin too.
He went to live in Paris.

**2** Quickly read the rest of the biography. Match paragraphs A–D to the descriptions.

☐ an evaluation of his achievements
☐ the end of his career
☐ his continuing success
☐ how he built his reputation

# Robert Capa photographer

**A** DURING HIS FIRST years in Paris, Capa worked mainly on local photo stories. It was not until 1936 that he got his big break. He was sent to cover the Spanish Civil War and, as a result, his work started to appear regularly in top magazines and newspapers. It was his picture of a Loyalist soldier falling to his death which brought him international repute and became a powerful symbol of war.

**B** In 1939, shortly after the Spanish Civil War, Capa worked in New York for a while. However, he quickly returned to Europe on the outbreak of World War II and stayed there for six years. His photographs of the Normandy invasion became some of the most memorable war photographs in history, and he received the Medal of Freedom Citation for his work.

**C** Capa's job as a war photographer often put him in great personal danger, but despite the risks his motto was always: 'If your pictures aren't good enough, you aren't close enough.' However on 25 May 1954, Capa's luck ran out. He was working on an assignment in French Indochina when he stepped on a land mine. He was killed instantly.

**D** Today Robert Capa is considered one of the finest war photographers of all time. He was an exceptional photojournalist who used his camera to express and record the horror of the events around him. Not surprisingly Capa hated war, especially his often passive role in it. 'It's not always easy to stand aside and be unable to do anything except record the sufferings around one,' he said.

**3** Read the biography again and answer the questions.

1 How did Robert Capa get his 'big break'?
2 What do you think he was trying to achieve through his pictures? How did he feel about his work?
3 Did any of the facts about his life surprise you? What do you think was the most interesting fact?
4 How does the writer use direct quotes? What effect do they have?
5 Do you think Robert Capa was a brave man? Would you describe him as a 'hero'?

**4** Write your own biography. Either write about someone who interests you, or use the notes about Isabel Allende below. Use the paragraph plan to help you.

# ISABEL ALLENDE

**Paragraph 1: The early years**
- 1942: born in Lima, Peru – moved to Chile when she was three
- worked as a secretary, then a journalist
- 1973: military coup – her uncle, President Salvador Allende, was assassinated
- went with her husband and children to Venezuela

**Paragraph 2: How she built her reputation**
- 1975–1984: worked as a journalist in Venezuela
- 1981: wrote letter to her dying grandfather – became her first novel *The House of the Spirits* – critically acclaimed

**Paragraph 3: Her continuing success**
- 1984–1985: wrote *Of Love and Shadows* and *Eva Luna* – bestsellers and made into films
- 1994: wrote *Paula* – inspired by the illness of her 28-year-old daughter

**Paragraph 1: An evaluation of her achievements**
- now lives in San Francisco with her second husband
- continues to write novels – also teaches literature
- one of most talented writers of her generation

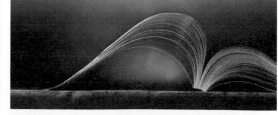

# Tapescripts

## Unit 1

**T 1.1**

1 I tried to repair my car, but I couldn't. I didn't have the right tools.
2 'You look awful. Why don't you see a doctor?'
'I have. He just gave me some pills and told me to take things easy.'
3 'It's a long journey. Take care on the motorway.'
'Don't worry. We will.'
4 I met your sister last night. She thought we'd met before, but we hadn't.
5 'Have you read this report?'
'No, I haven't, but I will.'
6 The weather forecast said that it might rain this afternoon. If it does, we'll have to call off the tennis.
7 My car's being mended at the moment. If it wasn't, I'd give you a lift. Sorry.
8 I'm so glad you told Sue exactly what you thought of her, because if you hadn't, I certainly would have!
9 I got that job I applied for, so I was delighted. I really didn't think I would.
10 'Come on, John! It's time you were getting up!'
'I am! I'll be down in a second.'
11 'I think I'll give Bob a ring.'
'You should. You haven't been in touch with him for ages.'
12 I went to a party last night, but I wish I hadn't. It was awful.
13 My boyfriend insists on doing all the cooking, but I wish he wouldn't – it's inedible!
14 'Aren't you going to Portugal for your holidays?'
'Well, we might, but we're still not sure.'
15 'Andy got drunk at Anne's party and started insulting everyone.'
'He would! That's so typical. He's always doing that.'

**T 1.2**

1 A Can you come round for a meal tonight?
B Thanks very much. I'd love to.
2 A Did you post my letter?
B Oh, I'm really sorry. I forgot to.
3 A I can't take you to the airport after all. Sorry.
B But you agreed to!
4 A Was John surprised when he won?
B He certainly was. He didn't expect to.
5 A Why did you slam the door in my face?
B It was an accident. I really didn't mean to.
6 A You'll be able to enjoy yourself when the exams finish.
B Don't worry. I intend to!

**T 1.3**   I = Interviewer, V = Vijay, B = Bhikhu

**Part one**

I What was it like, life in Eldoret then?
V It was a quaint little place ... very safe ... we had sunrise at six, sunset at six in the evening and that was the same all the year round simpl... that's because we were on the equator and 7,000 feet above the sea level, therefore the climate is excellent and do you know they claim that it was the best climate in the world ...
B Life was quite difficult in some respects ... erm ... the biggest tragedy of our life was we lost our father when we were quite young, I was s... eight I think my brother was six and ... er ... and in spite of the sort of safe community there, my mother had to bring us up so ... it was quite difficult really ... er ... to manage on a day-to-day basis but my mother made sure we had enough and she used to teach nursery school children... .

I Did you come to England together ... at the same time? ...
V Bhikhu is the older and I followed him ... it was a year after he came, a year and a quarter ... I was sixteen.
B I came here at the age of seventeen or eighteen, I think ... yeah.
I Now, what was it made you come to England?
B Well, in our case, certainly we were British citizens and we knew that we could educate ourselves, as well as work ... we knew as we could study and work we knew we would be fine ... we knew we had to work hard ... we did see it as a land of opportunity.
I It is said that you came here with just a few pounds in your pocket.
V That's absolutely true. Maybe Bhikhu had a pound more than me, but I honestly had five pounds of my own.
I So what about the steps then from that point to actually starting your business? What happened?
B It's a long way really, I mean ... er
V We could write a book ... [laughter]
B I mean when I first came, my ... my first and main ambition really was to study, get a university degree and so on, so I set about getting that sorted out and that was first of all ... er ... applying for...well doing A levels full-time and working part-time to sustain ourselves ... er
I This was in London?
B This was in London. I wanted to be an architect.
I Did you qualify as an architect?
B Yes, I did. I went to Bristol University and did seven years.
I But ... but you Vijay you didn't follow that path I mean architecture wasn't your ...
V [laughs] No, no it wasn't me, I haven't got the discipline of an architect, I think. I actually did my A levels and then went to a school of Pharmacy in Leicester and I did my degree in Pharmacy there. In the back of my mind I suppose was the fact that if you are in pharmacy you can go into business more than if you are a doctor and that's sort of what led me to do pharmacy.
I And that, of course there is the tradition among the Patels, certainly in East Africa of business, isn't there?
V Sure.
I And what I neglected to ask you, about your father, was he a businessman?
V He was a timber merchant. Yes, and ... er ... he ... he had actually only just started his business and within a year of him starting the business, which he did very well at, though he was there for a short time, but he passed away.

**T 1.4**   Part two

I So you started your business with ... er ... the equivalent of a corner shop except ... er ... it was a pharmacy ...
V Yes, it was a pharmacy, indeed, yes.
I Now, what was it in you two that made you go from that one corner shop to what we have now?
B Er ... well, I mean, what I did ... I mean, I qualified as an architect, worked in private practices and so on, and ultimately ... erm ... decided that was not for me. Erm ... so, thereafter I went into business, which was a couple of corner shops, newsagents, all my friends thought I was mad ... and so I went into business, in ... in East London in two newsagent shops, but then after a couple of years I left it erm ... so I came across to where my brother Vijay was ... and joined him and by then ... he had started his pharmacy business, made a success of it and by the time I joined him I think he had about three or four, quite a few shops and we decided to go together and ...
I Two brothers working in the same business could be a recipe for disaster – you know power struggles and all the rest of it but in your cases, what is it, what do you each bring that the other perhaps lacks?

V Bhikhu is a trained architect and, do you know, Bhikhu has a tremendously disciplined and a very high IQ mind, so I was building up a very, very successful enterprise, that's something I do have in me, the vision, the go, even if I say so myself, I have that in me to build a successful enterprise, I do lack the discipline to look after it ... and hence Bhikhu's strength really enhances my weakness tremendously, so the deal was, I make the wealth brother, you look after it. Today twenty or twenty-two, twenty-three years on, that stays.
B Yeah, so it works very well, I think basically we complement each other, and ... erm ... where we're different from other people perhaps ... er ... there isn't sort of ... er ... siblings rivalry ... a lot of it is sort of for the greater good of the family. A lot of Asian families are like that they look after the family as a whole and I think that comes across in our ... our relationships as well really. And that is important.
I On the subject of family you ... you mentioned earlier how much of a role your mother had in your early life, especially after your father died. What ... is she with you now?
V Indeed she is, and do you know she is a very strong person. She lives with me ... she's a very strong personality. I mean a truly great lady, she sacrificed her entire life. You know she just worked twelve hours a day, seven days a week for umpteen number of years 'til we were grown up enough to leave the nest, as it were.
I What about ... in England in achieving what you've achieved ...
V Sure ...
I ... did you come up against much racial discrimination?
V No, and I can safely and honestly and in my heart say that I have not come against any segregation as such ... in my business, in my working life.
B Yeah, I mean I came slightly earlier on and I had slightly different experiences when I first came to the UK. ... Erm I couldn't get a job despite all my qualification ... er ... and at that time, it was very apparent I couldn't because of my colour of my skin and this was going back to the sixties. Also as a newsagent I had a terrible time, where I was ... windows would be smashed, my shutters in the shops were ... were attacked, there were all sorts of harassment where I was ... it was terrible.

**T 1.5**   Part three

I You've just been nominated ... or named as joint entrepreneurs of the year ... what was it for?
V Well ... coming from where we did ... to actually build a successful business ... er ... and the other, other thing is to actually provide employment, we provide employment for six hundred people directly.
I Do you think success has spoiled the Patels?
V Speaking for myself and my brother, I don't think it has. We are not the sort of helicopter or yacht people in any sense. Er ... we ... I can say ... truly say ourselves that we do not see ourselves any different to what we saw ourselves as when we were younger. We ... in fact we've got the same friends as we had when we were children, same college and university friends, we still keep in touch with them and I would like to think that we're approachable so ... I would say it hasn't really spoilt or changed us. Yeah? I mean, clearly, in terms of luxuries in life one tends to sort of indulge oneself a little bit but not extraordinarily, I hope.
B No way extravagantly, because if I could go on the train somewhere rather than the car, then I would. Er ... that sums up our, you know, approach to life, we really ... I would rather do some philanthropic work rather than waste money.
I One final question. Young people starting out ... what sort of advice would you give to them?

**V** Shall I go first?

**B** Yeah do.

**V** Live your dreams. If you have an ambition go for it. Do not let little, small distractions or calamities stop you. Chase your dream and go for it and that's, that's exactly what I have done. That's where I would like to be a role model, for anybody who wants to be somebody tomorrow … er … to see what we have done and if I can touch one life, then my job in this life's done.

**B** Now what I would say is … er … with the dreams one needs a sl… dose of reality a lot of hard work and, as Vijay says, not to be set back by … by any temporary kind of difficulties.

**T 1.6**

**1 Eric**

Many people think of my country as a great big, frozen land of ice, up north, with eskimos and red-coated policemen but it's obviously a very different country from that, eh. It's a bilingual country, 40% of the population has French as a mother tongue and it has a very dispersed population, but 90% of it lives in a small ribbon of land just 90 kilometres from the US border, eh. In fact probably one of the biggest concerns we have is the effect of US domination on our unique culture, because of TV, sports and such like. I think many of us have an inferiority complex relative to the US. Here in Europe, a lot of the time people think we're American, it's annoying.

**2 Mary**

So our stereotype is that we're miserable, mean and dour and unhappy with our lot and that we're a proud people, maybe quite nationalistic, especially in sport – we'll support *any* team that's playing against England. Maybe there's an element of truth in all of this. I mean you do meet people who are mean but far more you meet people who are generous. I saw a guy collapse in the street and folk were running out the shops and bringing him a chair, and a glass of water and things and d'you know if somebody collapses in London, folk'll step over them, assume they're drunk or whatever. Oh, and as for whether people are miserable, well I remember standing at a bus stop and it was a gorgeous sunny day, real blue sky, you know you don't see many days like that here, not very often. And I said to the woman next to me 'Isn't it a gorgeous day?' And she said 'Aye, but we'll pay for it!' And I thought how can you be so pessimistic when it's such a gorgeous day.

**3 Julia**

Ah well, I think we have a very, erm, well-deserved reputation for being loud, we are certainly very loud, erm, everywhere, it doesn't matter where we are, we just talk all at the same time and quite loud. And we're also very disorganised, erm, people believe that we are, and another thing that is well-deserved. Erm, what else, we're very lazy, erm, I don't think that is true, erm, we used to sleep our siestas er, but I think we're a bit more European now and we all have the same sort of timetables. Erm, and then well, we're sociable and outgoing, erm, we're always with other people, we're rar… rarely on our own, erm, we tend to do lots of things at the same time, and, that's also because, there are so many places and they open until late, erm, it's a bit more relaxed atmosphere than in England.

**4 Zoltan**

Most foreigners seem to think that all our dishes are spicy and really hot, which is not exactly true … er … we use quite a lot of paprika but it's not hot at all especially not when it's compared to Asian dishes for example. And also the other thing that people think of is … er … horses and … er … the great plains … one in five live in Budapest which is a big city, and quite a lot of people live in smaller towns and smaller cities and not on the great plains at all and many … would not have seen a horse in their whole lives.

**5 Rosemary**

Erm … I think that there is a stereotype in the eyes of a lot of British. I think they consider them loud, they consider them in many cases arrogant. Remember they lost the rev… the revolutionary war, and they still have this attitude of being, 'we once ruled you'. And although that was two hundred years ago, I think there is still this attitude that they are the rebellious children, or the rebe… rebellious offspring of Great Britain. And -erm, I think it's, it's very silly as an attitude because I think there are, yes there are a lot, who are extremely narrow, they don't see beyond their border, they are very arrogant, but there are also an incredible amount who are very aware of what's goes on in the rest of the world.

**6 Tristan**

We're generally perceived as being quite cold and … er … really quite uptight as well and I know this from my own experience … erm … that they're perceived also as being somewhat hypocritical – two-faced, now I don't think that was in relation to me, I hope not anyway and I think now they also come across as incredibly yobbish, sort of heavy drinking, potentially violent, which is … erm not entirely my experience.

**T 1.7**

1 **A** Where do you live?
   **B** We've got a small flat. It's on the ground floor of a block of flats in the centre of town.
   **A** Have you got a garden?
   **B** No, we haven't, just a car park at the back.
2 **A** Where do you live?
   **B** We have a small apartment. It's on the first floor of an apartment building downtown.
   **A** Do you have a yard?
   **B** No we don't, just a parking lot in the back.

**T 1.8**

1 **A** Do you have the time?
   **B** Yeah, it's five of four.
   **A** Did you say five after?
   **B** No, five *of* four.
2 **A** What are you gonna do on the weekend?
   **B** The usual stuff. Play soccer with the kids, and sweep the yard.
3 **A** Did you enjoy the game?
   **B** Yeah, it was great, but we had to stand in line for half an hour to get tickets.
4 **A** Did you have a good vacation?
   **B** Yeah, real good.
   **A** How long were you away?
   **B** Five days in all. Monday thru Friday.
5 **A** Can you mail this letter and package for me?
   **B** Sure thing.
   **A** And can you stop by the liquor store and buy a six-pack of Michelob and some potato chips?
   **B** Is that all?
6 **A** Did you see *The Birds* on cable last night?
   **B** Sure, even though I've seen it two times before.
   **A** My third time. Isn't it just an awesome movie?
   **B** Sure is. One of my favorites.
7 **A** Did they bring the check yet?
   **B** Yeah. They just did. But I can't read a thing. It's lighted so badly in here.
8 **A** Do we need to stop for gas?
   **B** Yeah, why not? I need to use the restroom, anyway.

**T 1.9**

1 **A** Have you got the time?
   **B** Yeah, it's five to four.
   **A** Did you say five past?
   **B** No, five *to* four.
2 **A** What are you going to do at the weekend?
   **B** The usual. Play football with my kids, and do a bit of gardening.
3 **A** Did you enjoy the match?
   **B** Yeah, it was great, but we had to queue for half an hour to get tickets.

4 **A** Did you have a good holiday?
   **B** Yeah, really good.
   **A** How long were you away?
   **B** Five days altogether. From Monday to Friday.
5 **A** Can you post this letter and parcel for me?
   **B** Of course.
   **A** And can you call at the off-licence and buy a six-pack of Stella and some crisps?
   **B** Is that all?
6 **A** Did you watch *The Birds* on telly last night?
   **B** I did, even though I've seen it twice before.
   **A** My third time. Isn't it just a terrific film?
   **B** It certainly is. One of my favourites.
7 **A** Have they brought the bill yet?
   **B** Yeah. They just have. But I can't read a thing. The lighting is so bad in here.
8 **A** Do we need to stop for petrol?
   **B** Yes, why not? I need to go to the loo, anyway.

# Unit 2

**T 2.1**

1 What did you think of your brother's new girlfriend?
2 You've lost weight! What have you been doing?
3 When do we have to do that homework for?
4 Did you finish that crossword?
5 I've got nowhere to stay tonight.
6 What's wrong? You don't look very well.
7 The children look very guilty, don't they?
8 OK, that's it for today. Don't forget! The next meeting's Friday the 6th at 2.30.

**T 2.2**

1 What did you think of your brother's new girlfriend?
   She's lovely. I got on with her very well.
2 You've lost weight! What have you been doing?
   I've started working out every morning at the gym.
3 When do we have to do that homework for?
   We have to hand it in on Friday.
4 Did you finish that crossword?
   No, I gave up. It was too difficult.
5 I've got nowhere to stay tonight.
   Don't worry. We'll put you up.
6 What's wrong? You don't look very well.
   I feel dreadful. I think I'm going down with the flu.
7 The children look very guilty, don't they?
   Yeah. I wonder what they've been getting up to?
8 OK, that's it for today. Don't forget! The next meeting's Friday the 6th at 2.30.
   I'll put that down in my diary straight away.

**T 2.3** LB = Lady Bracknell, J = Jack

**LB** Do you smoke?
**J** Well, yes, I must admit I smoke.
**LB** I am glad to hear it. A man should always have an occupation of some kind. There are far too many idle men in London as it is. How old are you?
**J** Twenty-nine.
**LB** A very good age to be married at. I have always been of the opinion that a man who desires to get married should know either everything or nothing. Which do you know?
**J** I know nothing, Lady Bracknell.
**LB** I am pleased to hear it. I do not approve of anything that tampers with natural ignorance. Ignorance is like a delicate exotic fruit; touch it and the bloom is gone. What is your income?
**J** Between seven and eight thousand a year.
**LB** In land, or in investments?
**J** In investments, chiefly.
**LB** That is satisfactory.

**J** I have a country house with some land, of course, attached to it, about fifteen hundred acres, I believe; but I don't depend on that for my real income. In fact, as far as I can make out, the poachers are the only people who make anything out of it.

**LB** A country house! You have a town house, I hope? A girl with a simple, unspoiled nature, like Gwendolen could hardly be expected to reside in the country.

**J** Well, I own a house in Belgrave Square.

**LB** What number in Belgrave Square?

**J** 149.

**LB** The unfashionable side. Now to minor matters. Are your parents living?

**J** I have lost both my parents.

**LB** To lose one parent, Mr Worthing, may be regarded as a misfortune; to lose both looks like carelessness. Who was your father? He was evidently a man of some wealth.

**J** I am afraid I really don't know. The fact is, Lady Bracknell, I said I had lost my parents. It would be nearer the truth to say that my parents seem to have lost me. I don't actually know who I am by birth. I was …, well, I was *found*.

**LB** Found!

**J** The late Mr. Thomas Cardew, an old gentleman of a very charitable and kindly disposition, found me, and gave me the name of Worthing, because he happened to have a first-class ticket for Worthing in his pocket at the time. Worthing is a place in Sussex. It is a seaside resort.

**LB** Where did the charitable gentleman who had a first-class ticket for this seaside resort find you?

**J** In a handbag.

**LB** A handbag?

**J** Yes, Lady Bracknell. I was in a handbag – a somewhat large, black leather handbag, with handles to it – an ordinary handbag, in fact.

**LB** In what locality did this Mr. James, or Thomas, Cardew come across this ordinary handbag?

**J** In the cloakroom at Victoria Station. It was given to him in mistake for his own.

**LB** The cloakroom at Victoria Station?

**J** Yes. The Brighton line.

**LB** The line is immaterial. Mr. Worthing, I confess I feel somewhat bewildered by what you have just told me. To be born, or at any rate, bred in a handbag, whether it had handles or not, seems to me to display a contempt for the ordinary decencies of family life. As for the particular locality in which the handbag was found, a cloakroom at a railway station might serve to conceal a social indiscretion – has probably, indeed, been used for that purpose before now but it could hardly be regarded as an assured basis for a recognized position in good society.

**J** May I ask then what you would advise me to do? I need hardly say I will do anything in the world to ensure Gwendolen's happiness.

**LB** I would strongly advise you, Mr. Worthing, to try and acquire some relations as soon as possible, and to make a definite effort to produce at any rate one parent, of either sex.

**J** I don't see how I could possibly manage to do that. I can produce the handbag at any moment. It's in my dressing-room at home. I really think that should satisfy you, Lady Bracknell.

**LB** Me, sir! What has it to do with me? You can hardly imagine that I and Lord Bracknell would dream of allowing our only daughter – a girl brought up with the utmost care – to marry into a cloakroom, and form an alliance with a parcel! Good morning, Mr. Worthing!

**T 2.4**

I never set out to pinch anyone's bloke, let alone Nina's. The day it all started, picking up a bloke was the last thing on my mind. Even I don't go out on the pull in manky old combats and a sweater that's seen better days. All I was thinking of, on that drizzly afternoon, was finding a cab home. Having started off in mist-like fashion, the drizzle had moved up a gear, as if it were thinking about turning into proper rain. At this point I was just up the road from Covent Garden, with drizzled-on hair and a jumper starting to smell of a wet Shetland sheep. That was when I saw Nina coming out of a smart little restaurant, with a bloke on her arm.

If I can misquote Jane Austen here, it is a truth universally acknowledged that if you are fated to bump into someone like Nina when you haven't seen her for four years, you will be looking like a pig's breakfast. While she will be looking like a *Sunday Times* fashion shoot in silk and cashmere. Only about six paces away, she was talking and laughing in her silver-tinkle way to the bloke, who was holding her umbrella up to stop her getting wet. The last time I'd seen her (at a wedding four years back) she'd had some tall, dark specimen in tow. Although everything about him was theoretically perfect, I hadn't been particularly impressed – to me he'd seemed just a bit plastic, somehow. I don't quite know what it was with this one – he wasn't classically good-looking, exactly, but the spark hit me at once!

**T 2.5** See p26

**T 2.6**

1  She threw the ring into the bin with the rubbish.
2  Sorry we're late. We got behind a farmer with a herd of cattle in the lane.
3  We'll meet you outside the cinema at six o'clock.
4  Oh, how sweet of you to remember my birthday!
5  Speak up! I can't hear a word you're saying.
6  We saw some deer when we were walking in the mountains.
7  The cupboards are bare. We'll have to go shopping.
8  Those two are a right pair of troublemakers.
9  The children sat in orderly rows in the school hall.
10  Uncle Bill chews every mouthful of food twenty times.

# Unit 3

**T 3.1**

Halico enjoyed a steady rise in profits in January. Unfortunately they fell dramatically in February, then picked up in March and April when they went up gradually. May saw profits shooting up, but then the company suffered a substantial decrease in June. In July and August profits increased slightly, then went up steadily in the early autumn months of September and October, before tumbling sharply in November. They then evened out in December.

**T 3.2**

Becom's sales began the year healthily, with January figures in the mid five thousand units a month. They dropped dramatically in February and March, plummeting to one thousand. Sales picked up slightly in April, then shot up in the early summer months of May and June, at the end of which period sales were peaking at six thousand five hundred a month. There was a bit of a downturn in July, when sales dropped by eight hundred, but then they remained stable in August and September. October saw a substantial decrease, down to three thousand, before sales picked up in the build-up to Christmas, rising steadily to end the year at four thousand five hundred.

**T 3.3**  I = Interviewer, PM = Prime Minister

**I** We are very pleased to have with us in the studio tonight the Prime Minister. Prime Minister, we've been …

**PM** Good evening, Jeremy.

**I** Good evening, Prime Minister. Er … Prime Minister, we've been hearing endlessly in the media about the latest crisis that is facing your government.

**PM** May I just say straight away that this is *not* a crisis.

**I** Well, many people say …

**PM** No, Jeremy, I think not … polls distinctly show that the vast majority of the population strongly support us.

**I** With respect, Prime Minister, the poll I read only this morning in the *Daily Sun* …

**PM** But surely you don't believe a word you read in the tabloid press. No – my government fully deserves every penny of their pay rise.

**I** Prime Minister, you can hardly argue the case for Members of Parliament voting themselves, … yes, voting themselves a 40% pay rise when your government has offered nurses just 2.6%, teachers merely 1.7% and firefighters …

**PM** Let me say that I greatly respect our public sector workers, they work hard and carry heavy responsibilities. However, MPs also work very conscientiously and carry burdens which are just as heavy. Also …

**I** But, Prime Minister, how can you justify …

**PM** If I can just finish, Jeremy. The fact is that this pay rise is much nearer 20% when you take into account the many expenses which all politicians regularly incur.

**I** Such as?

**PM** Well, you know, … er … travel – air and rail fares, an entertainment allowance, their personal secretaries, all of these highly necessary for any MP. You can't expect them to travel second class, eat in third-rate restaurants *and* do a first-class job. You know, Jeremy, the fact of the matter is …

**I** The fact of the matter is, Prime Minister, that this pay rise is five times the rate of inflation, and lately you and your ministers have repeatedly urged workers to accept increases in line with inflation. It seems perfectly plain to me and many people that …

**PM** Jeremy, Jeremy, let me explain. We set up an independent review body to look into …

**I** As I understand it, Prime Minister, this so-called independent review body was made up of mainly Members of Parliament, who, with respect, can hardly be called independent.

**PM** Ah, but only MPs can appreciate the particular workload of a politician. And I have to tell you that the review concluded that the effectiveness of the nation's MPs is being severely hampered by lack of funds, and that their salaries are pathetically low compared to those people working in industry, banking and the like.

**I** And what about your own pay rise, Prime Minister? Is there any truth in the rumour that you will be getting a rise of 50%?

**PM** Ah now, Jeremy, I came on your programme to talk about MPs' salaries, my own salary is being reviewed separately *and* it will be reviewed fairly. And, as you know, I believe passionately in fair and just settlements for all working people and I include myself in that, Jeremy.

**I** Of course you do, Prime Minister. Prime Minister, thank you very much.

**PM** Thank *you*, Jeremy.

**T 3.4**  I = Interviewer, AR = Anita Roddick
**Part one**

**I** I wonder what it was in you that … that enabled you to have that kind of feeling about what business should be.

**AR** I think it's what, I think what's … gave this erm … whole edge is that I was saved by not going to business school, by not doing the traditional route.

**I** That's a terrible condemnation of business school.

**AR** It is because I don't believe … I believe they do an incredibly good job of developing people to understand financial science. You can't expect to raise an entrepreneur in a business school. Entrepreneurs are usually erm … outsiders. That's why immigrants, refugees make the best erm … entrepreneurs. My parents were economic immigrants. Whether you had the … you know … the Jewish immigrants in the beginning of the century, or the Italian immigrants in the mid-century, or the Pakistani and the Bangladeshi, and the Indian … or the Caribbean … they all had … they all dance to a different drum beat. They're not part of the system. They're outside the system. And when you're a young person, and you feel as an outsider … 'cos we were the first Italians in this town. You were just braver because you didn't know any different. Business school … would have polished my thinking into a much more disciplined way. Market, product development, finance, instead of saying 'Hey!', having a great idea, and thinking 'My God! If I make this idea really good, people will buy it from me, hopefully give me a profit.' And it became, it was a notion of trading, which … entrepreneurs are manic traders. We're buyers and sellers … you know. And all we want to do is go into the market place for feedback on our ideas. And all the money we make is of no interest to us. This is what upsets the financial journalists because we don't give a darn about money. We just want the money to oil the wheels, to see how far this idea could go. And many of us feel fraudulent, because ideas just come out of our head like er … you know … like a genie in the bottle. We vomit ideas. But we are terribly, terribly bad at managing.

**I**  But as you … but … business needs, of course, all those other things …

**AR**  Of course it does.

**I**  … the structure, the management.

**AR**  Yeah, but that … it should be subservient. It's like … you need to breathe to stay alive, and if you keep on concentrating, breathing in … out, in out … What a life you're going to have if you concentrate only on profits. You're going to have a business that's going to die within a nano second because it's more than the profit. It's just the avenue, the engine for making you develop other ideas, or to invest in other things. So, you know, for me business school has never been … you know … has never been the sacred ground for it. It's always 'Have an idea. Learn.' And the best business people, entrepreneurs are people who ask questions. You know, I don't want to be the biggest retailer, you know, in the world. I have no interest in that. I just want to be the most idiosyncratic, the wildest, the bravest.

**Part two**
Anita Roddick is asked what she sees as the big dilemmas in business these days.

**AR**  You know, for me the big dilemma now in business is, are … businesses … businesses rule. That's the fact. Any institution …

**I**  Rule our lives?

**AR**  Rule our lives.

**I**  Rule the world?

**AR**  Rule the world. I mean, you can forget politics, and you can forget religion, as being the two most, foremost institutions. Business institution now has, because it's so wealthy, because it is so creative in many ways, it controls government thinking, it controls political thinking. And it controls our health, our safety, it controls what we eat, controls what we think. And it's because this whole growth in the global economy, and which really means corporate global economy. So this growth in corporations, multinational corporations which are … just bow down to nothing, no local laws, no national laws. They stop any environmental standards, any human rights standards if they deem it gets in the way

of trade. So they for me are the big enemy. So my messages now is 'Look for businesses that support local communities, because you keep the money in the local arena. Support local economic initiatives, support local farming, support local, anything local. And if we're working and trading internationally, let us trade with the grass roots. And let's trade in a way that is honourable. Let us pay living wages, and not slave … slave wages. Let us be penalized if we have human rights abusers within the products that we make or sell.' People are standing up and challenging those big brand names because they don't like their business practices.

**Part three**
Anita Roddick has announced that she has no intention of leaving her children any money when she dies.

**I**  You won't give your wealth, will you?

**AR**  To them.

**I**  To your children.

**AR**  No.

**I**  But in that mother role, shouldn't you be doing that?

**AR**  No. One of the biggest criticisms from the media is that my wealth is not going to go to them. And 'Oh!' they say 'Oh! What do your kids think about it?' My kids say 'I don't want to even talk about this, 'cos it means that my mum's going to be dead.' And number two, well 'What have we got already? We've got great homes, we've got our work.' And they're not poor. I mean, but they also know that if there's … if the wealth comes out at fifty or a hundred and fifty million quid, or whatever it is, what better thing to do than to give it away? What a great legacy, just you know with the building of the schools in Africa, the support of the community organisers, the human rights, this whole campaign I'm putting moneys into at the moment on the elimination of sweat shops and child labour and slave labour. I can't think of a better legacy. If all you're recognized for is the ability to accumulate money, then I think that is the next thing from being obscene. You know, the thing about wealth, it allows you to be generous. The sadness, one of the sadnesses about poverty, it doesn't allow you to be that.

**T 3.5**
1  We're in class learning English.
2  It's eight o'clock and time for a break.
3  I'm dying for a cup of coffee.
4  We've been in here for over an hour.
5  As a matter of fact, I think our teacher's asleep.
6  She doesn't understand that her English students are about to creep out.

**T 3.6**  See p36

**T 3.7**  See p36

**T 3.8**
1  **A**  Could I have your first name, please?
   **B**  It's Marc. That's M – A – R, and then C for Charlie, not K for Kilo.
   **A**  And the surname?
   **B**  De Weck.
   **A**  Could you spell that for me?
   **B**  Yes. It's two words. First D – …
   **A**  Is that T for Tango?
   **B**  No, D for Delta, and E for Echo. And then a separate word, WECK.
   **A**  Is that with a V for Victor?
   **B**  No, it's W for Whisky – E – C – K.
2  **C**  And your name, please?
   **D**  It's Pilar Asajani.
   **C**  Could you spell the first name for me?
   **D**  It's P – …
   **C**  B for Bravo?

**D**  No, P for Papa – I for India – L – A – R.
**C**  OK … Pilar. And your surname, please?
**D**  Asajani. That's A – S …
**C**  Was that F for Freddie?
**D**  No, it's A – S for Sierra – A, then J for Juliet – A – N for November, and I for India.
3  **E**  … And could I have the name of the other person who'll be driving the car?
   **F**  Yes, it's Ginny Dummet.
   **E**  Jimmy. You mean, J for Juliet – I – …
   **F**  No, it's G for Golf – I – double N – …
   **E**  Double M for Mike?
   **F**  No, double N for November, and Y.
   **E**  Was that I for India or Y for Yankee?
   **F**  Y for Yankee. And the surname is Dummet … D – …
   **E**  D for Delta?
   **F**  That's right. D for Delta – U – double M for Mike – E – T.

# Unit 4

**T 4.1**
1  A celebrity is a person who works hard all his life to become well known, and then wears dark glasses to avoid being recognized.
2  I don't want to achieve immortality through my work. I want to achieve it through not dying.
3  There is only one thing worse than being talked about, and that is not being talked about.
4  What goes up, must come down.
5  Winning isn't everything, but it sure as hell beats losing.
6  Whenever a friend succeeds, a little something in me dies.
7  Genius is one per cent inspiration, ninety-nine per cent perspiration.
8  If at first you don't succeed, try, try again.
9  Nothing succeeds like success.
10  Let me tell you about the rich. They are different from you and me.

**T 4.2**
All the A-list stars were there. That model, Angeline, I think it was Angeline, was there with her new boyfriend. They've been secretly going out for months. Oh, it was a glittering occasion. Stars everywhere and the crowds outside simply begging for autographs. I couldn't believe my eyes. And the dresses! I don't know how much they would have cost – a fortune, I imagine. All designer labels. The photographers were having a field day, and there were reporters everywhere, falling over each other to interview the biggest names. We didn't have the best seats, we were in the back row. We could still see everything. I was so busy star spotting that I didn't take in the plot. You'd have been the same. I'm not too keen on thrillers but it must have been good because at the end the whole audience rose to its feet and clapped. I'm not terribly sure what the story was about, but you really must go to see it when it's on general release. It was an amazing evening and to top it off we went to Quaglino's for supper afterwards and Sarah Jane Fox and Brad Brat were at the next table. How cool is that? Sarah Jane Fox has awful skin problems. Who cares about that when you've got that much money?

**T 4.3**
All the A-list stars were there. That model, Angeline, at least I think it was Angeline, was there with her new boyfriend. Apparently they've been secretly going out for months. Anyway, it was a glittering occasion. Stars everywhere and the crowds outside simply begging for autographs. Quite honestly I couldn't believe my eyes. And the dresses! I mean, I don't know how much they would have cost – a fortune, I imagine. All designer labels, naturally. The photographers were obviously having a field day, and of course there were reporters everywhere,

falling over each other so to speak, to interview the biggest names.

Admittedly we didn't have the best seats – as a matter of fact we were in the back row. Mind you, we could still see everything. Actually, I was so busy star spotting that I didn't take in the plot. No doubt you'd have been the same. To tell you the truth I'm not too keen on thrillers but it must have been good because at the end the whole audience rose to its feet and clapped. As I was saying, I'm not terribly sure what the story was about, but you really must go to see it when it's on general release.

All in all, though, it was an amazing evening and to top it off we went to Quaglino's for supper afterwards and guess what? Sarah Jane Fox and Brad Brat were at the next table. How cool is that? By the way, Sarah Jane Fox has awful skin problems. Still, who cares about that when you've got that much money!

**T 4.4**  A = Anna, B = Ben

A  Have you heard that Jan is thinking of marrying Paul?
B  Really? I don't know what she sees in him.
A  I know what you mean. Mind you, he is a millionaire.
B  Yes, I suppose having all that money does help.
A  Where did he get his money from?
B  Apparently, he made a fortune in I.T.
A  He's been married three times before. Did you know that?
B  Actually, it's just the once, I think.
A  I suppose they'll have a big wedding.
B  Of course they will. It'll be massive.
A  Oh, well. Good luck to them.
B  Absolutely. By the way, did you hear that Sara and Jeff had a car accident?
A  Oh no! What happened?
B  It wasn't serious. They skidded into a tree, but fortunately they weren't going fast. The car's a write-off, but at least no one was injured.
A  Thank goodness for that. I should get in touch with them, but I don't have their address.
B  As a matter of fact, it's in my diary. I'll give it to you.
A  Great. Thanks a lot. Anyway, I must be going. I'm meeting Jan for lunch.
B  Right. Nice to talk to you. Bye.

**T 4.5**  I = Interviewer, LM = Liza Minnelli

**Part one**

I  Now you know they wanted to keep it personal. It was the fourth marriage, after all. Just a few close friends. Elizabeth Taylor, Michael Jackson, Joan Collins, Martine McCutcheon. Coverage of the wedding of Liza Minnelli to David Gest has certainly been mesmerizing reading. While she honeymoons in London, Liza's returning to the London stage next Tuesday. After years of fighting alcohol and drug addiction, the problems which plagued her mother, Judy Garland, the appearance at the Royal Albert Hall marks something of a new chapter in her life. When I spoke to Liza as she was preparing for her concerts, she told me how much she was looking forward to performing for a British audience.

[Song extract from Cabaret]

LM  Oh, darling, this is truly my second home, and I'm crazy about so many people here. And the audiences in London are the very best in the world. You know, it's like a great tennis match to sing to people in London. They … they know how to react.
I  Why do you think of London as your second home?
LM  Because I lived here so long when I was a kid, and er … with my Mom, and my sister. And I went to school here. And my best friend was Katie Manning. I went to Miss Dixon and Miss Wolves' School for Young Ladies.
I  Did you learn how to be a young lady?
LM  Well, sort of. I mea… I did my best.

I  Now, you're on your honeymoon at the moment. How are you finding married life?
LM  Oh, I'm loving it. I just … I'm so happy. The world looks so beautiful to me right now. I've always found it beautiful, but it just … now it's like the inside of a diamond. You know it, it sparkles and glitters, and I notice everything. It's just miraculous.

[Song extracts]

**T 4.6**  **Part two**

I  We've certainly seen an awful lot of coverage about your wedding, all the people that were invited.
LM  I'll say.
I  Absolutely. Did it manage to still feel like a personal affair to you?
LM  Yes, it did, because … it's so funny but … the people that were invited are the people that are our friends. And the fact that they just happen to be famous … it's like if … if somebody in shipping, you know, got married, they'd have a lot of people who had to do with boats, there. Right?
I  Yeah, I think yours was a bit more glamorous, though, wasn't it? Than a shipping wedding?
LM  Well, I don't know. We had a good time.
I  There was also a bit of negative publicity around, that you had to deal with. Speculation about David's sexuality because of some reported remarks by … by Elton John. How did you cope with all of that?
LM  Well, you know Elton. I mean, you know, he was just kidding around. And Elton always talks on stage about the most newsworthy thing to say. And I guess we were the news that day, and er … He did an Elton, that's all. It didn't bother us. I mean, he's hilarious.
I  It was just an Elton. So you haven't fallen out with him over it?
LM  Oh, no! I … no! For goodness' sake! I know his sense of humour. He says that about everybody.

**T 4.7**  **Part three**

I  Was it always expected, growing up in the way that you did, that you would follow in your mother's footsteps?
LM  No. She was in the movies. I went directly to Broadway and made my mark. So while I … you know, I went off to New York on my own at sixteen. Never took another cent from my family.
I  Did your mother recognize your talent?
LM  Oh, she was hilarious about it. She said 'Oh, for God's sake, just go and do what you want to do. I know there's no way I can stop you, so just be good at what you do.'
I  And she must have been proud of you.
LM  She was very proud of me. And so was my father. And they were so supportive, and funny, and, and loving. You know I … sometimes I read this stuff that people write, and it's like … they want it to have been hard. Sure it was hard, but I don't think it was any harder probably than yours.
I  You clearly relish the performance in front of a live audience, but I have to say to you what I will always feel a sort of special recognition of is your film Cabaret, which … er … came out when I was a teenager. And you got us into a lot of trouble at school, because we went round saying 'Divinely decadent, darling!', and wearing green nail varnish. You got me expelled from gym class for wearing green nail varnish!
LM  Oh, I'm sorry! But I hope you enjoyed it!
I  Do you still look back at that film with fond memories?
LM  Oh, my God yes, because … you know … Marisa Berenson is my dear, dear friend. She was one of my maids of honour with Elizabeth Taylor, who's … I've also known since I was born, you know … and erm … There's so many people in that film that when … we still stay in

touch. We were banished to, to …er … Berlin, and kind of left on our own. They didn't know what we were doing. I don't think anybody was ever so surprised as the studio when this came out and was a big hit.
I  Can you still remember the songs? You couldn't give us a burst now!
LM  Oh, darling! Which ones do you like?
I  I like Cabaret.
LM  Oh, you do, do you?

[Song extracts]

I  The divinely decadent Liza Minnelli.

**T 4.8**

A  Liza Minnelli is just fantastic! Her concert was amazing!
B  It was, wasn't it? And she puts so much energy into her songs, doesn't she?
A  Yes, she does. Who wrote that song about marriage, and the way it changes the world?
B  She did. It's one of the few songs she ever wrote, actually.
A  So she can write as well as sing, can she? What a talent! Did you like her costumes?
B  Yes, I did. I thought they were fantastic. I've seen most of them before.
A  Have you? I haven't. She's playing again tomorrow, isn't she?
B  Yes, I think so. Let's go again, shall we?
A  All right. She's one of the all time greats, Liza Minnelli is.

**T 4.9**

1  A  You haven't seen my car keys, have you?
   B  No, I haven't. You had them this morning, didn't you?
   A  Yes, I did. If I can't find them, I'll be late for work, won't I?
   B  Panic over. Here they are!
   A  Well done. You're a star, you are!
2  A  You didn't like that meal, did you? You were pushing it around the plate.
   B  No, I didn't. Well, it hadn't been cooked properly, had it? Your steak was all right, was it?
   A  Yes. It was fine. Let's get the bill and go home, shall we?
   B  OK. We won't be coming back here in a hurry, will we?
3  A  You've forgotten the map, haven't you?
   B  Oh, dear. Yes, I have.
   A  But I put it next to the car keys.
   B  Well, I didn't see it, did I?
   A  You're blind, you are.
   B  Oh and you're perfect, are you?

**T 4.10**

1  Jeremy earns an absolute fortune!
   He does, doesn't he?
   Does he? I had no idea. How much?
   So he's rich, is he? Well, well, well.
   He's a rich man, Jeremy is.
2  Peter's new German girlfriend, Anna, is very beautiful.
   Yes, she is.
   Is she? She's not my type, actually.
   So she's German, is she?
   He's a lucky man, Peter is.
3  Jane and John are going to Florida on holiday.
   They're so lucky.
   They are, aren't they?
   Are they? I wish I was going.
   So they're going to Florida, are they?
   They're lucky, Jane and John are.
4  Zidane played really well in the match on Sunday, didn't he?
   He did, didn't he?
   Did he? I didn't think so.
   He's a great player, Zidane is.
5  Harrods is a great shop. You can buy everything there.
   You can, can't you?

Can you? I bet you can't buy a camel.
It's a wonderful shop, Harrods is.

6 I think our teacher is the best.
She is, isn't she?
Is she? I don't think she's as good as the one we had last year.
So you like her, do you?
She's a great teacher, Sylvia is.

7 Simon's a very experienced traveller. He's been everywhere.
He has, hasn't he?
Has he? I didn't realize.
He has, has he? I must ask him about it some time.
He's certainly been around, Simon has.

# Unit 5

**T 5.1** J = Jaap, M = Martine

J Well, it was nearly twenty-five years ago now …
M No, it was twenty-two.
J Oh, yes, twenty-two. And I was on holiday in Provence. A walking holiday. I'm from Holland – it's so flat – so the mountains here, here in Provence were irresistible, especially Mont Ventoux just here. It has wonderful walking trails.
M Yes, you see, I've lived in this village all my life. I was born here. Every day I've woken to the sight of the mountain rising up in front of the village. Every day it's the same, but a little bit different. It's so beautiful. The way the snowline ebbs and flows in the winter, or how the flowers cover the mountainside in spring. It's, it's entrancing.
J So, I was on holiday with a friend of mine, Rémi, and we'd walked to the summit of Mont Ventoux. It's a long climb, nearly five hours. We could see a village below us, a beautiful medieval perched village cascading down the hillside. It took us hours to reach it . . . and by the time we did we were exhausted and very thirsty. So, the first house we came to I knocked on the door to ask for a glass of water, and. . .
M Oh, I remember!
J … and the most beautiful girl opened the door!
M Oh, Jaap!
J And I fell in love. On the spot. That was it! My friend returned to Holland on his own.
M It's true! Poor Rémi.
J But lucky me.
M It was so unexpected. See, I am an artist, a potter, so my friends always believed I would marry a creative man, another artist or a poet. And in a way I have. You see Jaap was a physics teacher when I met him. But I have taught him how to work with the potter's wheel, to throw the clay, work with the kiln. He learned so quickly and became an expert – perhaps his science background helped. Friends say my pottery improved the very day I met Jaap, and now we've worked together for over twenty years. He throws the pieces, and I hand paint them.
J The studio where we work is attached to the house, and we have a small shop next to that. Whether we're working or not, we always have the view of Mont Ventoux to inspire us. We never grow bored of that, or each other.

**T 5.2**

1 I *do* do my homework immediately after class.
2 What it was, was love at first sight.
3 The thing most couples don't realize is how difficult married life can be.
4 It's the parents I blame for badly-behaved kids.
5 Not only are the values of society at risk but also the very survival of our nation is threatened.
6 Only then did I understand what she meant.
7 It was Sam that broke the blue vase!
8 I won't marry *any*body.

**T 5.3**

A What's your favourite holiday?
B We like walking in Scotland.
1 A We like going skiing in Austria.
 B What *we* like is walking in Scotland.
2 A What do you like doing on holiday?
 B *One* thing we *like* is *walking in Scotland*.
3 A You like walking in Wales, don't you?
 B *Scotland* is where we like walking.
4 A You like driving in Scotland, don't you?
 B It's *walking* in Scotland we like.
5 A Don't you just hate walking in Scotland?
 B Walking in Scotland is something *we like*.
6 A What do you like more than walking in Scotland?
 B There's *nothing* we like more than walking in Scotland.

**T 5.4**

1 What I can't *stand* about the Royal Family is that they're like a soap opera.
2 What surprises me *every* time the Queen speaks is the way she pronounces her vowels.
3 The thing that annoys me *most* about politicians is that they don't keep their promises.
4 What we did after class yesterday was race home to watch the football match on TV.
5 It's our *teacher* who knows all the answers.
6 Something I've *never* told you is that I've been married before.
7 What the *government* should do is come up with a better transport policy.
8 *Never* in my *life* have I heard such a ridiculous story!

**T 5.5**

1 A D'you know, when he left her, she threw all of his belongings out onto the street!
 B You know what they say – hell hath no fury like a woman scorned.
2 A They're back together again but their relationship's had a bumpy ride.
 B You know what they say – the course of true love never did run smooth.
3 A Go on then. I'll have one more. But that's the last one.
 B You know what they say – a little of what you fancy does you good.
4 A Good heavens! You? Going to cookery classes? You *must* be in love!
 B You know what they say – the way to a man's heart is through his stomach.
5 A But I don't want you to go off to Borneo for six months. How'll I survive?
 B You know what they say – absence makes the heart grow fonder.
6 A Ooh! Take your hands off my back! They're freezing!
 B You know what they say – cold hands, warm heart.

**T 5.6**

Shall I compare thee to a summer's day?
Thou art more lovely and more temperate:
Rough winds do shake the darling buds of May,
And summer's lease hath all too short a date:
Sometime too hot the eye of heaven shines,
And often is his gold complexion dimmed,
And every fair from fair sometime declines,
By chance, or nature's changing course untrimmed;
But thy eternal summer shall not fade,
Nor lose possession of that fair thou ow'st,
Nor shall death brag thou wander'st in his shade,
When in eternal lines to time thou grow'st;
So long as men can breathe, or eyes can see,
So long lives this, and this gives life to thee.

**T 5.7** P1 = Presenter 1, P2 = Presenter 2, O = Olive, B = Bob

P1 But as a matter of fact it'll be a rather sad St Valentine's Day for Olive Hodges. She's reached the remarkable age of 102 and she had been looking forward to her 77th wedding anniversary this year. Sadly her husband Fred died at the weekend but she told our reporter Bob Walker about their long relationship. Their first meeting was a brief one during the First World War. Their courtship began later after a chance meeting in a park.
O He was seventeen and a half at that time and six months later he was called up into the army. Er … There were many people who died, were killed by his side, he came through without a scratch. It was a miracle really.
Then just after the armistice when we were in the park and there was a band on a, on Sunday afternoon. This young man walked by and raised his hat then he went back and raised his hat, and he did this about six times. And I was very amused but I said to my friend, well, if he goes by again, I'll put him out of his misery. So the next time he went by I made some small remark to him and he came along and talked to us.
He used to come round and call for me to go for a walk so we were going for a walk one evening and he said 'I should like to marry you but I don't have any money.' And I said, 'Well we can wait.' I didn't see any need for a hurry and that was it.
B What was the secret of such a long and happy marriage?
O Well, we loved one another so intently and our, our attitude was that we wanted to make the other one happy.
B Now you were married almost 77 years. That's right? Was your love for each other as strong right up to the end?
O I think it was stronger. He didn't want to leave me and I didn't want to leave him. He wanted me with him all the time. I was pleased to be with him for that matter and he was always asking me if I still loved him as much as I used to and I had a job to reassure him that I *did* love him, but [*laughs*] he really loved me so much.
P2 Oh – what can you say? That was Olive Hodges.

**T 5.8** See p54

**T 5.9** See p54

# Unit 6

**T 6.1**

1 I must confess I don't buy a newspaper every day. When I do buy one, it tends to be *The Guardian*. It's well written, and it doesn't have a predictable political bias. It also has a crossword that is exactly the right level of difficulty for me.
2 I get *The Independent* every day, and *The Observer* on Sundays. They're the only newspapers I trust. They don't have the obvious political affiliations of some of the other dailies, they seem relatively impartial. They have interesting sections. I listen to the news all day long, so I tend to like the feature sections of newspapers rather than the news reporting. *The Independent* has good coverage of the arts – exhibitions, shows, concerts, reviews.
3 I get *The Mail*. It's pretty light-weight and readable. I find the broadsheets a bit too wordy for me. *The Mail* has articles on health, fashion, film stars, diets. I don't like its politics, however. It's a real right-wing rag. Anti-Europe, xenophobic, homophobic. I sometimes wonder why I buy it.

4   I'm a bit of a newspaper junkie. I read *The Sun*, *The Mirror*, *The Times*, and *The Financial Times*. I like to get a broad spectrum. *The Sun* tells me what's happening to celebs. *The Mirror* presents the left-wing conscience. *The Times* has some good features. And *The Financial Times* helps me with my investment portfolio.

5   I get *The International Herald Tribune*. It provides a good viewpoint of foreign affairs around the world. And it keeps me in touch with the States. I also get to find out what's happening in Major League Baseball, and see how my team the Yankees are faring.

**T 6.2**

Here is the news at eight o'clock.

News is coming in of an earthquake in southern China. Five hundred people are believed to have died, with over two thousand injured. International rescue teams have arrived in the area, and a huge humanitarian operation is underway. The earthquake is reported to have been 6.4 on the Richter scale.

A Monet painting has been stolen from the Louvre museum in Paris. Thieves are thought to have hidden themselves while the museum was closing, then escaped through a skylight. The painting is said to be worth $50 million.

The crisis over rising house prices seems to be settling down. Interest rates fell a further half a per cent last month. Government sources said that it is hoped that prices will level out to an overall rise of five per cent over the last twelve months.

**T 6.3**   I = Interviewer, SW = Simon Winchester

**Part one**

I   You've been described as a foreign correspondent of the more adventurous sort. Do you think that does you justice?

SW  I … it's a very flattering thing to say. I think what probably was meant by that is that I really don't like pack journalism. I'm … I'm not in the slightest bit interested in television, or waving a microphone in somebody's face. I … very much, you know, the man standing under the shadows of the bridge with the notebook in his hand and trying to be inconspicuous, and listening and observing. But going alone to unusual places. I think I find the off-beat more interesting. And although I was a White House correspondent for quite a long time, and so very much was in the thick of things during for instance the Watergate affair, with Nixon's resignation, generally speaking I have a happier time, I think, a more fulfilling time personally when I was based in India, with a patch to cover from Tehran to Bangkok, so wandering really in some of the most exotic countries in the world.

I   Is that something that you relish, that kind of exotic, slightly unknown, almost dangerous side to it?

SW  I've never made a particular virtue out of danger. I mean, I've covered a reasonable number of wars and skirmishes and things. But remote interests me. Remote islands and islands' people are fascinating. So I do … I tend to have been to nearly all the really strange, off-beat places.

**Part two**

I   Could you talk to me a little bit about how you think the foreign correspondent's role has changed during your career erm … whether they operate differently now to perhaps how they did when you began?

SW  Well, a lot of things have changed … the most notable is the general public's lack of interest in things foreign. It used to be, I think, as a … because of the residual, the sort of echoes of Empire … Britain particularly … in British newspapers, always had a very keen interest in the far away. That's not true any more, I think. And you look at foreign pages in newspapers

and they've shrunk savagely. *The New York Times* is more or less alone in maintaining a really strong collection of foreign correspondents. But even their editors acknowledge that foreign is an expensive luxury. Most readers aren't particularly interested. So it's changed in that degree in that the budgets are smaller, and foreign correspondents are much more constrained by not being able to spend the way they could. Secondly I think television has taken over to my way of thinking in far too … far too obvious a way, and that er … the man or woman looking for the … exotic, the faraway, the small story, the little essay which actually does illuminate brilliantly the inner workings of some distant place. There's no time for that because television leads the charge, television makes the story … We've lost the ability, the willingness, the interest to paint the subtleties of foreign … We go in … the blazing TV lights … for a short time, and then we go on to the next story. So the subtlety of abroad has disappeared, in terms of newspapers.

I   How did you use to approach that sort of situation?

SW  Well, I worked for *The Guardian* … in those days the foreign editor was keen to … it almost encouraged you to … to look behind the story, to leave the main story to the agencies. So I used to like doing that sort of thing. Nowadays you can't.

I   So is it the journalists' fault, or is it some sort of editorial control? Is it editors trying to satisfy budgets and political erm … ?

SW  Yes, I mean it's not the journalists' fault, I don't think. I mean, newspapers have become much more market-driven, and less of a public service. Erm … *The Guardian* seeks to make money, to increase its circulation, to outdo *The Independent*. And to do that it's got to spend its money, such as it has, in a more focused way. And that might mean more fashion coverage, or more social issues in England. And my friends who remain foreign correspondents now are not the sort of happy bunch that we were then.

I   Do they feel their hands are tied?

SW  Well, yes I think so. Newspapers particularly in their coverage of foreign have changed mightily, and in my view not for the better.

I   Do you think tabloid journalism has had anything to do with that? That sort of seeking out of sensationalism, and the ephemeral nature of the stories? Has that tarred all journalists with the same brush?

SW  No, I don't think that tabloid journalism has got much to do with it. I think the dominant reason for the change is television and budgets.

I   What have you personally got out of your career as a journalist?

SW  Enormous excitement, thousands of experiences, the years rushing past. It all does add up to a fascinating life.

**T 6.4**

1   A  Guess what! I won £5 million on the lottery!
    B  You're kidding! Really? That's amazing!
2   A  My grandfather died last week.
    B  Oh, no! I'm so sorry to hear that. You were very close, weren't you?
3   A  One of my students told me I was a lousy teacher.
    B  What a cheek! I hope you told him where to get off.
4   A  Here we are! Home at last.
    B  Thank goodness for that. I thought we'd never make it.
5   A  I'm broke since I bought all those designer clothes.
    B  Tough. It's your own fault. Serves you right.
6   A  Have you heard that Jim's leaving to go to another job?
    B  Good riddance. He was always useless.

7   A  I missed the last bus and had to walk home. I didn't get home till midnight.
    B  What a drag! You must have been really fed up.
8   A  When I get a job, I'm going to be a millionaire. I'll have three houses and ten cars.
    B  In your dreams. Fat chance you have of being able to afford a caravan and a bike.
9   A  I'm going on holiday to Barbados for two weeks with my girlfriend.
    B  Nice one! Can I come too?
10  A  My six-year-old daughter painted me a picture for Father's Day.
    B  Bless her! Isn't that sweet?
11  A  I'm fed up with revising. Let's go out for a beer.
    B  Now you're talking! A cold beer'd go down a treat.
12  A  Susan says she never wants to see you again.
    B  So what? I don't care. I wouldn't go out with her if she were the last person on earth.
13  A  My team lost again last weekend.
    B  Where's the surprise? They lose every weekend. They're rubbish.
14  A  Dad, I'm going to an all-night party. Is that OK?
    B  Over my dead body. You've only just turned twelve. No way!

**T 6.5**

1   My sister's been married seven times.
2   My dog died last night.
3   My teenage daughter told me she thought I was boring, stupid, and old-fashioned.
4   When I told little Katie that her grandma had gone to heaven, she asked when we could visit!
5   One day I'm going to be a famous film star, just you watch.
6   I can't come out tonight. My dad says I have to do my homework and tidy my room.
7   My girlfriend has dumped me! All because I said girls were stupid.
8   Dad. I know you don't like Malcolm, but I love him and I'm going to marry him.
9   I failed the exam because I overslept and missed half of it.
10  After last week's argument, my flatmate's decided to leave.
11  We've been given an extra week to hand in our essays.
12  My parents bought me a new car for my birthday.
13  How would you feel about going to the cinema this evening, then out for a pizza?
14  I'm going to tell the teacher what you said.

**T 6.6**

1   A  Pete. I crashed your car. Sorry.
    B  Great. That's all I needed. Thank you very much.
2   A  When you come on Saturday, we're going to have an ice-cream.
    B  Ooh! How exciting. I can't wait.
3   A  You know that guy Parkinson, the millionaire? Apparently he's been sent to prison for tax evasion.
    B  Well, ain't that a shame! My heart bleeds for him.
4   A  I have finally understood how this machine works.
    B  You're so clever, you are. I don't know how you kept it secret for so long.

# Unit 7

**T 7.1**  See p64

**T 7.2**

We have called you Daniel Patrick, but I've been told by my Chinese friends that you should have a Chinese name as well and this glorious dawn sky makes me think we'll call you Son of the Eastern Star. Your coming has turned me upside down and inside out. So much that seemed essential to me has, in the past few days, taken on a different colour. Like many foreign correspondents I know, I have lived a life that, on occasion, has veered close to the edge: war zones, natural disasters, darkness in all its shapes and forms. In a world of insecurity and ambition and ego, it's easy to be drawn in, to take chances with our lives, to gamble with death. Now, looking at your sleeping face, listening to your occasional sigh, I wonder how I could have ever thought glory and prizes were sweeter than life.

And it's also true that I am pained, perhaps haunted is a better word, by the memory, suddenly so vivid now, of each suffering child I have come across on my journeys. To tell you the truth, it's nearly too much to bear at this moment to even think of children being hurt and abused. And yet, looking at you, the images come flooding back. Ten-year-old Andi Mikail on a hillside in Eritrea, how his voice cried out, when the wind blew dust on to his wounds. The two brothers, Domingo and Juste, in Menongue, southern Angola. Juste, two years old and dying from malnutrition, being carried on seven-year-old Domingo's back. And Domingo's words to me, 'He was nice before, but now he has the hunger.'

Last October, in Afghanistan, when you were growing inside your mother, I met Sharja, aged twelve. Motherless, fatherless, guiding me through the grey ruins of her home, everything was gone, she told me. And I knew that, for all her tender years, she had learned more about loss than I would understand in a lifetime. There is one last memory, of Rwanda, where, in a ransacked classroom, I found a mother and her three young children huddled together. The children had died holding on to their mother, that instinct we all learn from birth and in one way or another cling to on until we die.

**T 7.3**  See p65

**T 7.4**

**1 Elaine**
This is something my father said to me the night before I got married and I always keep coming back to it. Dad said 'You know there are only three things in life of real importance – there's love, there's home, and there's work … and as long as two out of the three are OK you can deal with the third one. But lately I've been thinking that love and home are so intertwined it's a bit tricky, isn't it?

**2 Lizzie**
Actually this is something my ex-husband always said – he was quite a nice guy really … er … whenever we had a friend who irritated or annoyed us in some way, … er … someone who maybe was mean or who never listened and was always full of themselves and their own goings-on etcetera he, my ex, always said that before you cast people off and out of your lives you should allow them three faults. That way you get to keep most of your friends. Erm – I don't know what that says about our relationship – obviously there were a lot more than three faults on both sides!

**3 Justin**
This is an everyday piece of advice from me to me – something I've learnt from bitter experience – never go shopping in the supermarket when you're hungry! Always go shopping on a full stomach. It's absolutely fatal if you don't – you spend a fortune, get fat, and end up with loads of stuff in your fridge and cupboards that goes past its sell-by date!

**4 Claire**
Before I left Canada to work and travel in Europe, my grandmother told me that travel is the best education next to books and, well, that was something her mother told her when she was young. She also loved to travel and, you know, she was actually in England during the Second World War.

**5 Henry**
Oh my gran'pa is a real misery guts. And if … er … if me and my brothers ever get excited or happy about anything, like we're really looking forward to going on holiday or watching a football match, every time he says the same thing: 'Watch it boys – just remember it's better to travel hopefully than arrive.' Just how miserable is that? And we say 'Well, actually gran'pa when our team wins, it's better to have arrived!' D'you know I think the only thing that makes him happy is being miserable. How sad is that? I'm not going to be like that when I'm old.

**6 Simon**
Well, I think the words of wisdom I remember most are from my mother who was a hippy in the 1960s and she said 'always follow your heart especially with freedom and love.' And there we are.

**7 Fiona**
I remember my grandmother saying to me – I can't remember what exactly it was about, I was depressed about something, I was just a kid, and she said to me 'This too will pass'. I dunno something had happened at school, whatever, and she was just saying 'don't worry too much about it, it'll be over soon, it'll be a memory and this too will pass.' And I thought that was a really good way of looking at things – you know bad things – they do pass, but I think it's also true of good things. It's important to make the most of good things 'cos they too will pass. It's a good piece of wisdom, don't you think?

**8 Chris**
Well, these are not really *words* of wisdom, these are *letters* of wisdom, I suppose. The letters are WP, which stand for … er … willpower, which is something my grandmother repeats at regular intervals, mainly, it has to be said, to my grandfather. Basically she means that with willpower you can pretty much achieve anything, so if at first you don't succeed, keep persisting and eventually you'll get there. WP, WP!

**9 Sue**
Well something my mum used to say a lot is when I was younger – it's a little proverb I think and it's … er … 'Love many, trust a few, always paddle your own canoe.' And that's something I've remembered all my life and I suppose in a way I stick to it without really realizing that I am.

**10 Martyn**
It comes from an American actor friend of mine. He said this to me, I guess about 15 years ago, he just said 'Marty, dust it off!' And 'dust it off' essentially just means 'don't dilly-dally, just DO it.'

**T 7.5**

'You are old, Father William,' the young man said,
'And your hair has become very white;
And yet you incessantly stand on your head.
Do you think, at your age, it is right?'

'In my youth,' Father William replied to his son,
'I feared it might injure the brain;
But, now that I'm perfectly sure I have none,
Why, I do it again and again.'

'You are old,' said the youth, 'as I mentioned before,
And have grown most uncommonly fat,
Yet you turned a back somersault in at the door –
Pray what is the reason of that?'

'In my youth,' said the sage, as he shook his grey locks,
'I kept all my limbs very supple
By the use of this ointment – one shilling the box –
Allow me to sell you a couple?'

'You are old,' said the youth, 'and your jaws are too weak
For anything tougher than suet;
Yet you finished the goose, with the bones and the beak
Pray, how did you manage to do it?'

'In my youth,' said his father, 'I took to the law,
And argued each case with my wife;
And the muscular strength which it gave to my jaw,
Has lasted the rest of my life.'

'You are old,' said the youth, 'one would hardly suppose
That your eye was as steady as ever;
Yet you balanced an eel on the end of your nose –
What made you so awfully clever?'

'I have answered three questions, and that is enough,'
Said his father. 'Don't give yourself airs!
Do you think I can listen all day to such stuff?
Be off, or I'll kick you downstairs!'

**T 7.6**  See p68

# Unit 8

**T 8.1**

1  I suppose it's the eyes, really that first drew my attention. Not only are they the most extraordinary shade of deep, dark green, they also show how frightened she is. The photo was taken in 1985 by a guy called Steve McCurry, and it was the beginning of yet another war in Afghanistan. This girl had lost her parents and grandparents, she was living in a refugee camp, and the photographer just caught her as she was coming out of her tent. You can see the dust on her face and the torn clothes, and her face is slightly at an angle. It made a real impact on me, that photograph.

2  It was one of the first examples I came across of modern sculpture and I didn't really expect to like it. I think it's the combination of strength and gentleness which struck me most. All the lines of the mother's body are flowing, curved and soft. Yet the shoulders and arms surrounding the baby look big and strong, like a protective shield. I think it is a very accurate portrayal of motherhood, especially now that I have children of my own. I know what that fierce protectiveness towards your baby feels like.

3  From a distance it looks like a huge, white upturned fishing boat and when you get closer that's exactly what it is like – the sides curve upwards and seem to be made of white wooden slats. And, at regular intervals, along the sides, are long rectangular portholes, the windows, like long curved, glassed-in ladders. Inside, despite all the usual departure boards, shops, restaurants and the like, it still feels like a boat – long escalators transport you up to the ridge at the top and you walk out onto the platforms. It's visually stunning, and it all seems brilliantly suited to high-speed travel.

4  When I heard about all the fuss surrounding this art work I was curious to see it and when I did, my first thought was, 'God, she's messy!' The bed was unmade, the sheets dirty, there was all sorts of rubbish – cups, plates, magazines strewn everywhere. It was pretty revolting, really – particularly in a nice, clean, white gallery. Then my second thought was, 'Well, it's interesting, but I mean, what if someone sneaked in and made the bed while nobody was looking?! Would it still be art?'

5  The first thing that strikes is the serenity. There is a feeling that this scene has lasted forever and will continue to last forever. It's very peaceful – Parisians out enjoying themselves on a Sunday afternoon. The people appear to be frozen in

time. There is very little movement in the picture. The other thing that greatly interests me is the dappling of light through the leaves. When I first saw this picture, it was a moment of profound delight.

**T 8.2**  I = Interviewer,
JD = Joe Dudley Downing

**Part one    The early years**

I  Joe, have you always known that you wanted to paint?

JD  No, no not by any means. I had no knowledge of art until I was twenty-two … er … twenty-three years old. I grew up in … er … very rural area, in Kentucky, a village of only a thousand people. The village of Horse Cave … er …

I  Sorry?

JD  Yeah, Horse Cave, Kentucky … and there were no paintings of any kind in Horse Cave. No good paintings, no bad paintings … er … just no paintings, but what there was, was an immense amount of beauty. We had a farm and there were seven children but it was beautiful, there was nothing ugly in the house. We slept under the most beautiful patterned quilts, made by my mother and aunts and … er … cousins … er …

I  So … so, was your family quite artistic then?

JD  No, no that word couldn't apply to them – but they knew beautiful things, not just the quilts. I remember my mother calling me when she was shelling the beans that come in the fall, they were veined like marble, … er … blue, pale purple, you know, very, very beautiful and I remember her calling me and turning the beans in her hands in the sunlight and saying: 'Look, look at the colours!'

I  So, is it … erm … an idyllic childhood then?

JD  Well, except that at eighteen years old I was yanked out of my lovely country bumpkin life and thrown into the war – the Second World War and … er … I landed in France … er … had my nineteenth birthday in France, in Normandy, then we were sent to the front and I was engaged in the last year of the war in Germany and of course war … er … that really changes you.

I  Yes, yes, I can imagine, and did you stay in France after the war?

JD  … er … no, no I went back to America, to Chicago to study to be an optometrist.

I  An optometrist? How … er … ?

JD  Well, I had no real desire to be anything and I had to study something, and I loved Chicago. It's an enormously vital city. It was like a second birth for me to be plunged into city life – *big* city life and I met people, – writers, painters, interesting people, and early on, one of them took me to the museum in Chicago, which is just extraordinarily rich and beautiful and there … er … I was twenty-three – and having never seen a painting in my life, I stood in front of *La Grande Jatte*, by Georges Seurat and … er …

I  Oh, yes, isn't that Sunday afternoon on the banks of the Seine in Paris?

JD  Yeah, yeah – and to stand in front of *La Grande Jatte*, one of the most extraordinary paintings that ever existed, having never seen a painting before, was for me a remarkable experience. It reshaped my whole life.

I  So without that … er … you might never have become an artist?

JD  No – I don't think so really because I would eventually have gone to some museum and seen some painting, … I think.

**T 8.3**  **Part two    On being a painter**

I  But *your* painting is in an abstract style – *not* like Seurat – have you always painted like that?

JD  Oh, no, no in the beginning I didn't … er … er

… I didn't want to be an abstract painter but you must follow your bent or you're in trouble. You must forever follow where the painting leads you … er … more than *you* lead the painting. But … erm … in the beginning I did … erm … landscapes and still life, I love still life, I still love still life – and I did some portraits, perhaps two or three were worth saving! And then it started to become abstract.

I  And your studies? The, erm, optometry?

JD  No, no … er … oh no … I went back to France, to Paris and for seven years, in order to keep the pot boiling, I worked as a secretary for an American law firm and I was careful to be a good secretary so that they gave me some free time and I started doing collages and these were abstract. I did collages obsessively for four or five years and I think they became the foundation … er … for my whole painter's life.

I  So when you look back you can identify different stages in your painting?

JD  I've had, I guess, three, in retrospect. I've had three major exhibitions at different stages, the first in 1968 – and when you look back you can see a very strong thread, what the French call a *fil conducteur*, and that remains the same, but the style changes slowly and constantly and if it doesn't, a painter should be worried, because if it doesn't change, you'll wither.

I  And when you look back have you any regrets about the way your work has evolved?

JD  Oh no, no – you must do what your nature tells you to otherwise and … er … I've been enormously fortunate. Anyone who writes, who paints, who composes, any kind of artist knows how fragile it is – at any moment desire, the desire to do it can go.

I  I've noticed that one of the materials you work with, paint on, is leather, erm, small, small strips of leather. How did this come about?

JD  It's almost too ridiculous to tell. Erm … I was having dinner with friends and … er … an Italian friend from Milan had brought as a gift, a pasta-making machine and in order to show how the machine worked, she made green lasagne for dinner. And … it was so beautiful coming out of the machine – it was pale green and the … the flour made little valleys and mountains. It was just beautiful, velvety-looking and I said 'I'm sorry it's going to look like I'm showing off, but I really must paint on this'. So I made a tiny little landscape, a little rectangular painting on the lasagne, one for everybody at the table, including me, and at the end of dinner we all carefully took them home. And … er … the next day the phone rang and it was my friend and she was crying and I said 'Why are you crying?' and she said 'Well, haven't you seen your lasagne this morning?' So I ran to the kitchen and of course it had yellowed and cracked …

I  Ugh!

JD  … it looked awful, sick. So I said to my friend 'Look, quit crying, I'll make something that looks like green lasagne and I'll make you another painting'. So I spent two years looking and finally I came across that pale green leather that they use for making gardeners' gloves and I made her a little painting. And it was just wonderful!

I  It's a wonderful tale – it's a wonderful technique.

JD  Yes, and so the leather work began another stage in my painting. A new door opened.

**T 8.4**  **Part three    On living in the South of France**

I  I know you now live most of the time here in the village of Ménerbes, way south of Paris. How long have you lived here?

JD  I've been here thirty-three years.

I  It must have changed a lot in that time.

JD  Erm … yes and for the worse unfortunately … but that's true anywhere there's sunshine and olives and Roman tiles!

JD  This was, still is really, an agricultural village – they grow extraordinary asparagus, beautiful asparagus. It starts now, in March – after that there are cherries, peaches, peppers, and melons … they're famous for the melons so they really didn't need tourism. Of course, … er … I know that's ridiculous and selfish and mean to want to enjoy the extraordinary beauty of this place and want others *not* to come … but it would be terrible to destroy the perfume of this place, a place I've loved.

I  And how did you discover it all those years ago?

JD  Well, every summer when I was living in Paris, and … er … I can't drive …

I  Really! How do you get about?

JD  Oh, I just don't go anywhere. Anyways … every year, in summer, a friend, she would drive us down south, to the sea to swim … and one time we got down not far from here and she said 'I'm tired of lugging you two around. I do all the driving. This is a beautiful little place, let's stop and spend the night'. So there was a charming little hotel, gone now unfortunately, er … very pleasant. Next morning I got up much earlier than the others and … er … went out into the village and … er … there was a little dog, a young hunting dog and he started up a hill and I followed him and he brought me by, what is now, a house, and a farmer was sitting there and he'd written in the top of a shoe box, with a piece of chalk, he'd written 'RUINS FOR SALE' and so … er … I asked him how much he was asking and it was the only thing that I'd ever come across that we could afford to buy in the sun. So, … er … on the spot, I asked to buy it and it was very inexpensive 'cos it was total ruins, open to the sky, it'd been empty for thirty years. It took us four years before we could sleep here. So, anyway I went back to breakfast at the hotel and told them we all had a house! So that's the way it happened.

I  So you're back in a rural setting again?

JD  Yes, in a way it's odd that I should end up in a place that resembles so much where I grew up. Another farming community. Ménerbes has the same number of people as Horse Cave and the people even look the same.

I  A home from home then. And just finally, and this, this is a big question. If you could live your life again would you do anything differently?

JD  No, no – oh well … I think I might skip a war … but otherwise – no.

**T 8.5**  **Conversation B**

A  Hi, Annie! I haven't seen you for ages.

B  I know. Time flies, doesn't it?

A  It's true. Work as busy as ever, is it?

B  Yes, I'm slaving away as usual, but we're a bit snowed under at the moment. We're just about keeping our heads above water, but it isn't easy. How about you?

A  OK. Business was bad this time last year, and we really had to tighten our belts, but things have picked up since then. You've moved, haven't you? Where are you living now?

B  We've bought an old house in a sleepy little village. You must come and visit us.

A  I'd love to, but we're a bit tied up at the moment. Does it need much doing to it?

B  Everything. I hope we haven't bitten off more than we can chew.

A  You'll be fine. Anyway, I must dash. Lovely to see you again.

B  And you. Bye.

**A** I hear Pete's aunt left him everything.
**B** Absolutely right, he inherited a fortune out of the blue.
**A** He knew nothing about it then? How exciting!
**B** You bet! When he heard about it, he was over the moon.
**A** So what's his problem now?
**B** Well, he's in deep water because he spent the whole lot in a month and then his girlfriend walked out on him.
**A** You're kidding. I thought he'd asked her to marry him?
**B** He was going to ask her, and then he got cold feet.
**A** So what next?
**B** Looks like he'll have to pull his socks up and get a job.
**A** And a new girlfriend. What about that girl he used to work with? Mm… Miranda, Marilyn – no, that's not it, erm, her name's on the tip of my tongue.
**B** You mean Melissa. Whatever you do, *don't* mention Melissa! She told him he was a waste of space, money or no money.
**A** Oh dear, I'm glad you told me, otherwise I might have put my foot in it.

**T 8.7**   A = Amy, S = Seth

**A** Ugh! This hotel is horrible. I wish we hadn't come here. I've never seen such a dirty hotel in my life! It wouldn't be so bad if the bathroom was clean, but it's filthy. I wouldn't even wash my socks in it.
**S** I know, but it was getting late, and we'd been driving all day, and I wanted to stop. If we hadn't, we might not have found a hotel and we'd still be driving. That would have been awful. At least this is better than nothing.
**A** Well, I wish we'd set off earlier. Then we could have arrived in London today, and we'd have had a whole day to go round the galleries and museums. As it is, we won't get there till tomorrow lunchtime, and we'll only have a few hours.
**S** I'd have liked to spend more time in London, too, but I had to go to work this morning. If I hadn't, we'd be staying in a top London hotel now instead of this dump.
**A** I'd like to have seen a show, but we can't, so that's all there is to it. Anyway, it's time we thought about getting something to eat. If it weren't so late, I'd suggest going into town, but if we did, we might not find anywhere. It's quite late already.
**S** I wish you wouldn't moan about everything. I wouldn't mind, but you're so indecisive. If it were left up to you, we'd never do anything or go anywhere.
**A** OK, OK. I'm sorry. Let's go.

**T 8.8**

a 1 Can you help me?
  2 Could you help me?
  3 I wonder if you could help me?
  4 I was wondering if you could possibly help me? I'd be very grateful.
b 1 Do you mind if I open the window?
  2 Would you mind if I opened the window? It's so stuffy in here.
c 1 I want to speak to you.
  2 I wanted to have a word with you, if that's all right.
d 1 Dye it black.
  2 You could dye it black.
  3 If I were you, I'd dye it black.
  4 I'd have thought the best idea would have been to dye it black, but it's up to you.

**T 8.9**

1 **A** I'd like to book a table, please.
  **B** Certainly. What name was it?
2 **A** How old's Peter?

**B** I would think he's about 60.
**C** I'd say he's about 65.
**D** I'd have thought he was nearer 70.
3 **A** I was wondering if you'd like to go out tonight?
  **B** Mmm! What were you thinking of?
  **A** I thought we could try that new pasta place.
4 **A** What time will we be setting off on Monday?
  **B** I was thinking of leaving about 8.30.
  **A** Don't you think we should leave a bit earlier to avoid the rush hour?
  **B** That'd be fine.

**T 8.10**

1 Would you mind if I used your phone?
2 If I were you, I wouldn't paint the wall red.
3 Wouldn't it be better if we went in my car?
4 Would it be possible for you to ring back later? Could you possibly ring back later?
5 Don't you think we should phone to say we'll be late?
6 I was hoping you might give me a lift to the station.
7 I would think she's French.
   I'd have thought she was French.
8 I was wondering if you'd like to come to the cinema with me?
9 Would you mind filling in this form?
10 I wouldn't be surprised if it rained this afternoon.
11 I was thinking of going for a walk. Anyone interested?
12 I just thought I'd pop in to see if you needed anything.
13 I'd say it's a bad idea.
    I'd have said it was a bad idea.
14 I'd have said that apologizing to her would be the best idea.
15 I gave her a present. You'd have thought she could have said thank you.

**T 8.11**

1 **A** Hi, Jenny. You all right?
  **J** Uh huh. You?
  **A** Er … yeah. OK. Listen, Jenny. Are you doing anything tonight?
  **J** Gosh! Er … I don't know. Why?
  **A** Well, I was wondering if you'd maybe … you know … if we could go out somewhere … if you … if you'd like to.
  **J** Well, er … What did you have in mind?
  **A** Oh, I don't know. We could have a bite to eat, or we could take in a film. What do you fancy?
  **J** Well, that would be really nice. We could meet at the new bar on the High Street and take it from there. What do you think?
  **A** OK. Nice idea. What time …?
2 **A** Hello. The Bedford Hotel. Karen speaking. How can I help you?
  **B** I'd like to book a room, please.
  **A** Certainly, sir. I'll just put you through to reservations. It's ringing for you.
  **B** Thank you.
  **R** Reservations. Robert speaking. I understand you'd like to book a room.
  **B** That's right. For three nights starting Wednesday the fifteenth of this month.
  **R** For how many people?
  **B** Just me. I wonder if it would be possible to have a room at the back of the hotel. I'm afraid I can never get to sleep if I hear the traffic.
  **R** I'll just see what I can do, sir. Yes … that's certainly possible. Your name was?
  **B** Brown. Jonathan.
  **R** Thank you sir. Would you mind giving me a credit card number … ?
3 **A** So what do you think of it?
  **B** It's fantastic!
  **A** It needs a lot doing to it, though. What do you think of the colour scheme?
  **B** It's too dark. Browns and blues and reds. You could do with something brighter. If I were

you, I'd go for cream or white. You can't beat cream, it goes with everything.
  **A** Mm … maybe. What about the kitchen?
  **B** Well, this is a bit of a disaster area, isn't it? I'd have thought the best idea would be to rip it all out and start again. I know it would be expensive, but at least you'd end up with a kitchen that suited you. No?
  **A** Don't you think I should wait a bit before I do that?
  **B** Well, you could, but I wouldn't. I was thinking you could go to Ikea and get a whole new kitchen.
  **A** Wow! Would you come with me?
4 **A** Hello.
  **B** Hi. Can I speak to Amanda, please?
  **A** She's out at the moment. Sorry.
  **B** Ah, OK. Would you have any idea when she might be back?
  **A** I'd have thought she'd be back by 8.00. She usually is on a Tuesday.
  **B** Would you mind giving her a message? Could you say that Andy phoned, and I'll try her again after 8.00?
  **A** Fine.
  **B** Would that be OK?
  **A** Sure.
  **B** Thanks a lot. Bye.
  **A** Bye.

# Unit 9

**T 9.1**

… The day started -erm much like any other day I got on the subway. We came across the bridge and I remember noticing what a lovely day it was -er with the bright blue sky. I remember coming out of the subway as I normally did, and I saw a -erm saw a cloud, or what looked like a small cloud, white cloud and I remember thinking 'Gosh that's unusual because this sky is so totally clear' – but I didn't think much more of it and I set off walking to my office -er I didn't get far. I got to the -er first block, and on the corner there were a couple of people -erm looking up, staring up at the tower, -erm so I looked down on what they were looking at and -erm noticed that there, what seemed to be, to me, at the time, anyway, a small hole, and you could actually see a few bits of flame round the edge and I asked these two people what happened and -er one of them said that a plane had flown into it and I remember thinking -er ah no can't be true. As I walked there were more and more smoke coming out, but I made it to my office and -erm went up to the 16th floor. So I went into the office, and there were lots of my colleagues there. Obviously there was a lot of sort of confusion, so I went to one of these offices with the clearest view and I looked out and I remember thinking 'Gosh! I don't remember that, there's a hole in the other side'. Quite a few people who'd been in the office earlier than me that morning, they'd -erm they'd seen both of them, they started telling me about this second one that went down the river some sort of exploded towards them -erm because it came from the south. Erm, soon you could start to see – they obviously started to evacuate -er and there were just thousands of people walking straight up towards us, just pouring, pouring up towards us. Erm, I tried to phone family and friends but none of the phones seemed to work -er so I sent out an email, that seemed to be the one thing that was still working. I couldn't speak to any of my family in England. I did speak to my wife once when I first got in and told her to wake up and turn on the television and see what was happening. I was unable to get through to her. After that, these -er sort of surreal goings on, sending these emails backwards and forwards about what was happening -erm outside my very window. And it was while I was writing an email I heard some screams, and I ran round -er just to see sort of this huge, huge cloud of smoke and people just shouting and screaming 'It collapsed! It collapsed!' This huge cloud of dust came, you could see it pouring up the avenues, and it sort of burst out -erm through Battery Park, right out into the Hudson River -erm because I remember seeing lots of the ferries were all doing evacuations, taking people from every point they could, and they just got enveloped in this huge cloud of dust. There was so much dust you didn't know, you know whether – how much it had fallen, whether it was just the top. I suppose we were all expecting to see something still there. We could still see the other one standing because it had the big antenna, the big aerial on top of it. So as we stood there watching it, no idea how long for, and then of course, the -er other one collapsed. You could clearly see, there's a very particular design, these long, long sort of slightly ornate metal work. I remember seeing that sort of explode out and then you just saw the great big top with this giant aerial on, just drop straight down and you'd see all this other stuff just peeling away from the sides -erm you could see just each corner of it peeling back and this giant top just smashing down through it and obviously there was all the dust and everything and -erm more screaming. We all thought 'cos we'd seen so many, so many thousands of people walking north that maybe everyone had got out -erm because there was this you know non-stop procession of people. In fact I think our brains didn't even think about the fact that there were people inside it, you just sort of looked at it as a building, and you just assumed there was no one in it, you just don't actually want to think about that. It was, you know, unlike any feeling you've ever thought, there wasn't really – there was no panic in the office, and also a very clear acknowledgement that -erm something had changed had -er something had changed in the world today and we were sitting staring at it. It was quite the most incredible thing, and from what was just a normal lovely New York autumn day, it's just incredible how much changed in that morning.

### T 9.2

1 We're sitting at the back, in row 102.
We've had another row about our finances.
2 That was never him singing live. He was miming.
'Live and let live' is my philosophy.
3 Close that window! There's one helluva draught.
You're not close to getting the answer.
4 I soon got used to working the late night shift.
I don't trust used car-dealers. I'd never buy a car from one.
5 It's impossible to tear open this packet. Give me a knife.
A single tear ran silently down her cheek as she waved goodbye.
6 He always looks so content with his lot.
The content of your essay was excellent but there were rather a lot of spelling mistakes.
7 The headteacher complained to the parents about their son's conduct in class.
General MacIntyre has been appointed to conduct the next stage of the war.
8 Could you record the next episode for me? I'm out that night.
He's broken the Olympic world record for the 100 metres.

### T 9.3  A, B, C, D, F = British soldiers, E = German soldier

A Hey, listen!
B Yeah, they're coppin' it down Railway Wood tonight.
A Nah, not that. Listen. What is it?
C Singin' innit?
B It's those Welsh bastards in the next trench.
C That's Jerry, that is.
B Yeah, it is Jerry. It's comin' from over there.

D Sing up, Jerry! Let's 'ear yer!
C Oh nice, weren't it?
E Tommy? Hello Tommy!
B Eh! 'E 'eard us!
C 'Ello?
E Fröhliche Weihnacht!
C Eh?
B What?
E Happy Christmas!
ALL Oh! 'Appy Christmas!
F Hey, yeah, it's Christmas!

### T 9.4  I = Interviewer, GW = Graham Williams, HS = Harold Startin

**Part one**

I That scene from the West End musical of the 1960s Oh What a Lovely War! is a pretty accurate illustration of the kind of thing that happened in several places on the Western Front on that Christmas Eve of 1914. Listen to the account of someone who was actually there. Graham Williams, a rifleman with the London Rifle Brigade, was on sentry duty that night.
GW On the stroke of 11 o'clock, which by German time was midnight, 'cos they were an hour ahead of us, lights began to appear all along the German trenches, and er … then people started singing. They started singing Heilige Nacht, Silent Night. So I thought, 'Well, this is extraordinary!' And I woke up all the other chaps, and all the other sentries must have done the same thing, to come and see what was going on. They sang this carol right through, and we responded with English Christmas carols, and they replied with German again, and when we came to Come All Ye Faithful, they joined in singing, with us singing it in Latin, Adeste Fideles.
I So by the time you got to that carol, both sides were singing the same carol together?
GW Both singing the same carol together. Then after that, one of the Germans called out, 'Come over and see us, Tommy. Come over and see us!' So I could speak German pretty fluently in those days, so I called back … I said, 'No, you come over and see us!', I said, 'Nein, kommen … zuerst kommen Sie hier, Fritz!' And nobody did come that time, and eventually the lights all burned out, and quietened down and went on with the usual routine for the night. Next morning I was asleep, when I woke up I found everyone was walking out into no-man's land, meeting the Germans, talking to them, and … wonderful scene … couldn't believe it!
I Further along the line in the perfect weather, Private Harold Startin of the Old Contemptibles was enjoying that morning too. He couldn't speak any German, but that didn't stop him making friends.
HS We were 'Tommy' to them, and they were all 'Fritz' to us. They couldn't have been more cordial towards you, all sharing their goodies with you. They were giving us cigars about as big as your arm, and tobacco.
I Were you frightened at first? Were you suspicious at all? Because these were people …
HS No!
I … that you'd been trained to hate, weren't they?
HS No! There was no hatred, we'd got no grudge against them, they'd got no grudge against us. We were … we were the best of pals, although we were there to kill one another, there were no two ways about that at all. They helped us bury our dead, and we buried our dead with their dead. I've seen many a cross with a German name and number on and a British name and number on. 'In death not divided.'
I Did you do other work during the truce as well? Was it just burying the dead, or were there other things …

HS Oh, there was strengthening the trenches, borrowing their tools …
I You actually borrowed German tools to strengthen your trenches?
HS We borrowed German tools. They … then … they'd come and help you strengthen your defences against them.

**Part two**

I Not only was the truce more extensive than anyone has realized before, it also lasted much longer than has been believed until now. In some areas, the war started up again on New Year's Day, but in the part of the line where Harold Startin was, the truce lasted a lot longer than that.
HS Ours went on for six weeks. You can read in the history books about Sir John French, when he heard of it, he were all against it. But our truce went on for six weeks. And the Württemberg Regiment, they got relieved before we did, and they told us they thought it were the Prussian Guards goin' to relieve them, and if it was, we should hear three rifle shots at intervals, and if we only heard three rifle shots we should know that the Prussian Guards, that were opposite us then, and we'd got to keep down.
I Because they would be fiercer than …
HS Yes!
I … than the Württembergers?
HS Yes!
I Can you remember particular Germans that you spoke to? Over six weeks you must have made friends?
HS I spoke to one, Otto, comes from Stuttgart, 'as … 'as been over to England to see me.
I So you made friends during the truce and kept in touch after the war?
HS Made friends during the truce, and friends after.

*Goodbyee!* (Soldiers' song from the 1914–1918 war.)
Goodbyee! Goodbyee!
Wipe the tear, baby dear, from your eyee!
Though it's hard to part, I know,
I'll be tickled to death to go.
Don't cryee! Don't sighee!
There's a silver lining in the skyee.
Bonsoir, old thing! Cheerio! Chin-chin!
Au revoir! Toodle-oo! Goodbyee!

### T 9.5

1 'Oh great! I got the job!'
'Well done! I knew you would.'
2 'My car's making this strange rattling sound.'
'It sounds bad. You should really get it serviced.'
3 'Oh no! I've missed the last bus!'
'Don't worry. We'll give you a lift.'
4 'Will you lot stop making so much noise!'
'We're not. We're just talking quietly.'
5 'Don't worry, dad. I'll be home by midnight.'
'You'd better be, because if you're not, you're grounded for a week!'
6 'Did you make all this mess?'
'I'm sorry, really I am.'
7 'I get so nervous when I have to speak in public.'
'Take deep breaths before you start.'
8 'We climbed right to the top in record time.'
'Where's the proof?'

### T 9.6  See p90

### T 9.7  See p90

### T 9.8  See p90

# Unit 10

**T 10.1**

1 And they're coming into the straight, Cornichon leads from Pegasus who is being closely challenged by River Island. River Island has moved into second place. Cornichon's still going well. They're approaching the winning post. It's going to be a photo finish … Cornichon has beaten River Island, with Pegasus in third place. What a thrilling finish to this race!

2 Johnson receives the ball in his own half, passes to Mimosa. Mimosa dribbles past two defenders and shoots. Oh! The goalkeeper knocks it behind for a corner kick. The ball comes into the centre. The striker, Hughes, is in position and heads the ball into the back of the net! What a goal! Ambletown are now two–nil up!

3 It's deuce. Mintoff serves, Everett returns, but Mintoff's at the net, and volleys the ball deep. Everett runs and hits the ball cross-court, but Mintoff's got it covered and punches it down the line. Advantage Mintoff, and match point. She serves to her opponent's back-hand, Everett struggles to get the ball back, but it goes into the net. Game, set, and match to Mintoff, 6–4, 6–2.

4 There's the bell for round six and Manson's straight back into the centre of the ring. Buckley moves in slowly from his corner. Manson gets in a good punch, he's caught him on the chin and the Scot crumples to the canvas. The count starts, Buckley's trying to get up, 8, 9, 10 – he's not up! It's a knockout in Round 6. Manson takes World Heavyweight title back to the States!

5 The Giants are two runs down in the ninth inning. They have men on first and second base, a home-run now would win it. Jackson swings and misses the first and second pitches. He hits the third pitch cleanly. It looks good. It flies across the field and lands in the stands. A 3-run homer to Jackson and the Giants win the game 7–6.

6 The eighteenth hole is a par-three. Mallestro's first shot put him on the green, just two yards from the hole. Spink put his first in the lake, and has taken two shots to get to the green. If Mallestro putts from here he'll win. He strikes it well, the ball trickles to the edge of the hole, and yes, it's in. Mallestro wins the match and the tournament.

**T 10.2**

1 Annabel is very clever, but Sonia is absolutely brilliant.
2 I thought the book was really stupid, but the film was quite ridiculous.
3 The meal was very pleasant, and the company absolutely delightful.
4 My mother was quite upset, but my father was really devastated.
5 Their house was really unusual, but the garden was quite extraordinary.
6 Her shoes were quite expensive, but the dress was really exorbitant.

**T 10.3**

1 The holiday was quite good, but I wouldn't go back.
2 James is quite clever. Cleverer than me, anyway.
3 The answer is quite obvious. I'm surprised you can't see it.

**T 10.4**

1 Kate thinks maths is hard, and she's absolutely right.
  Kate thinks maths is hard, and she's quite right.
2 Personally I find maths totally impossible.
  Personally I find maths quite impossible.
3 She's absolutely terrified of dogs.
  She's completely terrified of dogs.

4 I was very pleased to hear you're getting married.
  I was terribly pleased to hear you're getting married.
5 I'm sure you'll be extremely happy together.
  I'm sure you'll be really happy together.

**T 10.5**

1 This wine is rather pleasant. You must try it.
2 I'm absolutely determined to lose weight.
3 The film was quite interesting. You should see it.
4 The restaurant was quite nice, but I wouldn't recommend it.
5 If you ask her, I'm pretty sure she'll say yes.

**T 10.6**   M = Mick, J = Jes

M D'you see all those medals?! You know he's a 'Sir' now?
J Sorry, … who's a what?
M Y'know Steve Redgrave … *Sir* Steve Redgrave the Olympic rower. There's an article here on him. He's the only guy to have won five consecutive gold medals at the Olympic games.
J Yeah 'course I know him, he's one of my sporting heroes, isn't he? Ever since I tried rowing in my first term at university and …
M I didn't know that you -er … rowing I mean.
J Yeah, yeah, gave it up, totally, absolutely, completely knackering – too whacked to make it down the pub afterwards … [*laughter*]. So, how does Steve Redgrave manage it?
M He says here it's all in the training – he's been training eight hours a day, seven days a week for 25 years -er started when he was 16, he says he pushes his body to the absolute limit, beyond the pain barrier – just like he does in every race. His body goes numb and his mind goes blank – he doesn't even hear the crowds cheering him on.
J Oh, boy, do I remember the pain barrier?! – Jeez, I was stiff the next day … had joints like an old man.
M Yeah – day in, day out Steve's down at the gym working out – working on leg, arm, back, shoulder muscles. Is that man focussed!? Doesn't sound like the kind of lifestyle you'd go for! [*laughs*]
J Hey, hang on … *he* doesn't have my health problems …
M Oh yeah?! And what may those be?
J Well, there's my bad back …
M Oh yeah … only if you're asked to get off it to do something like… -er
J Like what?
M Do the washing up! Tidy the flat! [*laughter*] Well, actu… in fact Steve Redgrave *does* have health problems – real ones – not imaginary ones…
J No?
M He's diabetic … says here he was diagnosed with diabetes at 35. Has to use insulin every time he eats, -er that's six jabs a day.
J You're kidding. I had no idea.
M Yeah, he drinks gallons of blackcurrant juice to quench his thirst when he's training. Doesn't sound much like your kind of drink. Hey, take a look at Steve's diet, he's the carbohydrate kid – porridge, pasta and potatoes, loadsa red meat and eggs … oh and he loves chocolate.
J Obviously doesn't have to watch his weight then …
M No, lucky so-and-so, and he has to keep up his strength, has to consume over 6,000 calories a day, all seventeen stone of him.
J Well, he's a helluva big guy, so dedicated to his sport he has to keep eating!
M Hey … but it says here all that dedication -er nearly cost him his marriage – too much time rowing, no time for his family -er and he's got three kids. His wife'd had enough of it all – do you know, she's an osteopath! How handy is that? Anyway, she felt that he was sacrificing his family to his obsession – so that's why …
J … he's not going for a sixth … no, no … I knew he was giving it all up.

M He sounds a really decent guy, actually – modest – he says being knighted was the ultimate accolade, he never expected it – and it was his greatest moment, after winning the fifth medal of course – and now he plans to make use of his fame by raising money for children's charities. He's running the London Marathon this year, he wants to raise £5 million eventually.
J Hey, I was thinking of doing that!
M What? Raising 5 million?
J Idiot … no, I thought I might try the Marathon.
M With your bad back!
J OK maybe next year.

**T 10.7**   A = Adelhaide, K = Kate

A C'mon Kate type in 'Darcey Bussell' and see what we get.
K OK, -er she must have her own website don't you think?
A Hey, yeah, just look there's loads of stuff here, some great pics, *and* an interview …
K Oh yeah – oh, goodness, she's just stunning looking, isn't she?
A I just think she's the most fantastic dancer. You know, she only started dancing 'cos her mum wanted her to improve her posture.
K Yeah, she says that here. Addey do you remember when we started?
A Do I! – I cried all the way through the first lesson – nearly didn't go back … Hey, but we were only three.
K Darcey says she didn't start 'til she was five and she only did it at first 'cos she liked all the pretty costumes – but by the time she was 11 she was *passionate* about it.
A Well, I'm passionate about it, *you're* passionate about it, but it doesn't make us dancers like Darcey!
K Don't I know it! D'you think we're the wrong shape? I mean, look at her – she's just so slender and lithe and we're …
A Come on, scroll down some more – she's talking about her diet. Oh, it's just not fair – look at what she eats – loads of carbohydrates -er pasta, baked potatoes, cereal … If I ate all that I'd look like …
K Well, you wouldn't look like Darcey Bussell! You know it takes real guts to be a ballet dancer – I mean, you have to give over your whole life to it – there's no way it's all pretty costumes and feathers.
A Feathers?
K *Swan Lake* – you idiot – there's loadsa feathers in *Swan Lake* – look she says she loves doing the classical ballets – *Romeo and Juliet* and *Sleeping Beauty* –
A Yeah, but I bet they're hugely strenuous to do. You just think how exhausted we are after a two hour lesson …
K That's true – do you know, she rehearses nearly ten hours a day and if she's not rehearsing, she still has to exercise for hours and have loads of massage and physio just to keep her limbs supple.
A It's crazy – I suppose she'd just seize up without all that. Er – you know I don't think I could be *that* dedicated about anything. How on earth does she do it?
K I dunno, I just think dancers get used to exhaustion and pain – she says every morning she wakes up to find some part of her body in agony, could be her back, could be her calves, bottom, and she's got tendonitis in her ankles at the moment …
A Tender… what?
K Tendonitis – 'sgot something to do with tendons I reckon, *and* her feet are all bloodied 'cos she's lost all her toenails.
A Ugh! I lost a toenail once, it turned black and in the end I pulled …
K OK, OK so you're a dedicated dancer too …
A No, actually Tanya's horse stood on it …
K Ouch! Why do you think she does it?
A Who, Tanya?
K No, silly, Darcey …

**A** Oh c'mon it must be fantastic – just imagine what it's like being centre stage at the Royal Opera House.

**K** Absolutely – look what she says – 'it's worth all the pain because of the amazing adrenalin rush when you're on stage and you feel the appreciation of the audience.'

**A** Oh yeah, and did you know sometimes she has whole ballets created 'specially for her? She says that's the best of all.

**K** Oh wow … what must that be like?

**A** Wouldn't you just love it – the curtsies, the bows, the bouquets, roses thrown by adoring fans, gorgeous blokes in evening dress …

**K** In your dreams!

**A** Hey, is Darcey married?

**K** Sure is. She's married to an Ozzie banker, called Angus and they have a little daughter – Phoebe. She says here she wants more kids soon.

**A** *She* has it all!

**K** Oh I dunno – she must be totally wiped out at the end of each day.

**T 10.8** **See p98**

**T 10.9**

1 Mum! Tommy's broken the vase!
Never mind. Accidents will happen.

2 I just need to go back in the house and make sure I've turned off the iron.
Good idea. Better safe than sorry.

3 It's been raining non-stop for weeks! Do we need some sunshine!
You can say that again.

4 Work's awful at the moment, and I have to go away on business this weekend!
Oh, well. A change is as good as a rest.

5 I got a card from Jerry a week after my birthday.
Oh, well. Better late than never.

6 We're having a complete break for a fortnight.
Sounds like just what the doctor ordered.

7 Took me ten years to build up my business.
Nearly killed me.
Well, you know what they say. No pain, no gain.

8 Larry's failed his exams, Amy's got chicken pox.
Whatever next?
Oh dear! They say these things come in threes, you know.

9 They've got ten kids. Goodness knows what their house is like.
The mind boggles. It doesn't bear thinking about.

10 Bob's a weird bloke. Have you heard he's going to walk across Europe?
It takes all sorts.

**T 10.10**

1 My uncle has never married. He lives in a caravan. He eats only cheese, and he has twenty-five cats.

2 James Herriot had three jobs and wrote non-stop for five years before his book became a bestseller.

3 Isn't it lovely when the kids are in bed, the house is quiet, and we can relax!

4 I finally got a date for my knee replacement operation. I've had to wait eighteen months.

5 I really wanted to stay at home for New Year, but my in-laws are insisting that we go to stay with them.

6 When I go abroad, I make sure I have life insurance, medical insurance, and personal possessions insurance.

7 We had a fabulous holiday. Two weeks sitting round a swimming pool, reading and relaxing.

8 I've spilt red wine on your carpet. I'm really sorry.

9 I've lost the car keys, I've burnt the meal, and the washing machine has packed up. How bad is that?

10 My daughter is on a cabbage soup diet. She eats nothing else.

# Unit 11

**T 11.1**

1 How old is the earth?
The current scientific estimate for the age of the earth is 4.6 billion years. There are numerous indicators that the earth was in existence billions of years ago but it still is impossible to prove exactly how many millions.

2 The earth is considered to have a maximum of seven continents. What are they?
A continent is one of several major land masses on the earth. These are Africa, Antarctica, Asia, Australia, Europe, North America, and South America. Many geographers and scientists now refer to just six continents, where Europe and Asia are combined (since they're one solid land mass).

3 How many countries are there in the world?
There are 193 countries in the world. East Timor is the most recent country, having gained independence from Indonesia in 2002.

4 Which continent has the most countries?
Africa is home to 53 independent countries, representing more than 25% of the countries of the world. The largest African country is Sudan.

5 What is the population of the world?
The population of the world is 6.1 billion people and it is growing all the time. Current research indicates that about five people are born every second, while two people die, leaving us with a population increase of three new human beings per second.

6 Which country has the largest population?
China. It is home to more than 1.2 billion people. India is currently the world's second most populous country with 1 billion people, but by 2040, India is expected to have the largest population.

7 What proportion of the earth is covered by water?
71% of the Earth's surface is covered in water, which maintains the temperature of the planet. Of the 71% , 97% is salt water, 3% is fresh water, of which 1% is drinking water.

8 How many oceans are there? What are they?
Most often the world is divided into four major oceans – the Pacific Ocean, Atlantic Ocean, Arctic Ocean, and the Indian Ocean. Some consider there to be five oceans – the fifth being the Antarctic Ocean.

9 How much of the earth's land surface is used to grow food?
Only 11% of the land surface is used to grow food. 31% is forest, 27% is desert and wilderness, 26% is pasture land. 5% is urban.

10 Where is the world's largest desert? What is it called?
The Sahara Desert in Northern Africa is the world's largest desert. At more than 9 million square kilometres, it is slightly smaller than the size of the United States.

11 What's the difference between a political and a physical map?
A political map shows human-created features such as boundaries, cities, roads, and railroads. Physical maps display the natural features of the earth – the location and names of mountains, rivers, valleys, ocean currents, and deserts. Most common maps and globes are combinations of political and physical maps.

12 Which is the world's largest island?
At 2,175,600 square kilometres, Greenland is the world's largest island. Australia also meets the definition of an island but it is large enough to be considered a continent.

**T 11.2**

1 He gave us some delicious, home-made, wholemeal bread, which was still warm from the oven.

2 A funny, little, old Irish lady arrived, wearing a big feathered hat.

3 I bought a gorgeous red and white striped silk shirt with gold buttons.

4 She's just had a lovely, fat, bouncing baby boy with lots of brown, tufty hair.

5 He showed me into a delightful, light, airy, high-ceilinged living room with all-white furniture and carpets.

6 I met a trendy, young Venezuelan art student who's living in London at the moment.

7 She's wearing shiny, tight-fitting, black, leather trousers with back pockets.

8 It's an exquisite, sweet-smelling apricot-coloured rose covering the whole wall.

**T 11.3**

**1 Sean**
I think the most unusual and interesting place that I've visited is … erm … a place called the *Salar de Uyuni*, which is in the south of Bolivia and it is … er … an enormous salt plain and … erm … we had to drive out of the nearest town and drive for two days … erm … without electricity or running water, those kinds of things . ,… erm … it's about 5,000 metres above sea-level, most of the time and most of it is almost completely white because it's covered in salt … erm … but because of the mineral content every now and again you get these incredible, strangely coloured lakes, like bright red and bright green lakes, and … erm … chocolate caramel covered mountains and things like that. Erm, I've got photos that when I look at them they look like trick photography of some sort because all the colours are so strange but that's exactly how I remember it.

**2 Lucy**
Erm … I went to Sydney last, last year in November. I went to, went on a little four-day tour and one of the places I stopped at was a little place called Nundle, and there was a sheep station and it was just out in the sticks and they had … they had a disco at night and you had the volume whacked up full because there was no one, no neighbours, in so many miles, and I just remember dancing and at the end of the night 'cos the toilets were outside so I was brushing my teeth and dancing away to the music that was still going on, under the stars, and it was absolutely gorgeous … it was really good. I really enjoyed that.

**3 Jerry**
Erm … I think the place that felt most sort of remote from– from normal life was Iceland where I went last year … erm … actually on a, on a bicycling trip … erm … which was incredibly empty, I mean really strange landscapes with lots of glaciers and volcanoes and strange volcanic smells … erm … and almost no people and constant very high wind, and it really felt like the end of the world.

**4 Claire**
I once visited a place called Moose Factory, which is a tiny island community … erm … in the middle of the Moose River in Canada and when the river freezes in the winter you can drive a car or a truck across the ice to get to the island but in the spring and autumn, when the ice is thin the only way to enter or leave the island is by plane and of course in summer the people travel across the river by boat.

**5 James**
The most farflung or unusual place that I've visited was … is probably … er … I went to … er … in Colombia, in the Sierra Nevada Mountains, I went to a place called the Lost City … Lost City, *La Ciudad Perdida* and it was a three day hike into the jungle, in the tropical rain forest, then a long hike up a basically kind of a hill and into a … erm … into this village, which was buried in the jungle up until

about fifty years ago, when treasure hunters were out looking for it … erm … it was consumed by the jungle … kind of like an Incan thing but that was a different tribe but it had all these beautiful rock terraces and … er … it was an amazing trip..... it was good, it was very kind of Indiana Jones.

**6 Belinda**

Right – the weirdest place that I've ever visited has to be underwater in Sardinia, because I'd never actually snorkelled before, so I put on the mask looked below and realized that we only really live on half of the planet, and I just could not believe what I saw, I just felt really small. I was completely out of my depth in every sense, and … erm … it kinda put me in my place in a way, because it wasn't man's world and … er … I was shocked, I was terrified actually.

## T 11.4

Yes, that was a wonderful story. I was … there was a new railway line constructed across far western China, from a place called Urunchi, through a pass called the Zungarian Gate … into what is now Kazakhstan … and I thought it would be nifty to ride on one of the first trains, of course it's an extremely remote part of the world. So I go with a friend of mine called George Robertson, and the two of us go out from Urunchi, crossing the desert and now we're about 150 miles west of Urunchi and it's just sand dunes and nothing. And then suddenly the train stops and I look out and there's this 'halt'. I mean it's not a station, there's no town there's just a sort of watering tower, and so I say to the conductor 'Why have we stopped?' and he said 'Oh, we're taking on water' or something like that and we'll be stopped for half an hour. So I get out and stretch my legs in the blazing sun, sand dunes, camels until I go and talk to the engine driver and while I'm doing so, I hear a voice from the si.. behind me, saying in pretty impeccable English: 'Excuse me, do you speak English?' And I turn round and there is this vision of loveliness, this beautiful Chinese woman and I said 'Yes, I do actually,' and she said 'Good!' in a very sort of matter of fact slightly unsmiling way.

## T 11.5

She looked at her watch and she said 'This train is stopping here for another 27 minutes. Have you ever read the works of Anthony Trollope?' And I'm thinking, wait a minute this is really strange, but 'Yes, I like Trollope a lot.' 'Good,' she said. 'Would you be willing to discuss with me *The Eustace Diamonds*, particularly the character of Lady Glencora?' I'm thinking 'this is not happening', but I do my best, struggling, I mean I must have read *The Eustace Diamonds* twenty years before. I could just about remember odds and ends, so I struggle through a conversation with her and then the guard waved his green flag and blew a whistle and she said 'Quick, quick go back otherwise you'll miss your train.' So I … but I said 'You're beautiful. I love you, I want to live with you for the rest of my life' and she said 'Don't be so silly! Get in the train. Give me your business card.' So I didn't have one, but George had one so I scribbled my name and the train was moving. And the last vision I have of her was her scrabbling on her hands and knees to pick up my card while we went round the corner and I went back into the compartment and I said 'George, I've just had the most really strange experience … so we then went travelling all the over Siberia for the next couple of months and I arrived back in Hong Kong and there was a letter …

## T 11.6

… there was a letter and she said:
'Dear Mr Winchester, I just want you to know that meeting you that day was just one of the most extraordinary events of my life. I … am married to a cadre in the Chinese communist party and we were

… he committed some infraction and we were sent to this ghastly little town … it was called Kwi Tun. Nothing happens here. It's 30 miles away from the road and from the railway line. There's no one here that speaks English. I'm the only person, but I'm desperate not to lose my language, so the international train goes through every Tuesday and Thursday and I cycle all the way across the desert, down to the train station, wait for it to come in, knock on every compartment to see if there's anyone there that speaks English. Occasionally there's some sort of migrant worker … but one day I meet this man who not only can speak English, but is English and, my passion is Trollope. He knew all about Trollope. I was able to speak for 25 minutes about Trollope and it was like … you were like an angel from heaven. It was wonderful.'
Anyway we're the very best of friends. We have been for years.

## T 11.7

1 I don't like children who always have to be the centre of attention.
2 The journey from work to home, which usually takes half an hour, took over two hours yesterday.
3 Politicians who make extravagant promises aren't worth listening to.
  Politicians, who make extravagant promises, aren't worth listening to.
4 The Taj Mahal, which took twenty-two years to complete, is built from exquisitely carved white marble.
5 These are the photographs I was telling you about.
6 We docked at the small port on the coast of East Africa where my parents lived twenty years ago.
7 My cousin, who's a real thrill-seeker, went hang-gliding at the weekend.
  My cousin who's a real thrill-seeker went hang-gliding at the weekend.
8 We went on a cycling holiday in Wales, where there are some really steep hills.

## T 11.8

1 A I'm cleaned out! This new jacket cost the earth.
  B Come on! It's good to spoil yourself every now and then.
2 A Believe me, that guy's really going places.
  B Don't I know it! He landed that consultancy job that we all applied for.
3 A The holiday's over. It's back to the real world.
  B You can say that again. Back to earth with a bump!
4 A What? You're not coming out on Saturday night!
  B I can't. My dad caught me smoking and I've been grounded for two weeks.
5 A Hey! Great to see you! I thought you weren't going to be able to make it.
  B I nearly wasn't. I had to move heaven and earth to get here.
6 A We're throwing caution to the wind and emigrating to Oz.
  B Don't your folks already live down under?
7 A Come on, you know you want to go out with me really.
  B In your dreams. Not if you were the last man on earth!
8 A Can you follow these instructions? Where on earth do all these screws go?
  B Don't ask me. I was totally floored by the last lot I read.
9 A I don't want to drink, so I'll do the driving tonight.
  B Great! That suits me down to the ground.

# Unit 12

## T 12.1

We are immediately struck by the softness of the sunshine and the activities of the countryside. The everyday pursuits of the three common men pictured – the ploughman, the shepherd, and the fisherman – are being carried out with apparent pleasure.
It takes the viewer some time to realize the central event of the painting, the splash of a pair of legs as the fallen Icarus plunges into the sea. They are caught at the precise moment that this symbol of human pride is about to disappear forever. It is ironic that no one is paying attention. All of the movement in the picture is away from the main event. The ploughman and shepherd, oblivious, go about their business, as does the fully-rigged boat, also sailing away from the fallen figure.
*Landscape with the Fall of Icarus* can be interpreted as a warning against pride and ambition. The ploughman who labours on, ignoring the hapless Icarus, exemplifies the ideal of the common man, who remains content with his modest lot in life. We should not search for personal gain, nor have ambitions above our station in life. Bruegel will have known the Flemish proverb 'No plough stops for the sake of a dying man'.
In the painting we also see life as a process of continuation. No matter what momentous events are happening in the world, near to you or far away, despite wars, death, natural disasters, famine, plagues or earthquakes, life goes on.

## T 12.2  See p111

## T 12.3

Salvador Dalí was born in 1904 in a small town, Figueres, in Catalunya, north east Spain, where his father was a prestigious notary.
Wanting to study art, Dalí went to the Royal Academy of Art in Madrid, but he was expelled from the Academy twice, as a result of which he never took his final examinations.
In 1928 he went to Paris, where he met the Spanish painters Pablo Picasso and Joan Miró, and established himself as the principal figure of a group of surrealist artists, whose leader was André Breton.
By 1929 Dalí found the style, consisting of the world of the unconscious recalled during our dreams, that would make him famous.
In 1927 he met Gala, a Russian immigrant ten years older than Dalí.
Although she was married to a French poet at the time, she decided to leave her husband as she wanted to stay with Dalí.
In 1940 Dalí went to the United States, where he stayed for eight years until 1948, when he and Gala returned to Europe, spending most of their time in Spain or Paris.
When Gala died in 1982, Dalí became deeply depressed, and moved to Púbol, a castle he had bought for Gala.
He lived in his castle for the rest of his life, dying there in 1989 of heart failure.

## T 12.4  Part One

RP We're in the central square of Lourdes, and there's literally thousands of people, most of them fairly elderly, -er congregating here. A lot of them have brought their own chairs to sit on. It's very quiet, given what a large crowd there is here. And people don't seem to be talking to each other. They seem to be er … almost reverential. A lot of them have heads bowed. Very introspective atmosphere. And you feel that when you're talking, you should really be whispering.
  Lourdes must be the strangest tourist destination in the world. A hundred thousand

seriously ill people come every year, many in wheelchairs or borne on stretchers, to mingle with millions of able-bodied pilgrims, and camera-carrying tourists. There are 30,000 hotel beds in a town of just 15,000 permanent residents. But in the midst of it all lies the sanctuary, several square kilometres of ring-fenced holy ground, containing three churches, and the famous grotto, where Bernadette Soubirous saw visions of the Virgin Mary, over 140 years ago.

Any pilgrims looking for spiritual guidance amidst a maze of garish souvenir shops can turn to Father Liam Griffin, who's sort of the official tour rep for English speaking visitors … Father Griffin, -er we're walking in the sanctuary here at the moment. There're thousands of people here today. How important is Lourdes –er within the Catholic Church?

**FG** Lourdes is a place of pilgrimage. It is a place where the Blessed Virgin Mary appeared to Bernadette Soubirous back in 1858, and in that way it is an important place of prayer. According to our statistics about six million people come here every year.

## Part Two

**RP** What is it about this place, this experience, that attracts so many people? Lourdes has long been associated with the miraculous. The spring which Bernadette discovered in 1858 is said to have healing properties, and the place has been linked with sudden dramatic cures of the seriously ill. But in the twenty-first century, I'm puzzled as to why more and more people are coming to Lourdes each year. Are they looking for something that modern science can't offer?

**AW** We've gone through a much more intellectual, rational age, where science is perhaps the dominant discourse in academic life these days. And it seems to proclude miracles. And modern Christians are divided as to whether they still occur, or whether they only existed in the past.

**RP** Andrew Walker is Professor of Theology, Religion and Culture at King's College, London.

**AW** The whole of Christianity, rightly or wrongly, is based on an idea that a man was also God raised from the dead. You can't get anything more miraculous than that. But it doesn't alter the fact that even if there were no miracles, I think from a sociological point of view, we do need to believe in the impossible, and you find it in Hinduism, and Christianity, and Judaism. There's a certain theatrical joy about the possibility that God can intervene in the world and change things.

## Part Three

**RP** In 1999 Jean-Pierre Bely became the most recent person officially confirmed to have been cured at Lourdes.

**JP** The illness began in 1971–72, at first very discretely. There were very minor symptoms, slight manifestations of disease, such as fatigue, a lack of suppleness and mobility in my hands, pins and needles in my fingertips. I work as a nurse in a hospital, so I just put it all down to stress. Over the years things got worse, but the actual diagnosis wasn't made until 1984, after a particularly violent attack that left me partly paralysed. It was after this that I went into hospital, and the doctors carried out a thorough examination. Afterwards the doctor, who I knew from my work as a nurse, said to me 'Jean-Pierre. Prepare yourself for the worst. I think you have multiple sclerosis.'

**RP** By 1987 Jean-Pierre was bedridden, receiving a one hundred percent state invalidity benefit, and he even had his house modified structurally to accommodate his extreme disability. Later that year he was persuaded to go on a pilgrimage to Lourdes, but whilst taking part in morning mass, he was overcome by a strange experience.

**JP** At that moment, everything was turned upside down, and I was sucked into a whirlwind of emotion, of joy, of peace, and an extraordinary feeling of serenity that came over me, which remains with me still to this day. The second part of the cure took place later that same day. I was back in the sick room, lying on the bed, and felt terribly cold, like an intense chill in my bones. But slowly it got warmer and warmer, until it felt like a fire burning through the whole of my body. I was overwhelmed by it. I heard this voice, like an order, 'Get up and walk!' And then, all of a sudden, I don't know how, I found myself sitting up on the bed, my legs dangling over the edge, and I started to touch the back of my hands. I realised I'd regained mobility and sensitivity in my spine and shoulders, which had been blocked for years. They were normal. In fact you could say I'd found normality again.

**RP** By the time Jean-Pierre, now able to walk again, returned home, all signs of his crippling illness had vanished. And remain so today.

## Part Four

**RP** It's perhaps no surprise that scientific research has confirmed what millions of pilgrims have always known, that visiting Lourdes profoundly improves your mental state. But this raises troubling questions for a doctor like myself. After all, I prescribe anti-depressants to my patients. Why not visits to Lourdes? What's stopping me? Well, personally I'm unhappy with the idea that just because something may seem inexplicable at the moment, that it means the only account left is a spiritual solution. Perhaps the key point about a miracle is that it is a mechanism for providing hope when in many circumstances, there is no hope. For me the danger of modern medicine is that when it runs out of technological answers, as it does for millions of the seriously ill, it turns its back and offers nothing else. Into this chasm of despair steps religion, miracles and hope. And Lourdes as a concrete place you can visit, provides an opportunity to renew your belief that something good can still come of catastrophe.

# Grammar Reference

## UNIT 1

### Avoiding repetition

To avoid repetition in many languages, it is common for words to be missed out. This is called ellipsis. In English it is common for the main verb to be missed out, leaving just the auxiliary, and this can cause problems.

### ▶ 1.1 Using auxiliaries to avoid repetition

**In short answers**

When a *Yes/No* question is asked, we use the auxiliary on its own when answering rather than repeating the whole verb form.

*'Will it rain this afternoon?' 'Yes, I think it will* (rain this afternoon).*'*
*'Should I revise for this test?' 'Yes, I think you should* (revise for the test).*'*

**Notes**

There is a difference in the short answers between *have* and *have got.*
*'Does she have to go?' 'Yes, she does.'*
*'Has she got to go?' 'Yes, she has.'*

**Commenting on given information**

When we make comments in conversation, we usually avoid repeating information that has just been given.
*'Mary's coming.' 'I know she is.'*
*'Angela can speak Russian and Hungarian.' 'She can't, can she?'*

**Note**

Where there is no auxiliary verb in Present and Past Simple positive statements, *do/does/did* is used to reply. This is to avoid repeating the full verb.
*'I adore Italy.' 'I do too, and so does James.'*
*'I thought the film was wonderful.' 'I didn't. I hated it.'*

**Responding with a different auxiliary**

To know which auxiliary verb to use, it is necessary to reconstruct the part of the sentence that is missing, and to consider carefully the meaning and the time of the events in the sentence.
*'I didn't see the film.' 'Oh, you should have* (seen the film). *It was great.'*
*'You must see the Renoir exhibition. It's superb!' 'I have* (seen it).*'*
*'I wish you'd lock the door when you leave.' 'But I did* (I locked it).*'*

**Using more than one auxiliary**

When there is more than one auxiliary, we can use one or more when responding.
*'He could have been lying.' 'Yes, he could/could have/could have been.'*
*'Would I have enjoyed it?' 'No, I don't think you would/would have.'*
We always use more than one if there is a change in auxiliary.
*'You should be given a rise.' 'Well, I haven't been.'*
*'She can't have told him yet.' 'She must have.'*

### ▶ 1.2 Reduced infinitives

We can use *to* instead of the full infinitive in replies.
*'Haven't you done the washing-up yet?' 'No, I'm just going to.'*
*'Are you coming for a walk?' 'No, I don't want to.'*
The verb *to be* is not usually reduced to *to.*
*She's less moody than she used to be.*
*I wasn't as impressed as I'd expected to be.*

## UNIT 2

### Phrasal verbs

### ▶ 2.1 Multiple meanings

Phrasal verbs can have multiple meanings.

a  *She worked out the plot of her book.* (= devise, plan)
b  *Work out how much I owe you.* (= calculate)
c  *I can't work out her handwriting.* (= understand)
d  *Their marriage didn't work out.* (= wasn't successful)
e  *I'm sure you'll work out your differences.* (= resolve)
f  *She works out at the gym every day.* (= do exercises, train)

### ▶ 2.2 Degrees of metaphorical use

There can be different degrees of metaphorical use.

a  *Take off your coat.*                                      Literal
b  *The sick sailor was taken off the ship.*
c  *They're taking 5p off income tax.*
d  *We're taking off a fortnight in the summer.*
e  *The plane took off.*
f  *His business is taking off.*
g  *He's a good mimic. He can take off the teacher perfectly.*  **Metaphorical**

Sentence f is an example of transference, in that it derives from the meaning of *take off* in sentence e. This is typical of the way in which the meaning and use of phrasal verbs grow and change.

### ▶ 2.3 Transferred or metaphorical meanings

The transferred (or metaphorical) meanings of phrasal verbs are often derived from the literal meaning.
*The court stood up when the judge came in.* (literal)
*You should stand up for what you believe in.* (transferred)
*Come round to my house.* (literal)
*She's coming round to my point of view.* (transferred)
*She gave away her money.* (literal)
*Don't give away my secret.* (transferred)

### ▶ 2.4 The grammar of phrasal verbs

There are four types of phrasal verbs.

**Type 1: verb + adverb (no object)**

a  *He **went out**.* (literal)
b  *I didn't put enough wood on the fire, so it **went out**.* (metaphorical)

**Type 2: verb + adverb + object (separable)**

a  *I **put up** the picture on the wall.* (literal)
b  *I **put up** my sister for the night.* (metaphorical)

Type 2 phrasal verbs are separable. The object (noun or person) can come between the verb and the adverb.
*I **put** the picture **up**.      I **put** my sister **up**.*
But if the object is a pronoun, it always comes between the verb and the adverb.
*I **put** it **up**.* (NOT *I put up it.*)      *I **put** her **up**.* (NOT *I put up her.*)
If the object is a long noun phrase, a noun with a qualifying clause, or a noun clause, the adverb comes immediately after the verb. This avoids the adverb being too far separated from the verb.
*They **turned down** the majority of the applicants for the job.*
*She **told off** the children who had stolen her apples.*
*You should **think over** what I've been talking to you about.*

### Type 3: verb + preposition + object (inseparable)

a  *She **came across** the street.* (literal)
b  *She **came across** an old letter while she was tidying her drawers.* (metaphorical)

Type 3 phrasal verbs are inseparable. The object (noun or pronoun) always comes after the preposition.

*She **came across** a letter.*
*She **came across** it.*    NOT ~~She came it across.~~

### Type 4: verb + adverb + preposition + object

*Don't just sit there! **Get on with** your work.* (Continue with it.)
*I've got to **cut down on** my spending.* (reduce)

Type 4 phrasal verbs are nearly all metaphorical. The object cannot change position.

*It cannot come before the adverb or the preposition.*
*I'm looking forward to it.*    NOT ~~I'm looking forward it to.~~

## Tense review

English tenses have two elements of meaning: time and aspect.

### Time

Is the action present, past or future? Does it refer to all time?

It is important to remember that *time* and *tense* are not always the same in English. Present tenses often refer to the present time, but not always; similarly past tenses do not always refer to past time.

*Your plane **leaves** at 10.00 tomorrow morning.* (present tense form referring to the future)
*In the book, the heroine **goes** back to her youth.* (present tense form referring to the past)
*I wish I **knew** the answer, but I don't.* (past tense form referring to the present)
*I **could** come tomorrow, if you like.* (past tense form referring to the future)

### Aspect

The three aspects add another layer of meaning to the action of the verb.

Simple       The action is seen as a complete whole.
Continuous   The action is seen as having duration.
Perfect      The action is seen as completed *before* another time.

### Choosing the correct tense

The choice of verb form depends on many factors, and not on a set of rigid grammatical rules.

1  **The nature of the action or event**
   Because English can employ its various aspects, events can be viewed with a multiplicity of implications. Look at this sentence:
   *I have been asking my husband to mend this door for two years.*
   In some languages this verb form is in the present – *I ask my husband* … – which indeed conveys the same basic message. But English has added on two aspects. The perfect aspect emphasizes both past and present, so that the enormity of this lack of DIY can be appreciated. The continuous aspect expresses the repetitive nature of the wife's requests. She hasn't asked once but a hundred times, every week for two years. Neither of these ideas are expressed by the present tense.

2  **How the speaker sees the event**
   Look at these sentences:
   a  *He always buys her flowers.*
   b  *He's always buying her flowers.*
   c  *I'll talk to Peter about it this afternoon.*
   d  *I'll be talking to Peter about it this afternoon.*
   In each pair of sentences, the actions are the same, but the speaker looks at them differently.
   In sentence *a*, the Present Simple expresses a simple fact. The Present Continuous in sentence *b* conveys the speaker's attitude, one of mild surprise or irritation.

In sentence *c*, *will* expresses a promise or a decision made at the moment of speaking. In sentence *d*, the Future Continuous is interesting for what it *doesn't* express. There is no element of intention, volition or plan. The speaker is saying that in the natural course of events, as life unfolds, he and Peter will cross paths and talk, independently of the will or intention of anyone concerned. It is a casual way of looking at the future, which is why we can find it in questions such as *Will you be using the computer for long?*, which is much less confrontational than *Are you going to be using the computer for long?*

3  **The meaning of the verb**
   In some cases, the choice of verb form might be suggested by the meaning of the verb. A verb such as *belong* expresses a state or condition that remains unchanged over a period of time. Other such verbs are *mean, understand, believe, adore, remember,* etc. It would therefore be more likely to find them in simple verb forms.
   *This house **belonged** to my grandfather. Now it **belongs** to me.*
   Similarly, verbs such as *wait* and *rain* express the idea of an activity over a period of time, and so are often found in continuous verb forms.
   *I've **been waiting** for you for hours!*
   *It's **raining** again.*

## ▶ 2.5  The simple aspect

The simple aspect describes an action that is seen to be complete. The action is viewed as a whole unit.

*The sun **rises** in the east.* (= all time)
*I've **read** the book and **seen** the film.* (complete)
*My father always **wore** a suit to work.* (habit)
*He **died** in 1992.* (action completed in the past)
*This shop **will close** at 5.30.* (simple fact)

Because the simple aspect expresses a completed action, we must use it if the sentence contains a number that refers to 'things done'.

*She's **written** three letters today.*    *I **drink** five cups of tea a day.*

## ▶ 2.6  The continuous aspect

Continuous verb forms express activities, or a series of activities, viewed at some point between their beginning and end. The continuous aspect focuses on the duration of an activity: we are aware of the passing of time. The activity is *not* permanent, and its duration is limited.

*I'm **staying** with friends until I find a place of my own.* (temporary)
*Why **are** you **wearing** that silly hat?* (in progress)
*I've **been learning** English for years.* (duration)

The activity may not be complete.

*I've **been painting** the kitchen.* (We don't know if it's finished.)
*He **was dying**, but the doctors saved him.*
*Who's **been drinking** my beer?* (There's some left.)
Compare: *Who's **drunk** my beer?* (It's all gone.)

The action of some verbs, by definition, lasts a long time, for example, *live* and *work*. The continuous aspect gives these actions limited duration and makes them temporary.

*Hans **is living** in London while he's learning English.*
*I'm **working** as a waiter until I go to university.*

The action of some other verbs lasts a short time. These are often found in the simple aspect.

*She's **cut** her finger.*    *He **hit** me.*

In the continuous aspect, the action of these verbs becomes longer or repeated.

*I've **been cutting** wood.* (for a long time)
*He **was hitting** me.* (again and again)

## 2.7 The perfect aspect

The perfect aspect expresses two ideas:

1 **An action completed before another time**
*I've read his latest book.* (some time before now)
*When I arrived, Mary had cooked the meal.* (some time before I arrived)
*I will have learned my lines before the play starts.* (some time before then)

2 **An action producing a result or a state of affairs relevant to a later situation**
*I've read his latest book.* (I know the story **now**.)
*When I arrived, Mary had cooked the meal.* (It was on the table **then**.)
*I will have learned my lines before the play starts.* (I'll know them **in time for the play**.)

An important characteristic of perfect verb forms, therefore, is that they explicitly link an earlier action or event with a later situation. If we want to direct attention specifically to the result or state produced by the earlier action without drawing attention to the activity that has produced that state, we don't use a perfect form.

*I know the book. It's good.* (present)
*The meal was ready. I ate it.* (past)
*I will know my lines. I'll give a good performance.* (future)

Another characteristic of perfect verb forms is that the exact time of the action or event is either irrelevant or disregarded. The important elements are not *time when*, but the occurrence of the action itself and the results or state of affairs produced by it.

## 2.8 Active and passive

The passive is frequently used in English to express ideas that require a reflexive or impersonal construction in other languages, and in many cases is also used where other languages use the active.

*English is spoken all over the world.*
*His books are sold in Europe.*

Passive sentences move the focus of attention from the subject of an active sentence to the object.

*Shakespeare wrote Hamlet in 1599.*
*Hamlet, one of the great tragedies of all time, was written in 1599.*

In most cases, *by* and the agent are omitted in passive sentences. This is because the agent isn't known, isn't important, or is understood.

*This house was built in the seventeenth century.*
*The escaped prisoner has been recaptured.*

Sometimes we prefer to end a sentence with what is new.

*'What a lovely painting!' 'Yes, it was painted by Canaletto.'*

In informal language, we often use *you* or *they* to refer to people in general or to no person in particular. In this way we can avoid using the passive.

*You can buy anything in Harrods.*
*They're building a new airport soon.*

## 2.9 Future forms

English has several forms which express future events, and which one the user selects depends on how he or she sees the event as much as its certainty or nearness to the present. The main forms are given here in order of frequency of use.

### will

*Will* can function as an auxiliary of the future in simply predicting a future event.

*The Queen will open the new hospital next Thursday.*
*Tomorrow will be warm and sunny everywhere.*

*Will* can also function as a modal auxiliary to express ideas of willingness and spontaneous intention.

*Will you help me for a minute?    What a lovely shirt! I'll buy it.*

### going to

*Going to* expresses a premeditated intention.

*I'm going to decorate the bathroom this weekend.*
*The Government is going to reorganize the entire Civil Service.*

*Going to* is also used to predict a future event for which there is some evidence now.

*Great news! I'm going to have a baby!*
*They're looking very angry. I think they're going to start throwing stones.*

### The Present Continuous

The Present Continuous is used to express an arrangement, usually for the near future.

*'What are you doing tonight?' 'I'm going out for a meal.'*

It is wrong to use the Present Simple in this sense. We cannot say ~~What do you do tonight?~~ or ~~Do you go to the party on Saturday?~~

The Present Continuous cannot be used to express an event that has not been arranged by human beings. We cannot say ~~It is raining tomorrow.~~ or ~~The sun is rising at 5.00 tomorrow morning.~~

### The Present Simple

The Present Simple is used to express a future event which is seen as being certain because of a timetable or calendar.

*What time does the film start?*
*My train gets in at 11.00.*
*The Cup Final takes place on April 13.*

### The Future Continuous

The Future Continuous expresses an activity that will be in progress around a specific time in the future.

*Don't phone at 8.00 – I'll be having supper.*
*This time tomorrow I'll be flying to Hong Kong.*

The Future Continuous also expresses an action that will occur in the natural course of events, independently of the will or intention of anyone directly concerned.

*In a few minutes we will be landing at Heathrow Airport.* (Of course the pilot has not just decided this!)
*Hurry up! The bus will be leaving any minute!*

The Future Continuous is often used to express a casual or polite question about someone's future plans. The speaker is trying not to impose his/her will in any way. This is related to the use of the Future Continuous described above, i.e. that it can express an action that will occur independently of the will or intention of the people concerned.
Compare:

*Will you bring Kate to the party?* (Perhaps a request.)
*Will you be bringing Kate to the party?* (I'm just asking.)

### The Future Perfect

The Future Perfect expresses an action that will have finished before a definite time in the future.

*I'll have finished my work by the time you get back.*
*Most of the leaves will have fallen by the end of November.*

## 2.10 The future in the past

Sometimes when we are talking about the past, we want to refer to something that was in the future at that time. This is called the 'future in the past', and it is expressed by *was going to*, the Past Continuous, or *would*. *Would* is very common in reported speech and thought.

*The last time I saw you, you were going to start a new job. Did you?*
*I was in a hurry because I was catching a plane that afternoon.*
*He said he'd give me a lift.*

The uses of these three forms are exactly parallel to *going to*, the Present Continuous, and *will* to refer to the real future.

*I'm going to start a new job.* (intention)
*I'm catching a plane this afternoon.* (arrangement)
*I'll give you a lift.* (offer)

The future in the past is often found in narratives.

*Alice smiled as she thought of the evening to come. She was meeting Peter, and together they were going to see a play at the Adelphi Theatre. She was sure the evening would be enjoyable.*

# UNIT 3

## Position of adverbs

### 3.1 Adverb + adjective

When an adverb qualifies an adjective or past participle, it comes immediately before it.

*The hotel is **completely full**.*
*We were **deeply disappointed** with his performance.*

### 3.2 Adverb + verb

When an adverb qualifies a verb + object, we do not usually put the adverb between the verb and its object.

*I like Mozart very much.* (NOT *I like very much Mozart.*)
*I usually have lunch at 1.00.* (NOT *I have usually lunch at 1.00.*)

### 3.3 Front, mid, or end position?

There are three normal positions within a sentence for adverbs.

1 Front (at the beginning of the clause)
   ***Today** we're studying adverbs. **Obviously** it's difficult. **However**, we're having fun.*

2 Mid (before the main verb, but after the verb *to be*)
   *I **sincerely** hope you can come to the party.     Pat and Peter are **always** late.*

3 End (at the end of the clause)
   *They told me the news **yesterday**.     She speaks three languages **fluently**.*

Different kinds of adverbs go in different positions, and many can go in all three. The rules about this are complicated, and you should consult a good grammar book for details. However, here are their common positions.

| | | |
|---|---|---|
| **Manner** (*quickly, sincerely, gently*) | end or mid | *She **quickly** tidied the room. She tidied the room **quickly**.* |
| **Place** (*here, outside, upstairs*) | end | *They're playing **outside**.* |
| **Point in time** (*tomorrow, yesterday, tonight*) | end or front | *We're going to Paris **tomorrow**. **Tomorrow** we're going to Paris.* |
| **Indefinite time** (*already, still, just*) Some indefinite time adverbs can go in the end position. | mid | *I've **already** seen the film. I **still** don't understand. I've seen the film **already**. I haven't seen it **yet**.* |
| **Frequency** (*always, never, seldom*) | mid | *I **always** drink tea in the morning.* |
| **Comment** (*clearly, obviously, naturally*) | front or mid | ***Obviously** I got it wrong. I **obviously** got it wrong.* |
| **Linking** (*however, so, although*) | front | *It was raining, **so** we went home.* |
| **Degree/intensifier** (*very, nearly, really*) | before the word they qualify | *I **really** like you. (before a verb) I'm **really** hot. (before an adjective) You **very nearly** killed me! (before another adverb)* |

**Notes**

1 Some adverbs can be both comment and manner. The position depends on which use it is.
   *I can see the boat **clearly**. (manner)*
   ***Clearly** you need to curb your spending. (comment)*
   *Many herbs grow **naturally** in hot climates. (manner)*
   ***Naturally**, I'll pay you back the money I owe you. (comment)*

2 Some adverbs express how complete something is. They come in mid-position.
   *I have **completely** forgotten her name.*
   *We have **almost** finished our work.*

3 If there is more than one adverbial in the end position, the normal order is manner, place, time.
   *He played **well yesterday**.*
   *I watched the sun rise **slowly above the horizon**.*
   *I was **at home yesterday**.*

### 3.4 Adverb collocation

Adverbs can go with certain verbs or adjectives because there is a link in meaning between the two. For example, emotions can be deep, so we often find the adverb *deeply* with words that express feelings.

***deeply** regret     **deeply** embarrassing     **deeply** hurt*
Here are some more examples.

| | |
|---|---|
| freely admit | desperately anxious |
| highly recommended | feel strongly |
| severely damaged | fully insured |
| walk briskly | easily confused |
| sadly missed | |

### 3.5 Adverbs with two forms

Some adverbs have two forms, one with and one without *-ly*. Sometimes the two meanings are connected:

*We were flying **high** over the ocean.*
*I think very **highly** of Joe and his work.*
*Hold **tight**! The train's going to move.*
*We control our expenditure **tightly**.*
Sometimes the two meanings are not connected:
*We work **hard**. (a lot)*
*I **hardly** recognized her. (= almost not)*
*Turn **right** round. (= completely)*
*If I remember **rightly**, they live here. (correctly)*

### 3.6 just

*Just* has several meanings.

| | |
|---|---|
| exactly | This house is just right for us. |
| only | He isn't a man. He's just a boy. |
| a short time before | I've just tried phoning you. |
| right now | I'm just getting dressed. |
| simply, only | I just want you to go. I'd just like an egg for breakfast. |
| equally, no less | You're just as bad as David. |

*Just about* means *almost*.
*'Are you ready to go?' '**Just about**.'*
It can express something that is nearly not possible.
*I can **just** reach the top shelf.*
Sometimes it doesn't mean very much. It just emphasizes what you're saying!
***Just** what do you think you're doing?!*
*It's **just** incredible!*

# UNIT 4

## ▶ 4.1 Discourse markers

Discourse markers are words and expressions that show how a piece of discourse is constructed. They can:

- show the connection between what is being said now to what was said before.
- show the connection between what is being said now to what is about to be said.
- show the speaker's attitude to what has been said.
- show the speaker's attitude to what he/she is saying.
- clarify, direct, correct, persuade, etc.

This list is not exhaustive.

---

**Basically**, you're spending too much money.
*(This is the most important point.)*

You think I'm wrong, but **actually** I'm right.
*(I'm correcting you as gently as possible.)*

**Quite honestly**, you need a better job.
*(I'm going to speak to you sincerely.)*

**Apparently**, there are good jobs in the City.
*(I've heard this, but I don't know if it's true.)*

**Admittedly**, you'd have to move.
*(I know this point weakens what I'm saying.)*

**Surely** you can understand what I'm saying?
*(I don't know why you don't agree with me.)*

**After all**, I gave you good advice before.
*(Don't forget this. It explains why I'm right.)*

**As a matter of fact**, I saved your company.
*(This is a fact which might surprise you.)*

**Mind you/Still**, that was a long time ago.
*(It occurs to me that this contrasts with what I just said.)*

**Actually**, you didn't thank me then, either.
*(I'm adding some new information to what I just said.)*

**I mean**, why should I bother about you?
*(I'm trying to make things clear to you.)*

**Obviously**, you aren't going to take my advice.
*(This fact cannot be doubted.)*

**At least**, I doubt if you will.
*(I'm correcting or changing what I just said.)*

**Naturally**, you'll do what you think is best.
*(Of course this is what I would expect.)*

**Anyway**, it's up to you.
*(I'm concluding, and not talking about that any more.)*

**All in all**, finding an interesting job isn't easy.
*(I'm considering every part of the situation.)*

The ball's in your court, **so to speak**.
*(I'm using words that don't have their usual meaning.)*

**By the way**, can you lend me some money?'
*(This isn't connected to what we've been talking about.)*

---

## Tags and replies

It has been said that a solid grasp of the systems of auxiliaries is essential to mastery of spoken English.

## ▶ 4.2 Question tags

### Falling intonation

With a falling intonation on the tag, this is not a real question. It means 'Agree with me, talk to me.'

*It's a lovely day, isn't it?*

*The film was great, wasn't it?*

### Note

We can reply to a statement with a question tag.
*'Lovely day today!' 'Yes, it is, isn't it?'*
*'You're filthy!' 'Yes, I am, aren't I?'*
*'Their kids have got good appetites.' 'Yes, they have, haven't they?'*

### Rising intonation

With a rising intonation on the tag, we really want to know something because we aren't sure of the answer.

*You didn't say that to him, did you?*

*They wouldn't take my car away, would they?*

### Notes

Notice the auxiliaries in these questions tags.
*Let's go, shall we?*
*Give me a hand, will you?*
*Don't forget to post my letter, will you?*
*Nobody phoned, did they?*
These question tags can be used in requests.
*You couldn't lend me a tenner, could you?*
*You haven't seen Peter anywhere, have you?*

### Same way tags

These occur after affirmative sentences. The tag is positive and the intonation rises. The speaker repeats what he/she has just heard and uses the tag to express interest, surprise, concern, or some other reaction.

*So you're Kevin's sister, are you? I've heard a lot about you.*

*So you like rap music, do you? Well, just listen to this.*

### Reinforcement tag

There is no inversion in the tag and the intonation rises. The tag emphasizes the idea in the main clause by repeating it, and these tags are used to express that the speaker knows exactly what he/she is talking about.

*She's a clever girl, she is.     You're blind, you are.*

It's possible to introduce the subject of the sentence in the tag. In this case, there can be inversion.
*She's a lovely dancer, Jane is.*
*Likes his food, does Malcolm.*

## ▶ 4.3 Replies

### Short answers

Short answers are used in reply to *Yes/No* questions.
*'Did you have a good time?' 'Yes, I did. It was great.'*
*'Have you been to Russia?' 'No, I haven't, but I'd like to.'*

### Reply questions

We use reply questions to show interest, and to show we're listening.
*'I had a terrible day today.' 'Did you, dear?'*
*'The boss was in a foul mood.' 'Was he?'*

### Avoiding repetition

This was dealt with in Unit 1.
*'Who wants an ice-cream?' 'I do.'* (I want an ice-cream.)
*'Who came to the party?' 'Everybody did.'*

# UNIT 5

## Adding emphasis

### ▶ 5.1 Structures which add emphasis

Sentences can be emphasized by adding certain structures. They are called cleft or divided sentences. Look at this base sentence.

*Lucy moved to London.*

We can emphasize different parts of the sentence according to which element is the most important:

**What** *Lucy did was move to London.* (*What* = the thing which/that)
**Where** *Lucy moved to was London.* (*Where* = the place which/that)
**Why** *Lucy moved to London was because …* (*Why* = the reason why)
**It was** *Lucy* **who/that** *moved to London.* (*who* = the person who/that)

Or we can emphasize the whole sentence:

| *What happened was that* | |
| *What surprised me was the fact that* | *Lucy moved to London.* |
| *What interests me is why* | |

### ▶ 5.2 Negative inversion

Sentences can be given emphasis by negative inversion, which can take place …

1 after negative adverbials such as *never, nowhere, not for one minute, not since, not until, never again, rarely*. It is mainly used in written English but can also be used to emphasize points in more formal spoken English such as when making speeches.
   **Never** *had he eaten such a huge meal.*
   **Nowhere** *will you come across a more hospitable nation.*
   **Nothing** *do they appreciate more than a trip to the country.*
   **Not until** *1918 did British women get the vote.*
   **Rarely** *do you meet a man of such integrity.*

2 in certain established sentence patterns.
   **Hardly** *had he begun to speak* **when** *the majority of the guests departed.*
   **No sooner** *had we sat down to dinner* **than** *the doorbell rang.*
   **Little** *did anyone realize the seriousness of the situation.*

3 after expressions with *only* and *no*.
   **Only** *when I myself became a parent did I realize the value of my parents' advice.*
   **Not only** *did she write short stories,* **but** *she was* **also** *a painter of talent.*
   **At no time** *was I ever informed.*
   **In no way** *can this government deny its guilt.*
   **On no account** *will I compromise my ideals.*

### ▶ 5.3 Pronunciation

Of course a major way of adding emphasis in spoken English is by stressing individual words. In English a change of word stress changes the meaning of a sentence. Look at this base sentence:

*John likes the brown shoes.*
**John** *likes the brown shoes.* (Tom doesn't.)
*John* **likes** *the brown shoes.* (He doesn't hate them.)
*John likes the* **brown** *shoes.* (Not the black ones.)
*John likes the brown* **shoes.** (Not the brown sandals.)

**Note**
It is possible to stress the word *the* (pronounced /ðiː/) when it means that something is so superior to the alternatives, it can be considered the only real choice.
*If John wants brown shoes, Jimmy Choo shoes are* **the** *brown shoes to buy.*

### ▶ 5.4 Emphatic *do, does, did*

*Do, does,* and *did* can be used to give emphasis in positive statements in the Present and Past Simple, and also in the imperative.
*John* **does** *like the brown shoes.* (You were wrong!)
**Do** *come with us on holiday. We'd love you to.*
*I* **do** *love you, really I do.*
*He* **does** *seem rather upset.*
*They* **did** *question him very thoroughly, didn't they?*

# UNIT 6

## Reporting with passive verbs

We can report words and actions using the passive in various ways.

### ▶ 6.1 *It* + passive verb + *that* clause

*It is* **said** *that Bet Molam, the writer, earns $1m a year.*
*It is* **reported** *that she is living in a rented house in Malibu.*
*It has been* **alleged** *that she married her third husband last week.*
*It is* **known** *that she has been working on a new book.*
*It is* **said** *that the book is based on her experiences in the Far East.*
*It is* **understood** *that she has been given an advance of $500,000.*

Other verbs that follow this pattern are:

| agree | calculate | discover | hope | show |
| allege | claim | estimate | know | suggest |
| announce | consider | expect | presume | suppose |
| assume | decide | fear | propose | think |
| believe | declare | feel | recommend | |

With some verbs we can use an infinitive instead of a *that* clause.

*It was* **agreed** *to buy the company for €500 million.*
*It is* **hoped** *to find a solution to the problem soon.*
*It has been* **decided** *to relocate.*
*It is* **planned** *to move our premises to Scotland.*

### ▶ 6.2 Subject + passive verb + *to* infinitive

*Bet Molam is said* **to earn** *$1m a year.* (Present Simple infinitive)
*She is reported* **to be living** *in Malibu.* (Present Continuous infinitive)
*She is alleged* **to have married** *her third husband.* (perfect infinitive)
*She is known* **to have been working** *on a new book.* (perfect continuous infinitive)
*The book is said* **to be based** *on her experiences.* (present passive infinitive)
*She is understood* **to have been given** *an advance.* (perfect passive infinitive)

Other verbs that follow this pattern are:

| allege | consider | know | say | think |
| assume | estimate | presume | suggest | understand |
| believe | expect | report | suppose | |

Notice this transformation with *there*:
*It is thought that there has been a plane crash this afternoon.*
**There is thought to have been** *a plane crash this afternoon.*
*It is estimated that there are one million unemployed.*
**There are estimated to be** *one million unemployed.*

## 6.3 *seem* and *appear*

We can use *seem* and *appear* to give information without stating categorically that we know it to be true.
They can be used in two patterns.

1  *It + seem/appear + that* clause
It **seems** *that she's upset.*
It **appears** *that she's crying.*
It **seems** *that I made a mistake.*
It **appeared** *that his car had been stolen.*

2  *Subject + seem/appear + to* infinitive
*She seems* **to be** *upset.*
*She appears* **to be crying***.*
*I seem* **to have made** *a mistake.*
*His car appears* **to have been stolen***.*

We can make the statement more tentative with the use of *would.*
*It* **would seem** *the problem has been nipped in the bud.*
*I* **would appear** *to have mislaid my wallet.*

# UNIT 7

## Modal auxiliary verbs

Modal verbs are a very rich and subtle area of the English language. They can *all* refer to the certainty, possibility, or probability of an event, and they can all refer to future time. Certain modals can also express other areas of meaning (see below).

## 7.1  Modals of probability in the present and future

The main modal verbs that express present and future probability are given here in order of degrees of certainty, *will* being the most certain and *might/could* being the least certain.

1  **will**
*Will* and *won't* are used to predict a future event which is seen as certain, a future fact.
*I'll be on holiday next week. I* **won't** *do any work at all.*
*Term* **will** *end on June 29th.*
*Will* and *won't* are also used to express what we strongly believe to be true about the present. They indicate an assumption based on our knowledge of people and things: their routine, character, and qualities.
*Is that the phone? It'll be John. He said he'd ring around now.*
*'I wonder what Meg's doing now?' 'It's 7.00. I suppose she'll be getting ready to go out.'*
*Don't take the meat out of the oven. It* **won't** *be ready yet.*

2  **must** and **can't**
*Must* is used to assert what we infer or conclude to be the most logical or rational interpretation of a situation or events. We have a lot of evidence but it is less certain than *will.*
*Wow, look over there! That* **must** *be John's new car.*
*You* **must** *be joking! I simply don't believe you.*
The negative of this use of *must* is *can't.*
*She* **can't** *have a ten-year-old daughter! She's only twenty-five herself!*

3  **should**
*Should* expresses what may reasonably be expected to happen. It also carries the meaning that we want whatever is predicted to happen, and is therefore not used to express negative or unpleasant ideas. It can also suggest a conditional: if everything has gone/goes according to plan, then (x) should happen.
*Our guests* **should** *be here soon. (if they haven't got lost)*
*This homework* **shouldn't** *take you too long. (if you've understood what you have to do)*
*We* **should** *be moving into our new house soon. (as long as all the arrangements go smoothly)*

4  **may**
*May* expresses the possibility that something will happen or is already happening.
*We* **may** *go to Greece for our holidays. We haven't decided yet.*
*We* **may not** *have enough money to go abroad this year.*

5  **might**
*Might*, like *may*, expresses possibility, but in a more tentative way.
*It* **might** *rain. Take your umbrella.*
*I* **might not** *be back in time for supper, so don't wait for me.*

6  **could**
*Could* is used in a similar way to *might.*
*It* **could** *rain, but I doubt it.*
*That French film* **could** *be worth seeing, but it didn't get very good reviews.*
The negative, *could not,* is NOT used to express future possibility. **Might not** is the negative of *could* in this use.
*It looks like it could rain, but it* **might not***.*
*He* **might not** *come.*
The negative *couldn't* has a similar meaning to *can't* in 2 above, only slightly weaker.
*She* **couldn't** *have a 10-year-old daughter! She's only 25 herself!*

7  **can**
We use *can* to express what is generally and all-time true, and logically possible.
*Cycling in town* **can** *be dangerous.*
*Can* cannot be used to predict future possibility. We must use *will be possible* or *will be able to.*
*In years to come it'***ll be possible** *to have holidays on the moon.*
*We'***ll be able to** *travel by space ship.*

## 7.2  Modal auxiliaries in the past

All the modal verbs given above are also used with *have +* past participle (the perfect infinitive) to express varying degrees of certainty about the past. Again, *will/would* is the most certain and *might/could* the least certain. *Can* is a special case (see below).
*You met a man with a big, black moustache? That* **would have been** *my Uncle Tom.*
*It* **won't have been** *Peter you met at the party. He wasn't invited.*
*It* **must have been** *Simon. He looks very like Peter.*
*It* **can't have been** *a very interesting party. No one seems to have enjoyed it.*
*Where's Henry? He* **should have been** *here ages ago! He may have got lost.*
*He might have decided not to come. He* **could have had** *an accident.*
*He* **can hardly have forgotten** *to come.*
*Can have* is only used in questions or with *hardly, only,* or *never.*
*Where* **can he have got to***?*
*They* **can only have known** *each other for a few weeks.*

## 7.3  Other uses of modal auxiliary verbs, present and past

### Obligation

*Must* is used to express strong obligation. The past is expressed by *had to.*
*You* **must** *try harder!*    *I* **had to** *work hard to pass my exams.*
*Should* is used to express milder obligation. The past is expressed by *should have* (+ past participle).
*You* **should** *rest.*    *You* **should have** *taken it more seriously.*

### Permission

*Can* and *may* are used to ask for permission. *May* sounds more formal than *can.*
**Can** *I ask you a question?*
**May** *I ask what the purpose of this visit is?*

The past of *may* and *can* is expressed by *was allowed to*. *Could* can only be used to report permission.

I **was allowed to** do whatever I wanted when I was young.
My parents said I **could** stay out until after midnight.

### Ability

*Can* is used to express general ability; the form in the past is *could*.

I **can** swim. I **could** swim when I was 6.

To express a particular ability on one occasion in the past, *could* is not used. Instead, *was able to* or *managed to* is used.

The prisoner **managed to** escape by climbing onto the roof.
I **was able to** give the police a full description.

### Willingness

*Won't* expresses a refusal, by either people or things. The past is *wouldn't*.

The car **won't** start.
He was angry because she **wouldn't** lend him any money.

### Characteristic behaviour/habit

*Will* is used to express characteristic behaviour. The past is expressed by *would*.

He**'ll** sit for hours staring into the fire.
My grandma **would** always bring me a little present when she came to visit.

If *will* is stressed, it suggests criticism and irritation.

David **will** leave his homework until the last minute. It's infuriating.

### Past forms of *need*

*Need* has two past forms.

*Needn't have* (+ past participle) expresses an action that was completed but that wasn't necessary.

You **needn't have bought** any butter. We've got lots.

*Didn't need to* (+ infinitive) expresses an action that was not necessary, but we do not know if it was in fact completed or not. The context usually makes this clear.

I **didn't need to do** any shopping because I was eating out that night.

# UNIT 8

## ▶ 8.1 *would*

*Would* can express past habits.

When I was a kid, we**'d** go looking for mushrooms.
My grandfather **would** sit in his armchair and nod off.

If *would* is stressed, it suggests criticism and irritation.

My sister **would** borrow my clothes without asking. It really annoyed me.

Stressed *would* can also be used to criticize a single past action. The meaning is 'that's typical of you/him/her'.

Did she say I hit her? She **would** say that. I hate her.

*Would* is used to express the future in the past (see p78). It reports speech and thoughts.

You promised you**'d** help me.
I knew you **wouldn't** like it.

*Would* can express a refusal on a particular past occasion.

I asked him if he was going out with anyone, but he **wouldn't** tell me.
The printer **wouldn't** stop printing, so I turned it off at the mains.

## Real and unreal tense usage

### Introduction

English tense usage can be divided into two categories: tenses used to refer to fact, and those used to refer to non-fact. Fact is what is considered to be real or quite possible; non-fact is what is supposed or wished for, which is either unreal or improbable.

| Fact | I work in a restaurant, but I don't earn much. |
| | If I find a better job, I'll take it. |
| Non-fact | I wish I had a lot of money. |
| | If I had a lot of money, I would open my own restaurant. |

Tenses used to refer to fact are related to real time. For example, a past verb form refers to the past.

I **had** a lovely holiday in Spain last year.

Tenses used to refer to non-fact are not related to real time. Generally speaking, this unreality is expressed by shifting the verb form 'backwards', for example, from present to past.

If I **had** a car, I **could** visit my friends.

Here the past verb form does not refer to the real past, but to the 'wished for' present and future. It has the effect of distancing the meaning from reality.

## ▶ 8.2 Type 1 conditional sentences (real)

It is important to understand this difference between fact and non-fact when discussing conditional sentences.

- Type 1 conditional sentences are based on fact in real time. They express a possible condition and its probable result.

  If it rains, I'll get wet.
  If he doesn't come soon, we'll miss the bus.

- *Will* is not usually used in the condition clause. However, it can appear when *will* expresses willingness (or in the negative, refusal), or insistence.

  If you**'ll wash** the dishes, I'll put them away. (if you are willing to)
  If Peter **won't give** you a lift, I will. (if Peter isn't willing to)
  If you **will smoke**, of course you'll get a cough. (if you insist on smoking)
  When *will* expresses insistence, it is stressed and never contracted.

- *Should* and *happen to* can be used in the condition clause to suggest that something may happen by chance, but is unlikely.

  If you **should come across** Pearl, tell her to give me a ring.
  If you **happen to find** my book, pop it in the post to me.

- There are several other links with meanings similar to *if* that can introduce Type 1 conditional sentences.

  Provided/Providing I have the time, I'll give you a hand to fix it.
  Supposing you miss the plane, what will you do?
  I'll come tomorrow unless I hear from you before. (if I don't hear from you)

## ▶ 8.3 Type 2 conditional sentences (unreal)

Type 2 conditional sentences are not based on fact. They express a situation which is contrary to reality in the present and future; a hypothetical condition and its probable result. This unreality is shown by a tense shift 'backwards':

Present → Past, *will* → *would*

If I **were** taller, I'd join the police force. (In reality I am not, and never will be, tall enough to join the police force.)
If you **saw** a ghost, what would you do? (I don't believe in ghosts, so I don't think you will ever see one.)

The difference between Type 1 and Type 2 conditional sentences is not related to time. Both can refer to the present or the future. By using a past verb form in Type 2, the speaker suggests that the situation is less probable, or impossible, or imaginary.

Compare the following.

*If it rains this weekend, I'll …* (Said in England, where rain is common.)
*If it rained in the Sahara, the desert would …* (This would be most unusual.)
*If there is a nuclear war, we will …* (I am a pessimist. Nuclear war is a real possibility.)
*If there was a nuclear war, we would …* (I am an optimist and I think nuclear war is very unlikely to happen.)
*If you come to my country, you'll have a good time.* (Possible.)
*If you came from my country, you'd understand us better.* (Impossible – you don't come from my country.)

### Notes
*Were* is often used instead of *was*, especially when the style is formal. It is also commonly used in the expression *If I were you …* when giving advice.
*If he **were** more honest, he would be a better person.*
*If I **were** you, I'd cook it for a little longer.*
The Type 2 conditional can make a suggestion sound less direct and hence more polite.
*Would it be convenient if I called this evening around 8.00?*
*Would you mind if I opened the window slightly?*
*Would* is not usually used in the condition clause. However, as with *will* in Type 1, it can appear when it expresses willingness. Again, it makes a suggestion sound more polite.
*I would be grateful if you **would** give this matter your serious attention.*
*Were to* can be used in the condition clause to suggest that something is unlikely to happen.
*If you **were to find** that your neighbours were drug smugglers, what would you do?*

## 8.4 Type 3 conditional sentences (unreal)

Type 3 conditional sentences, like Type 2, are not based on fact. They express a situation which is contrary to reality in the past. This unreality is shown by a tense shift 'backwards':

Past → Past Perfect, *would* → *would have*

*If I had known his background, I would never have employed him.* (I didn't know his background and I did employ him.)
*If I hadn't seen it with my own eyes, I wouldn't have thought it possible.* (I did see it with my own eyes, so it must be possible.)

## 8.5 Type 2 and Type 3 mixed

It is possible for each of the two clauses in a conditional sentence to have a different time reference, and the result is a mixed conditional.
*If we had brought a map with us, we would know where we are.*
*If we had brought …* is contrary to past fact (we didn't bring a map).
*… we would know …* is contrary to present fact (we don't know).
*If I didn't love her, I wouldn't have married her.*
*If I didn't love her …* is contrary to present fact (I do love her).
*I wouldn't have married her …* is contrary to past fact (I did marry her).
Care needs to be taken when the Type 2 conditional refers to the future.
*I'd come to the party next Saturday if I hadn't arranged to go to the theatre.*
This conditional is sometimes 'unmixed' to regularize the tense sequence.
*I would have come to the party next Saturday if I hadn't arranged to go to the theatre.*

## Hypothesizing

There are certain other constructions that have a hypothetical meaning and, as in conditional sentences, the unreality that they express is again shown by shifting the verb form 'backwards'.
*I wish I knew the answer.* (But I don't know.)
*If only I hadn't behaved so badly.* (But I did behave badly.)

## 8.6 Hypothesizing about the present and future

The Past Simple tense form is used for present and future time reference. Notice that *were* is used instead of *was*, especially in formal style.
*I wish I **were** taller!     If only he **were** here now!*
*Supposing/suppose you **had** a million pounds? What would you do?*

### Present state v. present action or event

When we hypothesize about a present state, the Past Simple tense form is used.
*I wish you **lived** nearer.     If only I **had** a car!*
When we hypothesize about a present action or event, *would* is used.
*I wish you**'d help** more in the house.*
*If only she **wouldn't wash** her socks in the bath!*
*Would* here expresses willingness in the first sentence, and annoying habit in the second.

### *I wish/If only*

Notice that it is unusual to say *I wish/If only I wouldn't …* because we can control what we want to do. However, we can say *I wish/If only I could …*
*I wish I could remember where I put my glasses.*
*If only I could give up smoking.*
We can say *I wish/If only … would* to refer to a definite time in the future, but only if we think that the action will probably not happen.
*I wish she'd come with me tomorrow.*
*If only you'd fix the car this weekend, we could go for a drive.*
If it is possible that our wish will be realized, then a different structure such as *I hope* is needed.
*I hope it doesn't rain tomorrow.*

### Fact v. non-fact

Notice the difference between fact and non-fact in the following pair of sentences.
*He looks **as if he is** French.* (Fact – it is possible that he is.)
*He looks **as if he were** French.* (Non-fact – we know he isn't.)
The same distinction is found with other *as if/as though* structures.
*Why is that girl smiling at me **as though she knew** me?*
*He behaves **as if he owned** the place.*

### *It's time*

*It's time* can be followed by an infinitive.
*It's time to go to bed.     It's time for us to go.*
It is also possible to use a past tense.
*It's time we went home.     It's time I was going.*
When we want to say that it is time for someone else to do something, the past tense is often used.
*It's time you got your hair cut.*

### *would rather*

*Would rather* can be followed by an infinitive (without *to*).
*I'd rather have red wine, please.*
When *would rather* is followed by another person, the construction *would rather + person + past tense form* is used.
*I'd rather you kept this a secret.*
*She would rather you paid by cheque.*

## 8.7 Hypothesizing about the past

The Past Perfect tense form is used for past time reference.
*I wish she **hadn't been** so unkind.*
*If only the police **had looked** in the attic, they would have found him!*
*Supposing/Suppose we **had missed** the plane? What would we have done?*

### would rather

Would rather + the Past Perfect is possible, but it is more usual to express the same idea using *wish*.

*I'd rather you'd left.     I wish you'd left.*

### Fact v. non-fact

Notice the difference between fact and non-fact in the following sentences.

*He looked as if he **was** tired.* (Fact – this is probably how he felt.)
*He looked as if he **had seen** a ghost.* (Non-fact – very improbable.)

### would like

*Would like* can be used with a perfect infinitive to talk about things we wish we had done.

*I **would like to have lived** in the eighteenth century.*

This can also be expressed by *would have liked* followed by either an ordinary infinitive or a perfect infinitive.

| I would have liked to live<br>I would have liked to have lived | in the eighteenth century. |
|---|---|

The same forms can be used to refer to the present and the future if it is contrary to fact.

| I would like to have stayed in<br>I would have liked to stay in<br>I would have liked to have stayed in | tonight, instead of going out. |
|---|---|

## 8.8  Softening the message

We can make our message less direct by using certain constructions.

### A past tense

*I **wondered** if you were free tonight? I **thought** we could go to the cinema.*

### The continuous

*I **was hoping** you could tell me the answer. When **will** you **be arriving**?*

### would

*Would it be possible for you to come back tomorrow?*
*Wouldn't it be better if you did it my way?*
*I **would** say/think she's in her seventies.*
*I **would** have said/thought she was about 65.*
*I **wouldn't** be surprised if Jack didn't come soon.*
*I just thought I'd give you a ring to see if you were all right.*
*You'd have thought she could have remembered my birthday.*

# UNIT 9

## Verb patterns

## 9.1  Verb patterns with the gerund

The gerund or *-ing* form is used:

1  After certain verbs

| admit   deny   regret   suggest |
|---|

*He **admitted** stealing the money.*

2  After prepositions, prepositional verbs, and phrasal verbs
*After leaving school he joined the army.*
*She **apologized for arriving** late.*
*I've given up smoking at last.*

### Note

The preposition *to* (not *to* as part of the infinitive) can cause problems. This is because *to* + *-ing* seems a strange combination.

*I'm **looking forward to seeing** you.*

*I'm **not used to driving** on the left.*
*Do you **feel up to going** out this evening?*

## 9.2  Verb patterns with the infinitive

### Verb + infinitive + *to*

The pattern of verb + infinitive + *to* is used:

1  After certain verbs

| ask   agree   offer   promise   refuse   want |
|---|

*He **asked** to do it.*

2  After certain verbs + object

| ask   beg   encourage   order   persuade   tell   want |
|---|

*They **asked** him to do it.*

### Note

Some verbs can take both of the above patterns.

| ask   beg   want   help |
|---|

*She **wanted** to do it.*
*She **wanted** him to do it.*

### Verb + infinitive without *to*

| make   let   help |
|---|

*They **made** me do it.*

### Notes

1  All infinitive patterns are possible with *help*.
2  The passive of *make* takes *to*.
   *I was **made to** do it.*
3  The passive of *let* is *allowed to*.
   *I was **allowed to** do it.*

## 9.3  Verb + *that* + clause

In some (not all) of the above examples, a *that* clause can be used after the main verb in place of a gerund or infinitive. There is no change in meaning. *That* itself can be omitted.

*She **admitted (that) she had made** a mistake.*
*He **promised (that) he would do** it.*
*They **suggested (that) we should have** a long break.*

### Notes

1  *Suggest* has special problems. These constructions are also possible.
   *They **suggested (that) we have** a long break.*
   *They **suggested (that) we had** a long break.*
2  He ~~wanted that I do it~~ is a common mistake.

## 9.4  Verb + *-ing* or *to* with little or no change of meaning

The verbs *begin, start,* and *continue* can take either *-ing* or *to* and mean the same.

| It | started<br>began<br>continued | to rain.<br>raining. |
|---|---|---|

### Note

The choice may be governed by style or the nature of the following verb.

*It's just starting to rain.* (NOT ~~starting raining~~)
*He slowly began to understand the situation.* (NOT ~~began understanding~~)

Many verbs that express feelings and attitudes (*like, love, prefer, can't stand*, etc.) can be followed by either *-ing* or *to*, and the distinction in meaning is small.

*I **like travelling** by train.* (general truth)
*I **like to travel** by train when I go to my grandmother's.* (a little more particular)

*Like* + *-ing* can mean *enjoy*. *Like* + infinitive can express what you think is the right thing to do.

*I like **cooking**.     I like **to pay** my bills on time.*

**Note**
The infinitive is always used with *would like/prefer*, etc.
*I'd **like to travel** by train when I next visit her.* (one particular occasion)

### 9.5 Verbs + *-ing* or *to* with a change of meaning

1  After the verbs *remember, forget,* and *regret,* the gerund refers to an action earlier in time than the main verb; the infinitive refers to an action at the same time or later.
*I **remember giving** her the message when I saw her.*
*Please **remember to give** her the message when you see her.*
*I **regret saying** that because I upset her.*
*I **regret to say** we can't offer you the job.*

2  After the verb *stop* and the phrasal verb *go on,* the gerund refers to an existing action; the infinitive refers to a following action.
*He **went on repeating** the question.*
*He **went on to say** that he wanted my advice.*

3  After verbs of the senses *see, hear,* etc. + object the gerund signifies an action in progress; the infinitive a completed action.
*We **saw him cutting** the hedge.* (He was in the middle of doing it.)
*We **saw him cut** the hedge.* (We saw the whole event from start to finish.)

### 9.6 Perfect and passive forms

The gerund and infinitive also have perfect and passive forms.
*I **don't remember having said** that.*
*She **suffered from having had** a difficult childhood.*
*He **doesn't like being told** what to do.*

# Unit 10

### 10.1 Intensifying adverbs and verbs

As we saw in Unit 3, certain verbs and intensifying adverbs go together because there is a link in meaning.

*deeply regret     sincerely hope     desperately need*

However, in most cases of verb + intensifying adverb, there is no reason at all why some combinations are possible and some are not.

| Possible combinations | | Impossible combinations |
|---|---|---|
| totally<br>absolutely<br>quite | agree | ~~sincerely agree~~<br>~~quite disagree~~<br>~~totally remember~~<br>~~fully think~~<br>~~completely adore~~<br>~~fully destroy~~<br>~~strongly like~~ |
| totally | disagree | |
| completely<br>fully<br>perfectly | understand | |
| seriously<br>sincerely | believe | |
| completely<br>strongly<br>entirely<br>really<br>thoroughly<br>greatly | forget<br>disapprove<br>depend<br>like<br>enjoy<br>appreciate | |

### 10.2 Intensifying adverbs and adjectives

It is important to understand the difference between gradable and extreme (or limit) adjectives. Gradable adjectives express qualities that can exist in different strengths. For example, a person can be more or less intelligent, a room more or less dirty, a film more or less interesting. Limit adjectives express extreme qualities.

*a brilliant person     a filthy room     a fascinating film*

Look at these pairs of gradable and limit adjectives.

*angry / furious       big / enormous       important / essential*
*tired / exhausted     long / endless       tasty / delicious*
*happy / delighted     upset / devastated   surprised / amazed*

Different intensifying adverbs go with gradable and limit adjectives.

| Intensifying adverbs<br>+ gradable adjective | | | Intensifying adverbs<br>+ limit adjective | | |
|---|---|---|---|---|---|
| very<br>awfully<br>rather | extremely<br>terribly<br>fairly | really<br>pretty<br>quite | absolutely<br>completely<br>utterly | totally<br>entirely<br>pretty | really<br>simply<br>quite |

As with verbs, not all combinations are possible. There is no real reason why we can't say ~~totally essential~~, ~~entirely determined~~, ~~completely furious~~ – we just can't!

The only combinations that are always possible are *very* + gradable adjective and *absolutely* + limit adjective. *Really* can go with most adjectives, both gradable and limit.

*very happy/tired/big*
*absolutely enormous/delicious/delighted*
*really angry/surprised/amazed*

### 10.3 *quite*

*Quite* has three meanings.

1  With gradable adjectives, when the stress is on *quite*, it means 'down a bit'. It says 'OK, but not as good as I expected'. It is negative.
*The restaurant was quite good, but I wouldn't go back.*

2  With gradable adjectives, when the stress is on the adjective, it means 'up a bit'. It says 'It was better than I expected'. It is positive.
*The film was quite good. You'd really like it.*

3  With a limit adjective, it means 'up to the top'. There is stress on *quite* as well as the adjective, and the rising intonation is exaggerated.
*He's being quite ridiculous!     You're quite right.*
*Are you quite sure?*

# UNIT 11

### 11.1 Adjective order

Generally speaking, value adjectives (which indicate personal opinion) come first, followed by size, age, shape, colour, origin, and material. Compound nouns (e.g. *washing machine, coffee pot*) are never separated.

There are several examples below of noun phrases with adjectives in this order.

*two lovely black leather riding boots*
*a priceless nineteenth-century Impressionist painting*
*their huge circular swimming pool*
*my Swedish wooden salad bowl*
*the dirty old metal garden seat*
*one tiny L-shaped utility room*
*Jane's pretty Victorian writing desk*
*his charming whitewashed country cottage*

# Relative clauses

## Introduction

It is important to distinguish between defining and non-defining relative clauses. Defining relative clauses are an essential part of the meaning of a sentence and therefore they cannot be left out. They define exactly who or what we are talking about.

*There's the woman **you were telling me about**.*

Non-defining relative clauses add extra information of secondary importance, and can be left out of a sentence.

*Mrs Bottomley, **who was an extremely mean person while she was alive**, has left all her money to a cats' home.*

Non-defining relative clauses are mainly found in written English, where sentences are carefully constructed. In spoken English, they sound rather formal, and can easily be expressed by simpler sentences.

*Did you know Mrs Bottomley has left all her money to a cats' home? It's incredible, really. She was such a mean person.*

## 11.2 Defining relative clauses

These are the main forms used. The forms in brackets are possible, but not as common.

|  | Person | Thing |
|---|---|---|
| **Subject** | who (that) | that (which) |
| **Object** | — (that) | — (that) |

Notice that English likes to drop the relative pronoun when it defines the object of the clause.

*The doctor **who helped me most** was Dr Clark.* (subject)
*The doctor **I found most helpful** was Dr Clark.* (object)
*The treatment **that** helped me most was acupuncture.* (subject)
*The treatment **I liked best** was acupuncture.* (object)

Notice that there are no commas before and after defining relative clauses when written, and no pauses when spoken.

### that

*That* is usually used as subject after the following: superlatives, *all, every(thing), some(thing), any(thing), no(thing)*, and *only*.

*He wrote some of the best poetry **that's ever been written**.*
***All that's needed** is a little more time.*
*Don't take **anything that's valuable**.*
*The **only thing that matters** is that you're safe.*

We often omit *that* when it is the object.

*She's one of the nicest people I know.*
*Is there anything I can do to help?*

### Prepositions

Prepositions can come either before relative pronouns or at the end of the relative clause. In spoken English, it is much more common to put the preposition at the end (and to drop the pronoun).

*This is the book I was talking to you about.*
*The people I work with are very kind.*

### Second relative clause

A second relative, introduced by *and* or *but*, usually takes a *wh-* pronoun, not *that*.

*Someone that I greatly admire, but who I've never met, is Professor Keats.*

## 11.3 Non-defining relative clauses

These are the main forms used. The form in brackets is possible, but not as common.

|  | Person | Thing |
|---|---|---|
| **Subject** | … , who … , | … , which … , |
| **Object** | … , who … (, whom … ) | … , which … |

*Mr Jenkins, **who has written several books**, spoke at the meeting last night.* (subject)
*Peter Clark, **who the Prime Minister sacked from the Cabinet**, has become the chairman of Redland Bank.* (object)
*My favourite drink is whisky, **which is one of Britain's most profitable exports**.* (subject)
*I gave him a sandwich, **which he ate greedily**.* (object)

Notice that there are commas around non-defining relative clauses when written, and pauses before and after them when spoken.

### Prepositions

Prepositions can come at the end of non-defining relative clauses, but in a formal style they are usually put before the relative pronoun.

*The lecturer spoke for two hours on the subject of Weingarten's Theory of Market Forces, which none of us had ever heard **of**.*
*The privatization of all industry, **to** which this government is deeply committed, is not universally popular.*

### which

*Which* can be used in non-defining clauses to refer to the whole of the preceding clause.

*He passed the exam, **which** surprised everyone.*
*The lift isn't working, **which** means we'll have to use the stairs.*

### whose

*Whose* can be used in both defining and non-defining relative clauses to refer to possession.

*There's the woman **whose** son was killed recently.* (defining)
*ABC Airways, **whose** fares across the Atlantic were lower than anybody else's, has just declared itself bankrupt.* (non-defining)

### what

*What* is used as a relative pronoun instead of *the thing that* in some sentences.

*Has she told you **what**'s worrying her?*
*I have to do **what** I believe is right.*

### when and where

*When* and *where* can be used to introduce both defining and non-defining relative clauses. In defining relative clauses, *when* can be left out.

*Can you tell me the exact time (**when**) you hope to arrive?*

*Where* cannot be left out unless we add a preposition.

*That's the hotel **where** we're staying.*
*That's the hotel we're staying **at**.*

In non-defining relative clauses, *when* and *where* cannot be left out.

*We go swimming after 5.00, **when** everyone else has gone home.*
*He shops in Oxford, **where** his sister lives.*

### why

*Why* can be used to introduce defining relative clauses after the word *reason*. It can be left out.

*Do you remember the reason **why** we are arguing?*

We can also say *Do you remember why we are arguing?* where the clause beginning with *why* is the object of the verb.

## Participles

### ▶ 11.4 Participles as adjectives

Present participles describe an action which is still happening.
*He dived into the sea to save the **drowning** child.*
*They watched the **burning** forest.*
Past participles describe the result of an action that has happened.
*She looked at the **broken** chair.*
*The **completed** statue looked very lifelike.*

### ▶ 11.5 Participles as reduced relative clauses

When participles come after a noun, they are like reduced relative clauses.
*I met a woman **riding** a donkey.* (who was riding)
*The cash **stolen** in the raid was never recovered.* (that was stolen)
*The man **being interviewed** by the police is suspected of arson.* (who is being interviewed)

### ▶ 11.6 Participles in adverb clauses

1 Participle clauses can describe actions that are going on simultaneously.
   *She sat by the fire **reading** a book and **sipping** a mug of coffee.*
   *He went to the party **dressed** as a monkey.*
2 Participle clauses can describe actions that happen consecutively.
   ***Opening** his suitcase, he took out a revolver.*
   ***Released** from its cage, the lion prowled around.*
3 If it is important to show that the first action has finished before the second begins, the perfect participle is used.
   ***Having finished** lunch, we set off.*
4 Participle clauses can express the idea of *because*.
   ***Being** a mean person, he never spent more than he had to.* (Because he was a mean person …)
   ***Not knowing** what to do, I waited patiently.* (Because I didn't know …)
   ***Weakened** by years of bad health, she could hardly sit up in bed.* (Because she had been weakened …)
5 Participle clauses can express the idea of result.
   *It rained every day for two weeks, completely **ruining** our holiday.*
6 Participle clauses can express the idea of *if*.
   ***Taken** regularly, aspirin can reduce the risk of a stroke.*
• Participle clauses can be introduced by *while, when, after, by, on*, and *since*.
   ***While studying** at Oxford, he met the woman he was to marry.*
   ***When leaving** the plane, remember to take your belongings with you.*
   ***After saying** goodbye, he ran to catch the train.*
   *I paid my debts **by taking** on another job.*
   ***On entering** the room, I noticed that everyone was looking at me.*
   ***Since arriving** in London, I've made a lot of friends.*

**Note**
In all participle clauses, the subject of the clause and the subject of the main verb must be the same.

### ▶ 11.7 Participles after certain verbs

Many verbs can be followed by an *-ing* form.
*I **spent** the evening **decorating**.*
*He **spends** his money **gambling**.*
*Don't **waste** time **thinking** about what might have been.*
*Let's **go swimming**.*

## Linking devices

### ▶ 12.1 Result

#### *so* and *such*

*It was raining, **so** we went home.*
*The play was **so** boring **that** I fell asleep.*
*It was **such** a boring film **that** I fell asleep.*

#### *as a result, therefore,* and *consequently*

*As a result, therefore,* and *consequently* can also express the result of something.
*He worked hard all his life. **As a result**, he amassed a fortune.*
*The dollar has gone down against the yen. **Therefore/Consequently**, Japanese goods are more expensive for Americans.* (more formal)

#### Participles

As we saw in Unit 11, participles can also express result.
*He fell off his motorbike, **breaking** his leg and **injuring** his arm.*

#### *too* and *enough*

When result involves degree (*heavy, hot*) or quantity (*little, much*), we can express the result with *too* or *enough*.
*This table is **too** heavy for me to lift.*
*There are **too** many people to fit into this room.*
*I'm not strong **enough** to lift the table.*
*The room isn't big **enough** to fit everyone in.*

### ▶ 12.2 Reason

#### *as* and *since*

*As* and *since* are used when the reason is already known to the listener/reader, or when it is not the most important part of the sentence.
***As** it was getting late, we decided it was time to leave.*
***Since** he had very little money, James decided he should look for work.*
Both these clauses are quite formal. In an informal style, we would be more likely to use *so*.
*It was getting late, **so** we decided it was time to leave.*

#### *because*

*Because* puts more emphasis on the reason, and most often introduces new information.
***Because** she was getting frail in her old age, she went to live with her daughter.*
When the reason is the most important part of the sentence, the *because* clause usually comes at the end.
*I went to live in London **because I wanted to learn English**.*

#### *for*

*For* introduces new information, but suggests that the reason is given as an afterthought. A *for* clause could almost be in brackets.
*We should plan ahead carefully, **for** the future is almost upon us.*

#### *because of, due to,* and *owing to*

*Because of, due to,* and *owing to* can also express the cause of something.
*We had to stop playing tennis **because of** the weather.*
***Due to** the economic situation, fewer people are taking holidays this year.*
***Owing to** a lack of funds, the project will discontinue next year.*

**Participles**

As we saw in Unit 11, participles can also express reason.

*Being an inquisitive person, I love to start conversations with strangers.*
*Deprived of oxygen, the animal soon died.*

## ▶ 12.3 Purpose

### The infinitive

The infinitive on its own is the most common pattern in informal English.

| *I went to Spain* | *to learn*<br>*in order to learn*<br>*so as to learn* | *Spanish.* |

We cannot use the infinitive in the negative.

| *I tiptoed upstairs* | *so as not to*<br>*in order not to* | *wake anyone up.* |

### so that

We can use *so that* + *can/could* or *will/would* to express purpose.
*I left for work early **so that** I could avoid the rush hour.*
We also use *so that* when there is a change in subject.
*Henry booked a taxi **so that** his daughter would arrive on time.*

### in case

When we want to prevent what might happen, we can use *in case*.
*I phoned her **in case** she thought I was still angry with her.*
This is more common than *so that she wouldn't think I was …*

## ▶ 12.4 Contrast

*But* is the most common way of expressing contrast. *Even though* is more emphatic than *although*. *Though* is more formal than *although*.

| *There was a general strike,* **but**<br>**Although** *there was a general strike,* | *most people managed to get to work.* |

*Even though there weren't any trains, I was only an hour late.*
*The journey back home was all right, **though** it wasn't easy.*

*Though* can be used as a comment adverb.
*'That meal was expensive.' 'It was good, **though**.'*

*All the same* and *even so* express contrast informally, while *however* and *nevertheless* are more formal.

| *I know he's a difficult person.* | **All the same,**<br>**Even so,** | *I'm very fond of him.* |

| *Our task became more and more demanding.* | **However,**<br>**Nevertheless,** | *we persevered.* |

*In spite of* and *despite* can also express contrast.

| *We enjoyed our picnic* | **despite** *the rain.*<br>**in spite of** *the rain.* |

*Despite being over eighty, my grandmother enjoyed the party.*

## ▶ 12.5 Time

### Linkers

The following linkers are conjunctions of time.
**When** *I saw the time, I realized I was late.*
**As soon as** *I got up, I had a shower.*
**After** *I had a shower, I got dressed.*

| **As**<br>**While** | *I was getting dressed, I thought about the day to come.* |

**Before** *I went to work, I read the mail.*
**Once** *I'd seen the bills to pay, I left the house.*

| *I worked* | **until**<br>**till** | *I had finished my project.* |

*I've been working on this project **since** I joined the company.*

**Participles**

As we saw in Unit 11, participles can also express links of time.
*Grabbing my briefcase, I left to catch my train.*
*Having bought a ticket, I went onto the platform.*

## ▶ 12.6 Condition

The following linkers are used to express a condition.
*If you want a holiday, let me know.*

| **Providing**<br>**Provided**<br>**As long as**<br>**So long as** | *you look after it, you can stay in my flat.* |

**Even if** *I'm there, I don't mind.*
*I'll presume you're coming **unless** I hear from you.*
**Whether** *you come **or not**, it would be nice to see you soon.*
*I'll go **wherever** you want.*
*Come **whenever** you want.*
*Bring **whoever** you want.*

| **However** *late it is,*<br>**No matter how** *late it is,* | *just phone me.* |

*(no matter who/what/when …)*
**Supposing** *you ever ran out of cash, I could help.*